Apophatic Elements in the Theory and Practice of Psychoanalysis

CW01095850

How can the psychotherapist think about not knowing? Is psychoanalysis a contemplative practice? This book explores the possibility that there are resources in philosophy and theology which can help psychoanalysts and psychotherapists think more clearly about the unknown and the unknowable.

The book applies the lens of *apophasis* to psychoanalysis, providing a detailed reading of *apophasis* in the work of Pseudo-Dionysius and exploring C. G. Jung's engagement with apophatic discourse. Pseudo-Dionysius brought together Greek and biblical currents of negative theology and the *via negativa*, and the psychology of Jung can be read as a continuation and extension of the apophatic tradition. Henderson discusses the concept of the transcendent function as an apophatic dynamic at the heart of Jung's thought, and suggests that *apophasis* can provide the key to understanding the family resemblance among the disparate schools of psychoanalysis.

Chapters consider:

- Jung's discussion of opposites, including his reception of Nicholas of Cusa's concept of the coincidence of opposites.
- Jung's engagement with Neoplatonism and Pseudo-Dionysius.
- The work of Jung in relation to Deleuze, Derrida and other writers.
- How motifs in Pseudo-Dionysius' *Ecclesiastical Hierarchy* resonate with contemporary psychoanalytic psychotherapy.

The in-depth examination of primary sources in this comprehensive volume provides a platform for research into *apophasis* in the wider field of psychoanalysis. It will prove valuable reading for scholars and analysts of Jungian psychology studying religion and mysticism.

David Henderson is Senior Lecturer in Psychoanalysis at the Centre for Psychoanalysis, Middlesex University, London, UK. He is an analytical psychotherapist working in private practice and a founder of the Association of Independent Psychotherapists, UK.

Research in Analytical Psychology and Jungian Studies Series
Series advisor, Andrew Samuels
Professor of Analytical Psychology, Essex University, UK

The *Research in Analytical Psychology and Jungian Studies* series features scholarly works that are, broadly speaking, of an empirical nature. The series comprises research-focused volumes involving qualitative and quantitative research, historical/archival research, theoretical developments, heuristic research, grounded theory, narrative approaches, collaborative research, practitioner-led research and self-study. The series also includes focused works by clinical practitioners, and provides new research-informed explorations of the work of C. G Jung that will appeal to researchers, academics and scholars alike.

Books in this series:

Time and Timelessness
Temporality in the theory of Carl Jung
Angeliki Yiassemides

Apophatic Elements in the Theory and Practice of Psychoanalysis
Pseudo-Dionysius and C. G. Jung
David Henderson

C. G. Jung and Hans Urs von Balthasar
God and evil: A critical comparison
Les Oglesby

Apophatic Elements in the Theory and Practice of Psychoanalysis

Pseudo-Dionysius and C. G. Jung

David Henderson

Routledge
Taylor & Francis Group
LONDON AND NEW YORK

First published 2014
by Routledge
2 Park Square, Milton Park, Abingdon, Oxfordshire OX14 4RN

and by Routledge
711 Third Avenue, New York, NY 10017

First issued in paperback 2016

Routledge is an imprint of the Taylor and Francis Group, an informa business

British Library Cataloguing in Publication Data
A catalogue record for this book is available from the British Library

Library of Congress Cataloging in Publication Data
Henderson, David (Psychotherapist)
    Apophatic elements in the theory and practice of psychoanalysis:
    pseudo-dionysius and C.G. Jung/David Henderson.
    pages cm
    Includes bibliographical references.
    1. Psychoanalysis. 2. Jungian psychology. I. Title.
    BF173.H45 2014
    150.19′54—dc23
    2013017697

ISBN 13: 978-0-415-79175-5 (pbk)
ISBN 13: 978-0-415-85784-0 (hbk)

Typeset in Bembo
by Swales & Willis Ltd, Exeter, Devon

For Susan

Contents

Acknowledgements

I am grateful to Robert Burns, Brendan Callaghan and Roderick Main. They each served as thoughtful readers and discussion partners at different stages of this project. Judith Warren kindly read through the text carefully and provided important reflection.

I gratefully acknowledge the permission to use material from the following sources:

> Jung, C. G., Collected Works of C. G. Jung, 1977, Princeton University Press, reprinted by permission of Princeton University Press.
> Jung, C. G., Collected Works of C. G. Jung, 1977, Routledge, reprinted by permission of Taylor & Francis Books (UK).
> *Pseudo-Dionysius, Pseudo-Dionysius: The Complete Works*, 1987, Paulist Press, reprinted by permission of Paulist Press.

The publisher has made every effort to contact authors/copyright holders of works reprinted in *Apophatic Elements in the Theory and Practice of Psychoanalysis: Pseudo-Dionysius and C. G. Jung*. If we have been unable to trace any copyright holder than we welcome correspondence from those individuals/companies.

Chapter 1

Introduction

The lonely cells of the recluses of Egypt have been revealed, by the archaeologist, to have had well-furnished consulting rooms.[1]

In former times people went into monasteries. Were they stupid or insensitive people? – Well, if people like that found they needed to take such measures in order to be able to go on living, the problem cannot be an easy one![2]

The aim of this study is to identify apophatic elements in the theory and practice of psychoanalysis. It will do so by an examination of the works of the sixth-century philosopher Dionysius[3] and the twentieth-century psychoanalyst Carl Gustav Jung.

I am using 'apophatic elements' as an umbrella term to cover a range of concepts, images, metaphors and behaviour which are characterized by negation or denial. *Apophasis* can be translated literally as 'unsaying'. It is 'away from speech' or 'saying away'. *Apo* is 'from' or 'away'. *Phasis* is 'assertion', from *phemi*, 'assert' or 'say'. *Apophasis*, denial, stands in relation to *kataphasis*, affirmation. The *via negativa* and negative theology are concerned with the apophatic in philosophy and religion. 'Unknowing' as an epistemological problem and as an experience is at the heart of apophatic writing.

Freud described psychoanalysis both as a theory for understanding the mind and culture and as a therapy for neurosis. This mirrors the debate among the interpreters of the writings of Dionysius. Some interpret his work as philosophy, others interpret it as a description of personal experience. Lossky, perhaps, embraces both sides when he describes apophaticism as 'an attitude of mind which refuses to form concepts about God'.[4] Coakley asserts that this division, while having 'some remaining heuristic worth, is far too blunt a tool to account for the historic variety of Dionysian influences down the centuries'.[5] Psychoanalysis has had a similarly varied influence, albeit for a much shorter period of time. Grinberg observed that '[i]n spite of its tremendous impact on mankind, paradoxically enough, it has not yet been possible to place and classify psychoanalysis within any of the existing fields of knowledge'.[6]

The problem of unknowing is central to the theory and practice of psychoanalysis. One of the motives behind this research is to explore whether or not there are resources within the discourse of the *via negativa* and negative theology to help the psychotherapist to think about unknowing in the psychoanalytic setting. Does the apophatic literature provide tools for understanding the process of psychoanalysis? Is it possible that, in the words of Dionysius, 'If one considers these texts [his own and those of psychoanalysis] with a reverent eye one will see something that both brings about unity and manifests a single empathy?'[7]

Passing reference to the apophatic tradition has been made in a few histories of psychotherapy. Ellenberger[8] and Whyte[9] identify Dionysius as one of a number of philosophers who contributed to pre-Freudian concepts of the unconscious:

> Plotin and the neo-Platonic philosophers defined God by means of a negative approach: God is not at all what we conceive him to be; he is unimaginable to us. The great mystic known as Dionysios the Areopagite, gave to this concept a Christian formulation: 'The most godly knowledge of God is that which is known by unknowing.'[10]

Burke characterizes Freud's theory as a 'secular variant of negative theology'.[11] Sells and Webb have written a paper about apophatic elements in Lacan and Bion.[12] Goudsmit in a study of the *via negativa* in psychotherapy compares Merleau-Ponty's 'negative philosophy' and Nicholas of Cusa's 'learned ignorance'.[13] Anderson used the work of Thomas Merton to develop an apophatic approach to psychotherapy.[14] Dourley, in a chapter entitled 'Toward an Apophatic Psychology', explores Jung's understanding of Eckhart.[15] Karlsson observes that:

> One of the reasons that psychoanalysis as a science struggles with difficult epistemological problems is that its subject matter – the unconscious – is constituted in terms of negativity. What other science investigates something which is defined by the prefix un-?! The only resembling discipline, in this sense, may be the so-called 'negative theology', which claims that an understanding of God can only be reached by stating what God is not.[16]

Frank asserts that 'all "psychology" which really *sees* its object and really takes account of its peculiar character must be "negative psychology" (by analogy to negative theology)'.[17] If Karlsson and Frank are right, psychoanalysis and negative theology share a concern to clarify how to think about negation.

Psychoanalysis has been widely and effectively used as a tool to study religious experience and mystical thought. However, *Essai sur l'Introversion Mystique: Etude Psychologique de Pseudo-Denys l'Areopagite et de Quelques Autres cas de Mysticisme* is, as far as I am aware, the only sustained psychoanalytic study of Dionysius. It was written by Morel in 1918 and dedicated to Flournoy. In his introduction Morel references Charcot, Janet, Freud, Jung, Bleuler and Bergson. He concludes that:

> le 'systeme' de Denys offre cette double analogie essentielle avec la pensée autistique: 1. Il est égocentrique. 2. Le critère de la vraisemblance est totalment exclue et remplacé par le seul critère de la jouissance. [...] Or, cette confu-sion de la réalité objective interne et d'un égocentrisme métaphysique est une forme particulière et tres répandue de mythomanie: création, réalisation de fictions, et confusion pseudo-hallucinatoire de celles-ci avec la réalité.[18]

The approach taken here turns the tables on psychoanalysis. It asks what sort of a practice and theory is psychoanalysis, and where is it located within the history of the European contemplative tradition, by use of the concept of *apophasis*. It asks in what ways, if any, the language of apophatic writing can illuminate the theory and practice of psychoanalysis. This process necessarily alters our perceptions of both ancient *apophasis* and modern psychoanalysis. As Turner observes:

> One understands a tradition when one understands *how* that past lives in the present ... to call upon a tradition is *always* to reread it, that is to say, to access a tradition *is already to have changed it*. Therefore the past is alive *as* tradition in so far as we transform it, so the normativity of the tradition is the product of what it yields to us by way of given achievement in the past in conjunction with our present strategies of rereading those achieve-ments, that conjunction of past and present constituting its character and life *as tradition*.[19]

In addition to the theoretical and historical objectives and motives for this study, it has a philological dimension. In the section on Dionysius I will describe ways in which apophatic themes appear in his texts. This is the first time that these features of his writing have been identified in such detail. In the section on Jung, I can claim to have identified his use of the notion of opposites in a more thorough manner than has been attempted before.

Chapters 2 and 3 of this study focus on Dionysius, the sixth-century Syrian writer whose works are often portrayed as the zenith of apophatic thought. He brought together the Greek and biblical currents of negative theology and the *via negativa*. Apophatic elements can be found in the writings of Plato, Philo, the Gnostics, Plotinus, Augustine, Gregory of Nyssa and Proclus, all of whom predate Dionysius. Dionysius' thought has been interpreted and made use of in a variety of ways by philosophers and theologians from his own time up to the present, including Eriugena, Aquinas, Cusa, Eckhart and the author of the *Cloud of Unknowing*.

In the last thirty years there has been a resurgence of interest in apophatic literature. Mortley,[20] McGinn,[21] de Certeau,[22] Carabine[23] and Sells[24] have written historical studies of apophatic philosophy, theology and mysticism. In debates related to deconstruction and postmodernism, Derrida[25] and Marion[26] have written significantly about Dionysius. Yannaras[27] and Carlson,[28] who develops what he calls the 'apophatic analogy', have compared Heidegger and Dionysius. Boeve uses the concept of 'cultural apophaticism' to reflect on contemporary relations between theology and culture.[29] Fitzpatrick[30] and Walker[31] have used *apophasis* within the context of the social sciences. Zembylas[32] and Abunuwara[33] argue for the importance of 'the unknowable' in education. Wolosky has explored *apophasis* in Eliot, Beckett and Celan.[34] Franke has used the theme of *apophasis* to compile an anthology, which includes work from literature and the arts.[35] He observes:

> As a newly emerging logic, or rather a/logic, of language in the humanities, this new (though also very old) quasi-epistemic paradigm for criticism, as well as for language-based disciplines and practices in general, can help us learn to read in hither to unsuspectedly limber and sensitive ways.[36]

Saward developed the concept of 'apophatic anthropology' based on patristic texts, especially Gregory of Nyssa, which he links with Wittgenstein's 'silence'.[37] Independently, Bernauer described Foucault's 'apophatic anthropology'.[38] Carlson[39] and Otten[40] use the notion of 'negative anthropology'. Caputo argues for a 'generalized apophatics':

> So to the *theologia negativa*, one could add a *anthropologia negativa*, an *ethica negativa, politica negativa*, where of the humanity, or the ethics, or the politics, or the democracy to come we cannot say a thing, except that they want to twist free from the regimes of presence, from the historically restricted concepts of humanity, ethics and democracy under which we presently labor. Humanity, ethics, politics – or whatever, *n'importe* – would belong to a general apophatics [...] The effect of this *ignorantia* is to keep the possibility of the impossible open, to keep the future open, to have a future.[41]

While these varied uses of *apophasis* are not referred to explicitly in what follows, they provide part of the wider context of this study.

In the context of his discussion of the relationship between continental philosophy and the *via negativa*, Bradley asks whether the relationship is one of kinship or opposition:

> Is continental thought ... a philosophical *continuation* and *extension* of negative theology's critique of language, identity and ontology or is it a *rejection* or *reaction* against a negative theological tradition that, for all its subversiveness, remains deeply indebted to the metaphysical and ontotheological tradition from which it departs?[42]

I am asking a similar question about the relationship between psychoanalysis and *apophasis*. My argument is that psychoanalysis, in this case the psychoanalysis of Jung, can be read as a continuation and extension of the apophatic tradition.

Chapter 4 examines apophatic elements in the work of Jung. The limits of consciousness, reason and language are ubiquitous themes in Jung's writings. In his view the unconscious is simply 'the unknown'. The inner and the outer worlds are ultimately both unknowable. Subjectivity and matter are both mysteries:

> The relation of a psychic content to the ego forms the criterion of its consciousness, for no content can be conscious unless it is represented to a subject. With this definition we have described and delimited the *scope* of the subject. Theoretically, no limits can be set to the field of consciousness, since it is capable of indefinite extension. Empirically, however, it always finds its limit when it comes up against the *unknown*. This consists of everything we do not know, which, therefore, is not related to the ego as the centre of the field of consciousness. The unknown falls into two groups of objects: those which are outside and can be experienced by the senses, and those which are inside and are experienced immediately. The first group comprises the unknown in the outer world; the second the unknown in the inner world. We call this latter territory the *unconscious*.[43]

The symbol is the most appropriate way of expressing a content that is ultimately unknowable. Jung felt that the writings of the Gnostics and the alchemists prefigured the paradoxical findings of psychoanalysis:

> Paradox is a characteristic of the Gnostic writings. It does more justice to the *unknowable* than clarity can do, for uniformity of meaning robs the mystery of its darkness and sets it up as something that is *known*. That is a usurpation, and it leads the human intellect into hybris by pretending that it, the intellect, has got hold of the transcendent mystery by a cognitive act and has 'grasped' it. The paradox therefore reflects a higher level of intellect and, by not forcibly representing the unknowable as known, gives a more faithful picture of the real state of affairs.[44]

Fear of the unknown inhibits personality development and is a source of resistance in psychotherapy:

> In studying the history of the human mind one is impressed again and again by the fact that its growth keeps pace with a widening range of consciousness, and that each step forward is an extremely painful and laborious achievement. One could almost say that nothing is more hateful to man than to give up the smallest particle of unconsciousness. He has a profound fear of the unknown. Ask anybody who has ever tried to introduce new ideas! If even the allegedly mature man is afraid of the unknown, why

shouldn't the child hesitate also? The *horror novi* is one of the most striking qualities of primitive man. This is a natural enough obstacle, as obstacles go; but excessive attachment to the parents is unnatural and pathological, because a too great fear of the unknown is itself pathological.[45]

The unknown within the context of psychoanalytic therapy is not solely the result of repression. The attitude of not knowing is an important element of analytic technique:

> There are naturally cases where the doctor sees something which is undoubtedly there, but which the patient will not or cannot admit. As the truth is often hidden as much from the doctor as from the patient, various methods have been evolved for gaining access to the unknown contents. I purposely say 'unknown' and not 'repressed' because I think it altogether wrong to assume that whenever a content is unknown it is necessarily repressed. The doctor who really thinks that way gives the appearance of knowing everything beforehand. Such a pretence stymies the patient and will most likely make it impossible for him to confess the truth.[46]

Jung argues that 'there are four methods for investigating the unknown in the patient'[47] – the association method, symptom analysis, anamnestic analysis and analysis of the unconscious.

These quotations from Jung, which I have cited at length, exhaust the explicit references to the 'unknowable' and the 'unknown' in the *Collected Works* Volume 20. However, I will demonstrate that apophatic motifs saturate Jung's theory and practice. I examine references in the *Collected Works* to writers and concepts from the Platonic tradition, with special attention to their apophatic elements. In Chapter 5 there is a systematic review of all references to Dionysius in Jung's work. There is a detailed analysis of Jung's writing on opposites, including *coincidentia oppositorum, complexio oppositorum, coniunctio oppositorum* and the union of opposites. I examine Jung's appropriation of Nicholas of Cusa's concept of the coincidence of opposites. Jung's concept of the transcendent function is discussed in Chapter 6.

I have already made reference to the contemporary discussions within a number of fields about the status and role of apophatic discourse. In Chapter 7 I use the work of a number of contemporary writers to reflect on apophatic themes in Jung. Aside from the intrinsic interest this may hold, it functions here to dispel the suspicion that Jung's preoccupation with the unknown is anachronistic or that it represents a regressive feature in his theory.

A first group of writers, Sells, Milem and Rorem, have provided interpretive frameworks with which to understand negative theology. I will identify elements of Jung's work which resonate with these schemas. A second pair of writers, Deleuze and Derrida, are of interest because aspects of their work can be read with an apophatic lens and compared with Jung's. Finally, the discussions about unknowing in two contemporary Jungian theorists, Dourley and Tacey, are examined.

In Chapter 8 there is an extended and impressionistic comparison of the process of psychotherapy and the liturgical practices described by Dionysius in the *Ecclesistical Hierarchy*. While it is not unusual to discuss psychotherapy in light of ritual processes described in anthropological literature, I hope to demonstrate that bringing to bear on the psychoanalytic process images and concepts from liturgical studies offers an additional insight into the nature of psychoanalysis. This highlights the performative and social dimensions of *apophasis* in the texts of Dionysius and Jung.

Philo of Alexandria, 2000 years ago in *On the Contemplative Life*, described a community of men and women who lived in solitude:

> They are called therapeutae and therapeutrides, either because they process an art of medicine more excellent than that in general use in cities (for that only heals bodies, but the other heals souls which are under the mastery of terrible and almost incurable diseases, which pleasures and appetites, fears and griefs, and covetousness, and follies, and injustice, and all the rest of the innumerable multitude of other passions and vices, have inflicted upon them), or else because they have been instructed by nature and the sacred laws to serve the living God, who is superior to the good, and more simple than the one, and more ancient than the unit.[48]

Analysts could be considered contemporary hermits. They dwell within the solitude of their consulting rooms and meet their clients in a liminal space.[49]

Hans Jonas comments ironically that the Gnostic writer of the Apocryphon of John displays:

> the kind of emphatic and pathetic verbosity which the 'ineffable' seems to have incited in many of its professors ... [the] effusive description devoted to the very indescribability of the divine Absolute – expatiating on the theme of His purity, boundlessness, perfection, etc. being beyond measure, quality, quantity, and time; beyond comprehension, description, name, distinction; beyond life, beatitude, divinity, and even existence – are a typical example of the rising 'negative theology', whose spokesmen did not tire for centuries of the self-defeating nature of their task.[50]

Despite this warning about 'the self-defeating nature' of my task, I hope to show that there are significant parallels between the apophatic thought of Dionysius and the work of Jung.[51] Indeed, perhaps the very 'self-defeating nature' of apophatic discourse provides us with another parallel with psychoanalysis, 'the impossible profession'.

Turner uses the concept of 'recursive contradictoriness' to describe 'a structure of an individual or social practice within which there is a built-in and systemic conflict between the elements which constitute it; a conflict which is not resolvable within the practice itself, for it is from its structural features as such that the conflict arises'.[52] Reflecting on the dilemmas of teaching Dionysius within the academy, he describes the conflict between an accurate appreciation of the ecclesial experience presupposed in the *Corpus Dionysiacum* and the requirements of the secular academic 'doctrine of decontextualization'.

Within psychoanalysis there is a similar conflict between the experiential knowledge of psychoanalysis available to the patient or the therapist, and the academic disciplines of psychoanalytic studies. These tensions contain an apophatic dynamic as the language and practices of the experiential and the academic constantly challenge, undermine and amplify each other. I attempt to be alive to these tensions throughout this study.

Notes

1 Brown, Peter (1982), 'The Rise and Function of the Holy Man in Late Antiquity', in *Society and the Holy in Late Antiquity*. London: Faber and Faber, p. 135.
2 Wittgenstein, Ludwig (1980), *Culture and Value*. Chicago: University of Chicago Press, p. 49, quoted by David M. Hay (1998), 'The Veiled Thoughts of the Therapeutae', in *Mediators of the Divine: Horizons of Prophecy, Divination, Dreams and Theurgy in Mediterranean Antiquity*, Robert M. Berchman (ed.). Atlanta, GA: Scholars Press.
3 Dionysius has been variously referred to as Pseudo-Dionysius, Dionysius the Pseudo-Areopagite, Pseudo-Denys etc. For the sake of simplicity I will refer to him as Dionysius throughout, unless I am making a direct quotation from another author. Further comments on his identity can be found in Chapter 2. All quotations, unless otherwise indicated, are from Colm Luibheid (trans.) (1987), *Pseudo-Dionysius: The Complete Works*, P. Rorem (foreword, notes, trans. collaboration), R. Roques (preface), J. Pelikan, J. Leclercq and K. Froehlich (introductions), New York: Paulist Press. They follow established convention whereby the name of the work is indicated in initials followed the line number. I will indicate the name of the work the first time it appears. Thereafter it will appear as an initial, i.e. *The Divine Names* line 893B is DN 839B.
4 Lossky, Vladimir (1957), *The Mystical Theology of the Eastern Church*. Crestwood, NY: St Vladimir's Seminary Press, pp. 38–9.
5 Coakley, Sarah (2008), 'Introduction: Re-Thinking Dionysius the Areopagite', *Modern Theology*, 24(4): 537.
6 Grinberg, Leon (1969), 'New Ideas: Conflict and Evolution', *International Journal of Psychoanalysis*, 50: 517.
7 *The Ecclesiastical Hierarchy*, EH 432B.
8 Ellenberger, Henri (1970), *The Discovery of the Unconscious: The History and Evolution of Dynamic Psychiatry*. New York: Basic Books.
9 Whyte, L. L. (1978), *The Unconscious Before Freud*. London: Julian Friedmann, p. 80.
10 Ellenberger, Henri (1957), 'The Unconscious before Freud', *Bulletin of the Menninger Clinic*, 21(1): 4.
11 Burke, Kenneth (1969), *A Grammar of Motives*. Berkeley: University of California Press, p. 317.
12 Sells, Michael A. and James Webb (1997), 'Lacan and Bion: Psychoanalysis and the Mystical Language of "Un-Saying"', *Journal of Melanie Klein and Object Relations*, 15(2): 243–264.
13 Goudsmit, Arno L. (1998), *Towards a Negative Understanding of Psychotherapy*. PhD thesis. Rijksuniversiteit Groningen.

14 Anderson, S. Michael (1984), *Therapy as Self-Emptying: Doing Pastoral Psychotherapy From an Apophatic Perspective*. DST dissertation, Emory University.

15 Dourley, John P. (1992), *A Strategy for a Loss of Faith: Jung's Proposal*. Toronto: Inner City Books.

16 Karlsson, Gunnar (2000), 'The Question of Truth Claims in Psychoanalysis', *Scandinavian Psychoanalytic Review*, 23(1): 4.

17 Frank, S. L. (1983), *The Unknowable: An Ontological Introduction to the Philosophy of Religion*. Athens, OH: Ohio University Press, p. 108.

18 Morel, Ferndinand (1918), *Essai sur l'Introversion Mystique: Etude Psychologique de Pseudo-Denys l'Areopagite et de Quelques Autres cas de Mysticisme*. Geneve: Librairie Kundig, pp. 136–7: '[…] the "system" of Dionysius offers this essentially double analogy with autistic thought: 1st It is egocentric. 2nd The criteria of plausibility is totally excluded and replaced by the sole criteria of pleasure. […] Therefore, this confusion of objective internal reality with a metaphysical egocentricity is a particular and very common form of mythomania: the creation and fulfillment of illusions, and quasi-hallucinatory confusion of these with reality.' (my translation).

19 Turner, Denys (2005), 'How to Read the Pseudo-Denys Today?', *International Journal of Systematic Theology*, 7(4): 434–5.

20 Mortley, Raoul (1986), *From Word to Silence: I The Rise and Fall of Logos, II The Way of Negation, Christian and Greek*. Bonn: Peter Hanstein.

21 McGinn, Bernard (1992), *The Foundations of Mysticism: Origins to the Fifth Century*. London: SCM Press; (1995), *The Growth of Mysticism: From Gregory the Great to the Twelfth Century*. London: SCM Press; (1998), *The Flowering of Mysticism: Men and Women in the New Mysticism – 1200–1350*. New York: Crossroads.

22 de Certeau, Michel (1992), *The Mystic Fable*. Chicago: University of Chicago Press.

23 Carabine, Deirdre (1995), *The Unknown God: Negative Theology in the Platonic Tradition: Plato to Eriugena*. Louvain: Peeters Press.

24 Sells, Michael A. (1994), *Mystical Languages of Unsaying*. Chicago: University of Chicago Press.

25 Derrida, Jacques (1992), 'How to Avoid Speaking: Denials' and 'Post-Scriptum: Aporias, Ways and Voices', in *Derrida and Negative Theology*, Howard Coward and Toby Foshay (eds), Albany, NY: SUNY Press.

26 Marion, Jean-Luc (2001), *The Idol and Distance*. New York: Fordham University Press.

27 Yannaras, Christos (2005), *On the Absence and Unknowability of God: Heidegger and the Areopagite*. London: T & T Clark, originally published in Greek in 1967.

28 Carlson, Thomas, A. (1999), *Indiscretion: Finitude and the Naming of God*. Chicago: University of Chicago Press.

29 Boeve, Lieven (2004), 'Cultural Apophaticism: A Challenge for Contemporary Theology', in *Rethinking Ecumenism: Strategies for the 21st Century*, Freek L. Bakker, et al (eds). Zoetermeer: Meinema; (2002), 'The Rediscovery of Negative Theology Today: The Narrow Gulf between Theology and Philosophy', in *Theologie Negative* (Biblioteca del' 'Archivio di Filosofia', 59), M. Olivetti (ed.). Rome: CEDAM; (2000), 'Christus Postmodernus: an attempt at apophatic Christology', in *The Myriad Christ: Plurality and the Quest for Unity in Contemporary Christology*, T. Merrigan and J. Haers (eds.), BETL, 152. Leuven: Peeters.

30 Fitzpatrick, Sean Joseph (2000), *Saying and Unsaying Mysticism: The Problem of Defining Mysticism in the Social Sciences*. PhD thesis Rice University.

31 Walker, Andrew George (1979), *Two versions of Sociological Discourse: The Apophatic and Cataphatic Grounds of Social Science*. PhD thesis Goldsmiths College, University of London.

32 Zembylas, Michalinos (2005), 'A Pedagogy of Unknowing: Witnessing Unknowability in Teaching and Learning', *Studies in Philosophy and Education*, 24(2).

33 Abunuwara, Kimberley (1998), 'Drawing on Levinas to Redefine Education: Making the Unknowable the New Priority', *Education*, 119(1).

34 Wolosky, Shira (1995), *Language Mysticism: The Negative Way of Language in Eliot, Beckett, and Celan*. Stanford, CA: Stanford University Press.

35 Franke, William P. (2007), *On What Cannot Be Said: Apophatic Discourses in Philosophy, Religion, Literature and the Arts: Classic Formulations*. Notre Dame, IN: Notre Dame University Press; (2007), *On What Cannot Be Said: Apophatic Discourses in Philosophy, Religion, Literature and the Arts: Vol. 2, Modern and Contemporary Transformations*. Notre Dame, IN: Notre Dame University Press; see also (2004), 'A Philosophy of the Unsayable: Apophasis and the Experience of Truth and Totality', *Analecta Husserliana*, 83.

36 Franke, personal communication.

37 Saward, John (1974), 'Towards an Apophatic Anthropology', *Irish Theological Quarterly*, 41.

38 Bernauer, James (1990), *Michel Foucault's Force of Flight: Toward an Ethics for Thought*. Atlantic Highlands, NJ: Humanities Press International.

39 Carlson, Thomas A. (1998), 'The Poverty and Poetry of Indiscretion: Negative Theology and Negative Anthropology in Contemporary and Historical Perspective', *Christianity and Literature*, 17(2).

40 Otten, W. (1999), 'In the Shadow of the Divine: Negative Theology and Negative Anthropology in Augustine, Pseudo-Dionysius and Eriugena', *Heythrop Journal*, 40: 438–55.

41 Caputo, John (1997), *The Prayers and Tears of Jacques Derrida: Religion without Religion*. Bloomington, IN: Indiana University Press, p. 56.

42 Bradley, Arthur (2004), *Negative Theology and Modern French Philosophy*. London: Routledge, p. 20.

43 CW9ii 1–2. Quotations from Jung's *Collected Works* follow the convention of listing the volume and paragraph (i.e. *Collected Works* volume 9ii, paragraphs 1–2: CW9ii 1–2). The titles of particular essays appear in the main body of the text where they are integral to the argument. *The Collected Works of C. G. Jung*, 20 vols, Sir Herbert Read, Michael Fordham, and Gerhard Adler (eds), William McGuire (exec. ed.), R. F. C. Hull (trans.). Princeton, NJ: Princeton University Press.

44 CW11 417.

45 CW17 146.

46 CW17 173.

47 CW17 174.

48 Philo, http://www.earlychristianwritings.com/yonge/book34.html.

49 Henderson, David (1998), 'Solitude and Solidarity: A Philosophy of Supervision', in *Psychoanalytic and Jungian Supervision*, Petruska Clarkson (ed.). London, Whurr; (1999), 'From Shaman to Therapist', in *Therapy on the Couch*, Susan Greenberg (ed.), David Henderson (Consulting Editor). London, Camden Press.

50 Jonas, Hans (1963), *The Gnostic Religion*. Boston: Beacon Press, p. 199.

51 While the sense in which he uses the term, negative theology, is different, it is amusing to note another warning, which was delivered in 1857 by the Rev. Josiah Bateman. He preached a sermon in Manchester in which he said, 'One great cause of sin is the secret lurking hope of escaping with impunity from its consequences. This is a strong delusion; and upon it NEGATIVE THEOLOGY rears its superstructure, teaching that Holy Scripture does not mean what it has always been understood to mean – that God will not execute the threatenings He has pronounced, and that the punishment of the wicked will not be final nor eternal. Let us, then, attempt to illustrate this delusion, to trace its source, and to shew its fallacy.' 'Negative Theology', in *Things That Accompany Salvation: Nineteen Sermons, Preached in St. Ann's Church, Manchester*. London: James Nisbet and Co., p. 193.

52 Turner (2005), p. 437.

Chapter 2

The *Corpus Dionysiacum*

Dionysius' potent set of writings have had an influence that belies their size. The works that survive are the *Divine Names* (DN), the *Celestial Hierarchy* (CH), the *Ecclesiastical Hierarchy* (EH), the *Mystical Theology* (MT) and nine letters. The authenticity of a tenth letter is disputed. He refers to several other works: *The Symbolic Theology*, *The Theological Representations*, *Divine Hymns*, *Concerning Justice and the Judgement of God*, *The Soul* and *The Conceptual and the Perceptual*. There is no settled scholarly opinion as to whether these works are missing or are fictions. The *Corpus Dionysiacum* (CD) offers a rich tapestry of philosophical, theological, scriptural and liturgical references. As a rule these references are not cited directly, but have been identified by textual analysis. The author demonstrates a breadth and depth of reading and an acute sensitivity to contemporary debates. He stands at the confluence of Greek philosophy and biblical tradition.

No original manuscripts of the *Corpus Dionysiacum* survive. Dionysius wrote sometime between the death of Proclus in AD 485 and the death of Sergius of Reshaina in AD 536. His work incorporates important ideas and even verbatim extracts from Proclus. The earliest known manuscript is a Syriac translation by Sergius of Reshaina, which is at St Catherine's monastery at Mt Sinai. This particular manuscript dates from the end of the sixth century. There are several distinct manuscript traditions in Greek, Syriac and Arabic. Scholars are working to clarify the relationship between these manuscript traditions and to establish a reliable history of the translations.[1]

The earliest datable references to the *Corpus Dionysiacum* are in the writing of Severus of Antioch (d. AD 536). Severus refers to the works of Dionysius three times in writings, which can be dated between AD 518 and AD 528.[2] References by other writers proliferate throughout the sixth century. John of Scythopolis wrote his *Prologue* and *Scholia* to the *Corpus Dionysiacum* probably between AD 537 and AD 543.[3] The status of the work has been controversial from the beginning. The writings were used to bolster the arguments of different factions in theological disputes of the time. It is not always clear how much this was because of the apostolic authority claimed by the author and how much it was because of the cogency of his arguments. It has been observed, however, that given the supposed apostolic authority of the writings it is surprising that they were not quoted more often. 'The few appeals to Dionysius are almost inconsequential in comparison with the many thousands of times Athanasius, the Gregories, Cyril of Alexandria, or Basil the Great were introduced into the controversies of the first half of the sixth century.'[4]

Nevertheless, after an initial period of dispute he was accepted as reliable and during the Middle Ages became accepted as an authority:

> The fact must, indeed, appear remarkable that these very writings, though rejected outright by such an authority as Hypatius, were within little more than a century looked upon as genuine by Catholics, so that they could be used against the heretics during the Lateran Council in 649.[5]

In the West the *Corpus Dionysiacum* is fundamental to the work of Eriugena, Hugh of Saint-Victor, Albertus Magnus, Thomas Aquinas, Bonaventure, Dante, Grosseteste, Thomas Gallus, the author of the Cloud of Unknowning, Eckhardt and John of the Cross. In the East, Maximus the Confessor, John Damascene, Germanus of Constantinople, Nicetas Stethatos, Gregory Palamas, Barlaam the Calabrian and Nicolas Cabasilas developed and extended the Dionysian project in various directions. Remarkably, the *Corpus Dionysiacum* continues in our own time to feature in philosophical and theological arguments by writers such as Bataille, Voegelin, Derrida, Marion, Caputo, Carlson and de Vries, as well as the expanding literature on mysticism. According to Mortley:

> It is difficult to overestimate the importance of pseudo-Dionysius for the history of European culture, particularly for the Latin segment of it. The French in particular look back to the Areopagite for the explanation of much that is in their culture, in respect of theology and philosophy, but also in respect of political institutions. The notion of hierarchy in the Areopagite was to play a role in establishing and ordering the social structure of the Middle Ages.[6]

The search for the identity of Dionysius is one of the great detective games of late antique studies. He presents himself as a contemporary of the Apostles; however, the fact that he quotes extensively from Neoplatonic and patristic writers shows that he cannot have been a contemporary of Paul. I wonder, however, whether readers in late antiquity were all duped by his alleged fraud. Was it not a common practice to hide one's identity behind a pseudonym or to attribute one's work to a master or patron? Surely there were many sophisticated readers who recognized the crafted nature of the *Corpus Dionysiacum*. 'Adopting the persona of an ancient figure was a long established rhetorical device … less a forgery in the modern sense than an acknowledgement of reception and transmission.'[7]

The perilous political situation may also have contributed to his adoption of a pseudonym. Sergius of Reshaina at the end of his translation of the *Corpus Dionysiacum* writes of Dionysius:

Everything that one is not permitted to say, and *that which a man is prohib-ited from speaking about with elevation, in a marveling manner, and in public*, he has consigned to his holy books, because there he might speak divinely.[8]

Hathaway wonders whether given the closure of the academy the 'every-thing' that was not permitted was the philosophy of Proclus and Damascius. Dionysius presents himself standing within a tradition as a channel, rather than as a creative originator of a doctrine.

Hypatius responded to Severus' citation of Dionysius with the retort, 'Those quotations you claim to have come from the Blessed Dionysius the Areopagite – how can you prove that they are authentic, as you maintain? For if they do come from him, they could not have been unknown to Blessed Cyril?'[9] The authenticity of the writing was questioned in the fifteenth century by Lorenzo Valla.[10] In the nineteenth century Koch and Stiglmayr separately established beyond doubt the connection between the *Corpus Dionysiacum* and Proclus.[11]

E. R. Dodds described him simply as 'an unknown eccentric'.[12] According to Golitzin, 'Over the past fifty years Dionysius had been variously identified as Ammonius Sakkas, Dionysius the Great of Alexandria, a disciple of Basil of Caesarea in Cappadocia, Severus of Antioch, Peter the Iberian, Damascius last of the *diadochoi* and Sergius of Reshaina.'[13] Golitzin himself argues for Peter the Iberian. Arthur supports Sergius of Reshaina.[14] Stiglmayr proposed Severus of Antioch.[15] Perczel contends that 'Dionysius could be either a personal disci-ple or a (former) friend of Proclus'.[16] He also argues that the pseudonym was adopted to protect the writer from powerful political opponents. It would have been dangerous to publish his writings under his own name. According to Burns, 'perhaps we should not exclude the possibility that the name is a pseudonym for a nun, or Byzantine empress'.[17] Noutsoubidze and Honigman claimed that Dionysius 'was Petre Iberi, the fifth-century Georgian theologian, and Bishop of Mayum'.[18] Gersh believes that Dionysius was a student at the academy.[19] According to Kojeve, 'Damascius wrote the *Corpus Areopagiticum* as a retort against Christian criticisms of pagan philosophy.'[20] While not formally supporting his candidature, Hathaway outlines how Heraiscus the Egyptian, a student of Damascius and Proclus, fits the profile.[21] Mortley, while declining to offer a name, feels that 'the author seems to be working in a non-Arian, somewhat Gnostic, Christian, Athenian Neoplatonist tradition'.[22] As Golitzin observes, the choice of which candidate to champion often says as much about the agenda of the proposer as it does about Dionysius. The most common attribution is to an unknown Syrian monk.

The aspect of the *Corpus Dionysiacum* which is significant for this study is the triad: *kataphasis, apophasis, ekstasis* (affirmation, negation, ecstasy). This is one of a number of triads that can be identified within the writings. They are all based ultimately on the Neoplatonic structure of emanation and return: *monos, proodos, epistrophe* (remaining, proceeding, returning). For Dionysius, *eros* is the engine of this dynamic.

In the literature about the relationship between Dionysius' Neoplatonism and his Christianity, there is a considerable body of opinion that holds that he has used Neoplatonism to subvert Christianity. Others believe that Neoplatonism is subsumed by Christianity in his synthesis. It is not the purpose of this study to determine Dionysius' orthodoxy; to take sides in a struggle which has been raging since the work first appeared. Its aim is rather to use some concepts, images and metaphors which appear in the *Corpus Dionysiacum* to expand our understanding of the psychotherapeutic process and to reframe some elements of psychoanalytic theory. Nonetheless, in my view in his own mind Dionysius was using Christianity to expand and transform the Neoplatonic concept of providence. Divine providence embraces and permeates all aspects of the triadic structures of the *Corpus Dionysiacum*. The concept of providence can be compared to the concept of meaning in psychotherapy.

Dionysius was not writing from a position that assumed the eternity of the world, a position that would have been a given if he were defending Neoplatonism against Christianity. The sense of creation permeates all his work. In addition, if his intention were to subvert Christianity it seems hard to imagine why the work would be so steeped in biblical, liturgical and patristic references. It is a Christian project rather than pagan project. However one characterizes the work it seems clear from his style that it was undertaken in good faith.

Notes

1   Lilla, Salvatore (2001), 'Brief Notes on the Greek *Corpus Areopagiticum* in Rome during the Early Middle Ages', *Dionysius*, 59, 201–214; Treiger, Alexander (2004), *On the Arabic Version of Ps.-Dionysius the Areopagite's 'Mystical Theology'*. MA dissertation, Hebrew Union University, Jerusalem.
2   Rorem, Paul and John C. Lamoreaux (1998), *John of Scythopolis and the Dionysian Corpus: Annotating the Areopagite*. Oxford: Oxford University Press, p. 11.
3   Rorem and Lamoreaux, p. 39.
4   Rorem and Lamoreaux, p. 21.
5   Stiglmayr, J. (1909), 'Dionysius the Pseudo-Areopagite', *The Catholic Encyclopedia*. New York: Robert Appleton, p. 5.
6   Mortley, Raoul (1986), *From Word to Silence II: The Way of Negation, Christian and Greek*. Bonn: Peter Hanstein, p. 221.
7   Corrigan, Kevin and L. Michael Harrington, 'Pseudo-Dionysius the Areopagite', in *The Stanford Encyclopedia of Philosophy*, available at: http://plato.stanford.edu/entries/pseudo-dionysius-areopagite/, p. 2.
8   Hathaway, Ronald F. (1969), *Hierarchy and the Definition of Order in the Letters of Pseudo-Dionysius: A Study in the Form and Meaning of the Pseudo-Dionysian Writings*. The Hague: Martinus Nijhoff, p. 25.
9   Coles, Alasdair Charles (2003), *The Treatment of Matter and Divinisation Language in the Ecclesiastical Hierarchy of Pseudo-Dionysius as a Basis for Evaluating his Sacramental Theology*. PhD thesis, Heythrop College, University of London, p. 14.
10 Coles, p. 15.
11 Koch, H. (1895), 'Der pseudo-epigraphische Character der dionysischen Schriften', *Theologische quartalschrift*, 77; Stiglmayr, J. (1895), 'Der Neuplatoniker Proclus als Vorlage des sogen. Dionysius Areopagiten in der Laehre vom Ubel', *Historisches Jahrbuch*, 16.

12 Dodds, E. R. (1963), 'Introduction' in Proclus (1963), *The Elements of Theology*, translated by E. R. Dodds, Oxford: Oxford University Press, p. xxvi.

13 Golitzin, Alexander (1994), *Et Introibo Ad Altare Dei: The Mystagogy of Dionysius Areopagita, with Special Reference to its Predecessors in the Eastern Christian Tradition*. Thessaloniki: Analecta Vlatadon, p. 24.

14 Arthur, Rosemary A. (2008), *Pseudo-Dionysius as Polemicist: The Development and Purpose of the Angelic Hierarchy in Sixth Century Syria*. Aldershot, UK: Ashgate, p. 197.

15 Stiglmayr (1928), 'Der Sogennant Dionysios A. und Severus von Antiochen', *Scholastik*, 3: 1–27, 161–89, cited in Campbell, Thomas L. (1981), *Dionysius the Pseudo-Areopagite: The Ecclesiatical Hierarchy*. Lanham, MD: University Press of America.

16 Perczel, Istvan (2000), 'Pseudo-Dionysius and the Platonic Theology: A Preliminary Study', in *Proclus et la Theologie Platonicienne*, Segonds and Steel (eds). Leuven: Leuven University Press, p. 530.

17 Personal communication.

18 Chkheidze, Paata (1994), 'Morality and Ethics according to Shota Rustaveli's Epic "The Knight in the Panther's Skin"', in *National Identity as an Issue of Knowledge and Morality: Georgian Philosophical Studies I*, N. V. Chavchavdze, G. Nodia and P. Peachey (eds). Washington, DC: The Council for Research in Values and Philosophy, p. 301.

19 Gersh, Stephen (1978), *From Iamblichus to Eriugena: An Investigation of the Prehistory and Evolution of the Pseudo-Dionysisan Tradition*. Leiden: Brill, p. 1.

20 Gersh, p. 4.

21 Hathaway, pp. 28–9.

22 Mortley, p. 221.

Chapter 3

Apophasis in Dionysius

The *Corpus Dionysiacum* is a blend of late Neoplatonic philosophy[1] and Syrian Christian theology.[2] In Proclus' version of the Neoplatonic theory of emanation and return, 'every effect remains (*mone*) in its cause, proceeds (*prodos*) from it, and returns (*epistrophe*) to it'.[3] In the *Corpus Dionysiacum*, emanation represents the outpouring of the *thearchia* (divine source).[4] The return is described by Dionysius as the movement from the perceptual to the conceptual and, finally, beyond the conceptual to unknowing and silence. This journey of return is accomplished by negations (*apophaseis*). Dionysius presents a distinctive vision of the mutual ecstasy of the *thearchia*, the Christian community gathered in liturgical celebration, and the whole of the cosmos. The *thearchia* flows out of itself, so to speak, to be united with the community and the community turns toward the One. 'Emanation and return describe, respectively, divine and human ecstasy.'[5] *Eros* powers this dynamic union.[6] It 'is the "motor" of Providence ... The movement of love brings about love's diffusion ... He moves into creation because, simply, he desires it.'[7]

In addition to its distinctive approach, the *Corpus Dionysiacum* has features in common with other apophatic texts, which are part of the 'implicit logic and conventions of *apophasis* as a mode of discourse'.[8] Apophatic texts are commonly interpreted either as philosophical statements or as descriptions of mystical experience. To some extent this reflects the difference between the Greek, *theoria*, and the Latin, *contemplatio*.[9] Interpretations of the apophatic elements in the *Corpus Dionysiacum* tend to emphasize either a philosophical/epistemological or an experiential/mystagogical approach. Writers who emphasize an epistemological interpretation include Tomasic[10], Mortley[11] and Gersh.[12] The most comprehensive argument for interpreting the *Corpus Dionysiacum* from an experiential perspective is made by Blum and Golitzin.[13] Counet,[14] Yannaras[15] and Aberth[16] also highlight an experiential understanding of the *Corpus Dionysiacum*.

In this chapter I will review the use of some important concepts (including *kataphasis, anagou, apophasis, aphairesis,*) that characterize Dionysian apophatic discourse. These features have not been so extensively documented before.

Kataphasis

The effects of divine providence are described in a profusion of images and propositions drawn from scripture and philosophy. 'The cataphatic is, we might say, the verbose element in theology, it is the Christian mind deploying all the resources of language in the effort to express something about God.'[17] According to Dionysius:

> There are too those other sacred pictures used to represent God, so that what is hidden may be brought out into the open and multiplied, what is unique and undivided may be divided up, and multiple shapes and forms be given to what has neither shape nor form. All this is to enable the one capable of seeing the beauty hidden within these images to find that they are truly mysterious, appropriate to God and filled with a great theological light.[18]

Kataphasis (affirmation) and *apophasis* (negation) are not distinct moments in time, or two aspects of a linear process. In line with Neoplatonic philosophy, in the *Corpus Dionysiacum* they are simultaneous. According to Fisher, this language 'serves an epistemological-semiotic rather than ontological function'.[19] It was Eriugena who adapted these aspects of the *Corpus Dionysiacum* to fit an historical model of creation (*kataphasis*) and salvation (*apophasis*) and merged 'the Greek language of "procession and return" with the Latin language of "nature and grace"'.[20] It is this Latinized *Corpus Dionysiacum* which was used by Thomas Aquinas. Despite the fact that he cited Dionysius explicitly more than 1,700 times, 'Thomas does not make use of Dionysius' emphasis on God as beyond or above being, nor of union as our final goal.'[21]

Apophasis is often presented as a simple denial of *kataphasis*. This is the case in Aristotle, where *apophasis* is the denial of a proposition (*kataphasis*).[22] Within the *Corpus Dionysiacum*, however, *apophasis* has the effect of transcending the kataphatic not just cancelling it out. Negation is not the opposite of affirmation:

> Since it is the Cause of all beings, we should posit and ascribe to it all the affirmations we make in regard to beings, and, more appropriately, we should negate (*apophaskein*) all these affirmations, since it surpasses all being. Now we should not conclude that the negations (*apophaseis*) are simply the opposites of the affirmations, but rather that the cause of all is considerably prior to this, beyond privations, beyond every denial (*aphairesin*), beyond every assertion.[23]

Apophasis is at work at the heart of Dionysius' kataphatic celebrations of the divine:

> The very same things are both similar and dissimilar to God. They are similar to him to the extent that they share what cannot be shared. They are dissimilar to him in that as effects they fall so very short of their Cause and are infinitely and incomparably subordinate to Him.[24]

The anagogic interpretation of perceptible symbols negates their literal meanings and raises the meanings up to the conceptual level. 'It is the power of the divine similarity which returns all created things toward their Cause.'[25]

Anagou, anagoge

Within the *Corpus Dionysiacum* the terms *anagou*[26] and *anagoge*[27] are translated by Luibheid as 'uplifting'. They describe the apophatic element in the interpretation of symbols. 'The uplifting is not accomplished by the symbols in themselves, as if they possess any magical efficacy; it occurs in the process of interpreting them, in the contemplative movement from the perceptible "up" to the conceptual.'[28]

Iamblichus claims that theurgy 'connects the soul with the self-begotten and self-moved God, and with the all-sustaining, intellectual, and all-adorning powers of the God, and likewise with that power of him which elevates to truth'.[29] Rorem observes that 'by interchanging *anogoge* with *epistrophe* he [Iamblichus] fully harmonized this Chaldean rite with the late Neoplatonic doctrine of procession and return'.[30]

The movement of return starts in the realm of the perceptual with the most dissimilar and inappropriate symbols of the divine:

> Now you may wonder why it is that, after starting out from the highest category when our method involved assertions, we begin now from the lowest category when it involves a denial. The reason is this. When we assert what is beyond every assertion, we must then proceed from what is most akin to it, and as we do so we make the affirmation on which everything else depends. But when we deny that which is beyond every denial, we have to start by denying those qualities which differ most from the goal we hope to attain. Is it not closer to reality to say that God is life and goodness rather than that he is air or stone? Is it not more accurate to deny that drunkenness and rage can be attributed to him than to deny that we can apply to him the terms of speech and thought?[31]

The process of interpretation then moves 'up' from the most inappropriate images to those that seem to be more appropriate symbols of the work of providence, which nonetheless must in their turn be negated:[32]

> He modeled it on the hierarchies of heaven, and clothed these immaterial hierarchies in numerous material figures and forms so that, in a way appropriate to our nature, we might be uplifted (*anagou*) from these most venerable images to interpretations and assimilations which are simple and inexpressible.[33]

Aphairesis

Aphairesis (abstraction) plays an important role in the *Corpus Dionysiacum*. 'Denial (*aphairesis*) of all beings' is a way of praising or celebrating 'the Light beyond all deity'.[34] 'The negative (*aphairesios*) expresses excess.'[35] In some places *aphairesis* appears in relation to *thesis* (affirmation, proposition, position): 'the assertion (*thesis*) of all things, the denial (*aphairesis*) of all things, that which is beyond every assertion (*thesin*) and denial (*aphairesin*)'.[36] According to Golitizin, '*aphairesis* is a fundamental aspect of the creature's appropriation of the divine from the very beginnings of its ascent. It is therefore present at every stage of the Dionysian anagogy.'[37]

Even non-being, by its denial (*aphairesis*) of being or, in Luibheid's translation, 'repelling being', unwittingly shows its longing for the Good:

> And if it is reverent to say, even that which *is not* desires the all-transcendent Good and struggles, by its denial (*aphairesin*) of all things, to find its rest in the Good which verily transcends all being.[38]

Through its participation in *aphairesis*, non-being has a share not only in the Good, but also in the Beautiful:

> And I would even be so bold as to claim that nonbeing also shares in the Beautiful and the Good, because nonbeing, when applied transcendently to God in the sense of a denial (*aphairesin*) of all things is itself beautiful and good.[39]

At the other end of the spectrum, at the most simple conceptual level, *aphairesis* plays a part in the movement into unknowing (*agnosia*). Something about God can be known 'from the arrangement of everything', but 'we pass by the way of denial (*aphairesei*)' to unknowing.[40]

In Chapter Two of *Mystical Theology* Dionysius offers a paradoxical prayer:

> If only we lacked sight and knowledge so as to see, so as to know, unseeing and unknowing, that which lies beyond all vision and knowledge. For this would be really to see and to know: to praise the Transcendent One in a transcending way, namely through the denial (*aphaireseos*) of all things.[41]

He closes *Mystical Theology* with a flurry of apophatic intensity (what Kenny calls 'the shock of *aphairesis*'[42]) by invoking the negation of negation:

> It is beyond assertion (*thesis*) and denial (*aphairesis*). We make assertions (*theseis*) and denials (*aphaireseis*) of what is next to it, but never of it, for it is both beyond every assertion, being the perfect and unique cause of all things, and by virtue of its preeminently simple and absolute nature, free of every limitation beyond every limitation; it is also beyond every denial (*aphairesin*).[43]

Apophasis

There is a range of definitions of *apophasis*. It was used as a legal term from the fourth century BC.[44] Before this it had been used by Demosthenes.[45] Aristotle uses the term in his *Categories*. It started to be used in negative theology in the sense of denial or negation from the fifth century AD.[46] It appears in an English text in 1550.[47] Definitions in 1657 and 1753 bring out the aspect of irony.[48] Contemporary definitions include: 'The mention of something in disclaiming intention of mentioning it.'[49]; 'Denying one's intention to talk or write about a subject, but making the denial in such a way that the subject is actually discussed. *Apophasis* asserts or emphasizes something by pointedly seeming to pass over, ignore, or deny it.'[50]; 'Make an assertion while disproving it at the same time.'[51]; 'The *rhetorical* figure in which one states something while seeming to deny it.'[52]; 'Rhetorical device of emphasizing a fact, by pretending to ignore or deny it.'[53]; 'To say no.'[54]; 'To speak off, deny.'[55]

Sells translates *apophasis* as 'unsaying'. He distinguishes between apophatic theory and apophatic discourse. 'Apophatic theory affirms the ultimate ineffability of the transcendent.' Apophatic discourse describes those 'writings in which unnameability is not only asserted but performed'.[56] It seems to me that the *Corpus Dionysiacum* could be described, in Sells' terms, as apophatic discourse, because the text is trying to propel the reader towards unknowing. The *Corpus Dionysiacum* is not a simple statement of the proposition that the *thearchia* is ineffable.

Sells identifies three elements of apophatic writing:

> Classical Western *apophasis* shares three key features: (1) the metaphor of overflowing or 'emanation' which is often in creative tension with the language of intentional, demiurgic creation; (2) dis-ontological discursive effort to avoid reifying the transcendent as an 'entity' or 'being' or 'thing'; (3) a distinctive dialectic of transcendence and immanence in which the utterly transcendent is revealed as the utterly immanent.[57]

Citing Gersh, McGinn describes two types of apophatic theology – the subjective and objective. In the subjective form it is the limitations of the human that render the first principle unknowable and ineffable. (McGinn subdivides Gersh's category into three varieties of subjective apophaticism.) In the objective type the first principle is unknowable 'without reference to our mode of conceiving'.[58]

Another approach sees 'human self-ignorance as a reflection of divine unknowability'.[59] According to Gregory of Nyssa, 'Since the nature of our mind, which is according to the icon of the Creator, evades our knowledge, it keeps an accurate resemblance to the superior nature, retaining the imprint of the incomprehensible [fixed] by the unknown within it.'[60] Marion argues that the inability of man to conceive of the One is not a failure but that it links the incomprehensibility of man with the incomprehensibility of God in what he describes as the 'privilege of unknowing'.[61] Just as the One cannot be reduced to an object of thought, neither can the human. Hence apophatic thought is a guarantor of the dignity of the human.

Dionysius asserts that the 'preference is for the way up through negations (*apophaseon*), since this stands the soul outside everything which is correlative with its own finite nature'.[62] This resonates with Marion's statement that 'only the infinite and incomprehensible can comprehend man, and thus tell him of and show him to himself.'[63]

While it is appropriate when describing the One to name all the beings which it has created, it is necessary to unsay these positive statements. For Dionysius *apophasis* is not merely a denial of a proposition (*kataphasis*), as it is in the case of Aristotle. A properly apophatic approach requires the negation of negation:

> Since it is the Cause of all beings, we should posit and ascribe to it all the affirmations we make in regard to beings, and, more appropriately, we should negate (*apophaskein*) all these affirmations, since it surpasses all being. Now we should not conclude that the negations (*apophaseis*) are simply the opposites of the affirmations, but rather that the cause of all is considerably prior to this, beyond privations, beyond every denial (*aphairesin*), beyond every assertion.[64]

There is a link between love and negation. 'Every affirmation regarding Jesus' love for humanity has the force of a negation (*apophaseous*) pointing toward transcendence.'[65] The power of love simplifies and uplifts by negating all that is not the One.

Hoion

According to Sells, 'Plotinus uses the term *hoion* (as it were) to indicate that a name or predicate should not be taken at face value.'[66] The frequency of Plotinus' use of the term increases the higher the level of ascent he is describing. It is what Sells calls an 'apophatic marker'. Where this term appears in the *Corpus Dionysiacum* Rorem argues that it is a 'disclaimer', and that the 'qualification seems to apologize for Neoplatonic language'.[67] Luibheid translates it as, 'if one may put it so',[68] 'so to speak',[69] 'if I may express it this way',[70] and 'if one must put it this way'.[71] Sells is highlighting the positive use of this literary device to heighten the 'apophatic intensity' of the text, whereas Rorem is drawing attention to the context in which Dionysius was writing and his need to defend himself against accusations of heresy.

Hyper-

The prefix *hyper-* (above, beyond, super) is used well over 500 times in the *Corpus Dionysiacum*.[72] The most frequent use is in *hyperousios* (beyond all being, supra-essential, above being), which appears at least 116 times.[73] Other terms which occur frequently are *hypercosmos* (above the world, transcend-ent, supernatural, celestial), *hyperexou* (transcend), *hyperkeimai* (lie above, be placed above, transcend, excel) and *hyperphys* (transcending nature, super-natural).[74] This litany of *hyper*-s gives the entire *Corpus Dionysiacum* a peculiar intensity, which can disorient, overwhelm or repulse the reader. However, the concept of God beyond being is not original to Dionysius, since 'in many texts of the period, Platonic, Christian and Neopythagorean, God is formally beyond existence'.[75]

Exaireou

Exaireou (to be removed from, transcend)[76] is used over forty times in the *Corpus Dionysiacum*.[77] Its primary use is to describe the transcendence of the One, which 'surpasses by far (*exairemene*) every sacred thing'.[78] The emana-tion of the One proceeds from 'his transcendent (*exeremenou*) dwelling place … [and] his own transcendent (*exeremenes*) unity'.[79] The transcendence of the One appears to the human eye like sleep. 'The sleep of God refers to the divine transcendence (*exeremenon*) and to the inability of the objects of his providential care to communicate directly with him.'[80]

Given 'the fact that the Godhead transcends (*exeretai*) and surpasses every real and every conceivable power' Dionysius asks, 'in what sense do the theologians praise it as power when it is in fact superior to (*exeremeneu*) power?'[81]

The divine transcendence defines the limits of knowledge. 'Transcendently (*exeremenen*) it contains within itself the boundaries of every natural knowl-edge and energy.'[82] 'And if all knowledge is of that which is and is limited to the realm of the existent, then whatever transcends being must also transcend (*exeremene*) knowledge … although it is the cause of everything, it is not a thing since it transcends (*exeremenon*) all things in a manner beyond being.'[83]

Exaireou can be used to define difference. 'Evil will only be and be seen by contrast with what it opposes, for it will be distinct from (*exertetai*) them, since they are good.'[84] The seraphim are 'transcendent (*exeremene*) beings.'[85]

Dionysius calls upon the familiar Neoplatonic theme of the sculptor to describe one aspect of negation. 'We would be like sculptors who set out to carve a statue. They remove (*exairountes*) every obstacle to the pure view of the hidden image, and simply by this act of clearing aside they show up the beauty which is hidden.'[86] In the process of the sculpting the human hierarchy by the action of providence, 'not every participant is simply removed (*exeretai*) from the Holy of Holies'.[87]

Epekeina

Epekeina,[88] usually translated by Luibheid as transcendent or beyond, appears primarily in the *Divine Names*.[89] The One is the 'cause of existence, and therefore itself transcending (*epekeina*) existence'.[90] 'Its supremely individual identity beyond (*epekeina*) all that is, its oneness beyond (*epekeina*) the source of oneness.'[91]

Knowledge of the One is beyond the capacity of human beings to express. 'We therefore approach that which is beyond (*epekeina*) all as far as our capacities allow us',[92] because 'whatever transcends (*epekeina*) being must also transcend (*exeremene*) knowledge'.[93] 'Therefore when talking of that peace which transcends (*epekeina*) all things, let it be spoken of as ineffable and unknowable.'[94]

For Plato, Plotinus and Proclus the beyond (*epekeina*) was *outside* of being. Cranz argues that 'Plotinus takes Plato's beyond (epekeina) and applies it extensively',[95] but that it is Proclus who pushes the concept to new limits. The One is 'the not being which is beyond being (*epekeina tou ontos*)'.[96] Dionysius adopts Proclus' development of *epekeina*, but combines it with the Jewish sense of the beyond as 'the relation of Yahweh to His creature, *within* the symbolic structure itself'.[97] This simultaneous reference to the *outside* and the *inside* is, according to Sells, a feature of apophatic writing.

Exaiphnes

While *exaiphnes* (sudden or suddenly)[98] appears only twice in the *Corpus Dionysiacum*, it has profound resonance within Greek philosophy[99] and Christian scripture[100] and spiritual writing.[101] Mortley dismisses the importance of the scriptural references, but claims that Dionysius' use of the concept 'strikes a new note in the philosophy of classical antiquity', because it abolishes 'the cornerstone of Western philosophy … the famous principle of non-contradiction, or the excluded middle'.[102] While Golitzin acknowledges the significance of the philosophical dimension, he argues that the scriptural references are essential to a full understanding of what Dionysius means by *exaiphnes*. He also observes that in Syriac exaiphnes is translated as 'out of silence'.

In *The Celestial Hierarchy*, Dionysius compares the divine nature with fire. One attribute of fire is its sudden appearance:

> If ignored it does not seem to be there, but when friction occurs, it will seek out something; it appears suddenly (*exaiphnes*), naturally and of itself, and soon it rises up irresistibly and losing nothing of itself, it communes joyfully with everything.[103]

In the *Third Letter* he describes the revelation of Christ as 'sudden'. 'What comes into view, contrary to hope, from previous obscurity, is described as "sudden" (*exaiphnes*).'[104] It has been seen, but it cannot be known. Despite having come into view Christ is 'hidden even amid the revelation … What is to be said of it remains unsayable; what is to be understood of it remains unknowable.'[105]

According to Hathaway, the order and subject matter of Dionysius' nine letters mirror the nine hypotheses in Plato's *Parmenides*, thus the use of *exaiphnes* in the *Third Letter* echoes its appearance in the third hypothesis of the *Parmenides*.[106]

Golitzin links the use of *exaiphnes* in the *Third Letter* with discussion of the chrism in the *Ecclesiastical Hierarchy*, 'where Christ is both the way and the goal', and with Moses' ascent into the darkness at the summit of the mountain in the *Mystical Theology*. He describes the *Third Letter* as 'Dionysius in a nutshell: christological, liturgical, and – yes – mystical'.[107]

Ekstasis

The One is ecstatic (*ekstasis*[108] or *ekstatikos*[109]) both because it is beyond being and because it flows out of itself toward being. Human ecstasy consists in correctly interpreting the manifestations of the divine and rising above through the means of negations.

In the *Ninth Letter* Dionysius has an extended passage in which he uses the metaphor of drunkenness to describe the ecstasy of the One. 'Quite simply, as "drunk" God stands outside of all good things, being the superfullness of all these things. He surpasses all that is measureless and his abode is above and beyond all that exists.'[110] It is the ecstatic *eros* of the One that creates and sustains the universe:

> This divine yearning (*eros*) brings ecstasy (*ekstatikos*) so that the lover belongs not to self but to the beloved ... And, in truth, it must be said too that the very cause of the universe in the beautiful, good superabundance of his benign yearning (*eros*) for all is also carried outside (*ekstatikes*) of himself in the loving care he has for everything. He is, as it were, beguiled by goodness, by love, and by yearning (*eros*) and is enticed away from his transcendent dwelling place and comes to abide within all things, and he does so by virtue of his supernatural and ecstatic (*ekstatiken*) capacity to remain, nevertheless within himself. [111]

This capacity to 'abide within all things' and yet 'to remain ... within himself' is a further example of the simultaneity of transcendence and immanence which Sells describes as a feature of apophatic writing.

By interpreting scripture correctly, 'we should be taken wholly out of ourselves'.[112] Interpretation through negations leads from sense perceptions, to concepts and, finally, to union with the One. Each level of interpretation is ecstatically transcended:

> The human mind has a capacity to think, through which it looks on conceptual things, and a unity which transcends the nature of the mind, through which it is joined to things beyond itself. And this transcending characteristic must be given to the words we use about God. They must not be given the human sense. We should be taken wholly out of ourselves and become wholly of God.[113]

The *Mystical Theology* begins with a call to ecstasy. 'By an undivided and absolute abandonment (*ekstasei*) of yourself and everything, shedding all and freed from all, you will be uplifted to the ray of the divine shadow which is above everything that is.'[114] Jones' translation brings out a rather different flavour. 'By the irrepressible and absolving ecstasis of yourself and of all, absolved from all, and going away from all.'[115] The sense of absolution does not come through in Luibheid's translation. The word 'irrepressible' evokes the dynamism of the return.

Rist observes that Dionysius uses a Christianized version of Proclean triads to describe divine providence operating in a three-fold ecstasy. Providential *eros* flows from the higher to the lower, between equals and upliftingly from the lower to the higher. [116]

Perczel maintains that there are significant differences between the mysticism of Proclus and of Dionysius. For Proclus union is a prelude to knowledge, while for Dionysius it is the beginning of unknowing:

> Another difference between the two mystical doctrines is that for Proclus, reaching the summit – which means reaching the Principle of all things – is just a prelude and a necessary precondition for the unfolding of the metaphysical science. For Dionysius, reaching the summit is just a prelude for an ecstasis, in which the Principle still remains in a certain sense unreachable. Since this is so, it is perhaps logical that the ecstasis is not followed in the *Mystical Theology* by any kind of positive knowledge. Quite the contrary, all positive knowledge (the height of which is the vision of the 'hypothetical reasons') is merely a prelude for this experience.[117]

Golitzin claims that the *Mystical Theology* and the *Divine Names* are the least original of Dionysius' writing, not because they reflect Neoplatonic philosophy, as others have observed, but because they are consistent with the patristic tradition. In the *Mystical Theology* the knowledge of God is described as the result of reciprocal ecstasies. 'It is an out-going from self, a departure of "a union which exceeds the creaturely powers of intellect and intuition".'[118] Golitzin sees Dionysius' approach to ecstasy as 'one of Dionysius' fundamental, and Christian-inspired, adjustments of pagan thought':[119]

> We recall that the divine and creaturely *exstaseis* are reciprocal, and understand thus that the activity or *energeia* of the divine *exstasis* is the same divine love working in the creature to bring about the *exstasis* of the latter. God pours himself into immanence in order that the realm of contingent being may transcend itself in and through him. The circle imagery is indeed apt, suggesting both the process of divine activity proceeding outwards to bring all back to itself, and the principle of the double *exstasis* having its beginning and end in God.[120]

Corrigan agrees that Dionysius develops a distinctive view of *ecstasis*, but where Louth sees a 'radical opposition between the Platonic vision and Christian mystical theology',[121] Corrigan maintains that Dionysius 'transforms precisely the *Platonic* tradition ... in the spirit of a shared philosophic enterprise'.[122]

Buckley clarifies the difference between Plotinian and Dionysian ecstasy. For Plotinus, emanation is a by-product of the One's self-contemplation or self-desiring (*eros auton*). For Dionysius, however:

> it is from his excess of *erotic* goodness that God is moved to create. The explicit and essential connection between God himself as divine Eros and the Good's self-diffusion, therefore, a connection not made by Plato and Plotinus, is, under the influence of Proclus, established by Dionysius.[123]

Apeiria

Apeiria[124] and *apeiron*[125] are translated variously as infinite, infinity, unlimited or unbounded in the *Corpus Dionysiacum*. Dionysius describes the One as 'at a total remove from every condition, movement, being, rest, dwelling, unity, limit, infinity (*apeirias*), the totality of existence'.[126]

Lilla identifies three different ways in which Dionysius uses the concept of the infinity of the One.[127] Firstly, 'the "one" comprehends all things in itself *potentially*'. For example, in the *Divine Names* Dionysius writes, 'Even to speak of it as "present in everything" is inaccurate since this does not convey the fact that it infinitely (*apeirias*) transcends everything and yet gathers everything within it.':[128]

> In its total simplicity it shakes off all duplication and it embraces everything in its transcendent infinity (*apeirian*) ... He is the boundary to all things and is the unbounded infinity (*apeiria*) about them in a fashion which rises above the contradiction between finite and infinite (*apeirias*).[129]

The One's infinitude is also expressed by the fact that its generativity is endless:

> His power is infinite because all power comes from him and because he transcends all power, even absolute power. He possesses a superabundance of power which endlessly produces an endless number of other powers.[130]

A third sense of infinity is found in the statement that the One is totally unknowable. While the first two senses in which Dionysius uses *apeiria/apeiron* have roots in Plato, Plotinus, Proclus and Damascius, this third use follows Gregory of Nyssa and Aristotle:[131]

> Just as the senses can neither grasp nor perceive the things of the mind, just as representation and shape cannot take in the simple and the shapeless, just as corporal form cannot lay hold of the intangible and incorporeal, by the same standard of truth beings are surpassed by the infinity (*apeiria*) beyond being, intelligences by that oneness which is beyond intelligence.[132]

Hager traces the theme of divine infinity in Plotinus, Proclus and Dionysius. Plotinus and Proclus 'argue to infinity from simplicity', while Dionysius bases his argument on revelation.[133] However, for all three 'the infinity of God is a metaphysically/philosophically grounded position, and not at all an expression of a late antique or oriental, irrational conception of God'.[134]

In line with Plotinus, Dionysius asserts:

> the ascent from the realm of the Intellect and Reason up to the absolute Simplicity of the perfect One as the highest principle is more difficult than the climb from the corporeal world perceivable through the senses on up to the Intellectual World of Ideas ... Mere human abilities of thought and comprehension – which are capable of dealing initially with that which has limits, form and finiteness in the visible world, and then with that which has intelligible form – shrink back from the One in Its Infinity.[135]

Agnousia

Agnousia,[136] *agnoustos*,[137] *agnoustous*[138] and *hyperagnoustos* are used in the *Corpus Dionysiacum* to describe a simple lack of knowledge, an aspect of the relationship with the One or a feature of the One itself.

In the *First Letter* Dionysius gradually transforms the concept. He starts with the common sense statement that 'knowledge makes unknowing (*agnousian*) disappear'. Then he posits 'the unknowing (*agnousia*) regarding God'. This is unknowing *about* God. Finally he claims that 'complete unknowing (*agnousia*) is knowledge':

> Darkness disappears in the light, the more so as there is more light. Knowledge makes unknowing (*agnousian*) disappear, the more so as there is more knowledge. However, think of this not in terms of deprivation but rather in terms of transcendence and then you will be able to say something truer than all truth, namely, that the unknowing (*agnousia*) regarding God escapes anyone possessing physical light and knowledge of beings: His transcendent darkness remains hidden from all light and concealed from all knowledge. Someone beholding God and understanding what he saw has not actually seen God himself but rather something of his which has being which is knowable. For he himself solidly transcends mind and being. He is completely unknown and nonexistent. He exists beyond being and he is known beyond the mind. And this quite positively complete unknowing (*agnousia*) is knowledge of him who is above everything that is known.[139]

In the *Third Letter*, he reiterates the failure of speech and knowledge in relation to the One. 'What is to be said of it remains unsayable; what is to be understood of it remains unknowable (*agnouston*).'[140]

Interestingly, in the *Ecclesiastical Hierarchy agnousia* is only used in the conventional sense of lack of knowledge to describe the uninitiated who are unprepared to participate in the sacraments. Their 'lack of knowledge (*agnousian*)'[141] leaves them in 'the dark pits of ignorance (*agnousias*)'.[142] 'Those who do not participate in and know (*agnous*)[143] the divine things do not join in the thanksgiving.'[144]

In the *Celestial Hierarchy* Dionysius observes that symbolic imagery provides 'pictures [that] have to do with beings so simple that we can neither know (*agnoustoun*) nor contemplate them'.[145] The One is compared to fire, which 'in itself it is undetectable (*agnouston auto*)',[146] and with wind, which is 'unknowable (*agnouston*) and invisible'.[147] In the section of the *Celestial Hierarchy* dealing with Isaiah's encounter with an angel, Luibheid's translation reads:

> As for the powers of the second and last rank, together with our own intel-ligent powers, he concentrates his clear enlightenment for the unknown (*agnouston*) union with his own hiddenness, in proportion to the degree of distance from conformity to God.[148]

It is unclear whether the 'he' in this passage refers to the angel, Isaiah or God. Consequently it is unclear whether 'the unknown union with his own hiddenness' is the angel's, Isaiah's or God's. Perhaps it applies through analogy to all three.[149]

In the *Divine Names* Dionysius aspires to write about the divine names 'in a manner surpassing speech and knowledge (*agnoustois aphthegktus kai agnoustous synaptometha*)',[150] because 'the unknowing of what is beyond being (*hyperousio-tetos agnousia*) is something above and beyond speech, mind, or being itself'.[151] Eventually, 'in a way we cannot know (*agnoustois*)',[152] the reader will share with the disciples the experience of the transfiguration. Meanwhile, 'with these analogies we are raised upward toward the truth',[153] which is 'apart from all, beyond unknowing (*hyperagnouston*)'.[154] The One is known through the divine names, but the names must be transcended. 'He is known through knowledge and through unknowing (*agnousias*) ... the most divine knowledge of God, that which comes through unknowing (*agnousias*), is achieved in a union far beyond the mind.'[155]

The One is 'the unknown (*agnouston*) ... beyond all unknowing (*hyperag-noustou*) and ... unknowable (*agnoustoi*).[156] The idea of the incarnation 'cannot be enclosed in words nor grasped by any mind (*agnoustos*)'.[157] The power,[158] the depth[159] and the peace[160] of the One are unknowable. The One is unknowable in itself.[161]

The *Mystical Theology* opens with a prayer to God to 'lead us up beyond unknowing (*hyperagnouston*) and light'[162] and an exhortation to 'strive upward as much as you can toward union with him who is beyond all being and knowledge (*agnoustous*)'.[163] Moses is portrayed as the exemplar because 'he plunges into the truly mysterious darkness of unknowing (*agnousias*). Here, being neither oneself nor someone else, one is supremely united to the com-pletely unknown (*agnoustou*) by an inactivity of all knowledge, and knows beyond the mind by knowing nothing.'[164] Dionysius encourages the reader to aspire to the 'unknowing (*agnousias*) which lies beyond all vision and knowledge'[165] and 'that unknowing (*agnousian*) which itself is hidden from all those possessed of knowing'.[166]

Hathaway observes that although Dionysius presents himself as Paul's disciple, present at Paul's attack on the Athenian 'unknown god'[167], in the *Corpus Dionysiacum* he 'defends, with the help of an Athenian philosopher [Proclus], the claim that God is *the* unknown'.[168] According to Rolt it is 'possible that the word "Unknowing" was a technical term of the Mysteries or a later Greek Philosophy, and that this is the real explanation and interpretation of the inscription of the Athenian altar: "To the Unknown God"'.[169]

Rolt compares Dionysius with Bergson in their approach to the 'transcendence of knowledge', but cautions that the concept of unknowing in Dionysius should not be confused with Spencer's concept of the unknowable. '[Spencer] teaches that Ultimate Reality is, and must always be, beyond our reach; [Dionysius] that the Ultimate Reality at last becomes so near as utterly to sweep away (in a sense) the distinction which separates us for It.'[170]

Henousis

Henousis[171] is used in a variety of ways in the *Corpus Dionysiacum* to describe unity or union. It refers to an attribute of the One, the relationship between a being, or beings, and the One, a quality of relationship between elements of a hierarchy, an aspect of mind or, finally, the process of unification.

The 'simplified unity (*henousin*)'[172] of the One empowers beings to rise toward union with itself. The unity of creation is a reflection of the 'absolute similarity' of the One.[173] Creatures are drawn into 'a unity reflecting God (*theomimeton henousin*)'.[174] Creation is 'the good procession of his own transcendent unity (*henouseous*)'.[175] The One is also 'something above unity itself (*auten hyperairon ten henousin*)'.[176]

The hierarchies provide a means through which to 'strive upward as much as you can toward union (*henousin*)'[177] with the One. They enable beings 'to be at one with him (*henousis auton*)'.[178] They allow for the return of creation 'to be united (*henousin*)'[179] with the One. Union with the One is accomplished through likeness.[180] Union with the One is 'like a fire'[181] and 'a blazing light'.[182]

'Communion and union (*koinounia kai henousis*)'[183] are the result of proper order between beings or between levels of hierarchy. In the Eucharist, the participants 'are made perfectly one (*henousei*)'[184] and it 'grants us … union (*henousin*) with the One'.[185] The catechumen, while not yet 'initiated into complete union with (*henouseous*) and participation in God', can rely on the support of others to carry him in the right direction.[186]

Under the influence of the One, minds are unified within themselves and with other minds. The 'untroubled mind' has 'a suitability for union (*henousin*) with God'.[187] 'Godlike unified (*hypertheon phous henousis*) minds who imitate angels' are 'enlightened after this blessed union (*makarioutates henouseous*)'.[188] The mind can 'concentrate sightlessly and through an unknowing union (*henouseous agnoustou*)'[189] on the divine light. Beyond conceptual thought the mind has access to intuitive or empathic knowledge. 'The human mind has a capacity to think, through which it looks on conceptual things, and a unity (*henousin*) which transcends the nature of mind, through this it is joined to things beyond itself.'[190] Through this 'sympathy' Hierotheus, Dionysius' teacher, had a 'mysterious union (*henousin*)' with 'the divine things'.[191] The power of the spirit enables 'a union (*henousin*)' beyond 'the realm of discourse or of intellect'.[192] Knowledge of the One is 'achieved in a union (*henousin*) far beyond mind'.[193]

In Chapter Two of the *Divine Names* Dionysius explains 'divine unity (*theias henouseos*) and differentiation'[194] in the Trinity and in creation. In the 'divine unity (*henouseis*) beyond being', there are no differentiations.[195] 'The divine unities (*henouseis*) are the hidden and permanent, supreme foundations of a steadfastness which is more than ineffable and more than unknowable.'[196] The differentiations which do exist in the divine are benign. Divine unities and differentiations as higher terms within the hierarchical process of emanation contain 'certain specific unities (*heouseous*) and differentiatiations'.[197] In Chapter Four Dionysius observes that the intelligible beings, the angels, 'have their own orders beyond the cosmos, their own unities (*henouseis*), their mutual relationships, their unconfused distinctions'.[198]

He uses the example of the light in a house coming from several lamps to demonstrate the notion of 'distinction in unity (*henoumena*) and ... unity (*henousei*) in distinction'.[199] The 'total union (*henousis*) of light' from the individual lamps cannot be differentiated.[200] The 'unity beyond being (*hyperousion henousin*)' surpasses 'not only the union (*henouseoun*) of things corporeal, but also the union[201] of souls, and even that of minds themselves'. Minds are in union to the degree in which they participate in 'the unity which transcends all things (*pantoun hyperermenes henouseous*)'.[202] Dionysius uses the images of the circle and the seal to illustrate the relationship between unity and differentiation. In a circle, all the radii share the centre point.[203] All the substances that receive the impression of a seal share the one seal:

> There are numerous impressions of the seal and these all have a share in the original prototype; it is the same whole seal in each of the impressions and none participates only in a part ... The substances which receive a share of the seal are different. Hence, the impressions of the one entire identical archetype are different.[204]

Participation is described in the *Divine Names*, not only as a means to achieve unity but as founded on the divine unity, because 'in the divine realm unities (*henouseis*) hold a higher place than differentiations'.[205] All beings owe their existence to their participation in the Good:

From it derives the existence of everything as beings, what they have in common (*hai henouseis*)[206] and what differentiates them (*hai diakriseis*), their identicalness (*hai tautotetes*) and differences (*hai heterotetes*), their similarities and dissimilarities, their sharing of opposites, the way in which their ingredients maintain identity.[207]

The Good is 'the unity underlying everything (*hai pantos plethous henouseis*)'.[208] Even those who pursue illusory goals participate in 'a distorted echo of real love and real unity (*henouseous*)'.[209]

The integrity of individual beings is assured by the unity of the One, which gives 'to all things their definitions, their limits, and their guarantee, allowing nothing to be pulled apart or scattered in some endlessly disordered chaos ... away from their own unity (*henouseous*) and in some total jumbled confusion'.[210]

In Chapter Five of the *Divine Names*, on the divine name Being, Dionysius claims that 'the laws governing each individual are gathered together in one unity (*henousin*) with which there is no confusion'[211] and that 'the exemplars of everything preexist as a transcendent unity (*henousin*),[212] in the One. Therefore all things are 'joined together in one transcendental unity (*henousin*)'.[213]

In Chapter Nine of the *Divine Names* the One is called 'same' because 'he is totally, uniquely, and individually like himself'.[214] It is also called 'similar'. 'All the similarity in the world is similar to a trace of the divine similarity so that all creation is thereby made a unity (*henousin*).'[215]

In Chapter Eleven of the *Divine Names* Dionysius discusses the divine name, peace. The One 'is still and tranquil ... in an absolutely transcendent unity (*henousin*) of self, turning in upon himself and multiplying himself without ever leaving his own unity (*henouseous*)'.[216] It draws creation together in 'a unity (*henousin*) without confusion'.[217] Dionysius invites his reader to 'contemplate the one simple nature of that peaceful unity (*heouseous*) which joins all things to itself and to each other',[218] ultimately in 'a unity (*henousin*) beyond all conceptions'.[219]

Golitzin describes *henousis* as 'the capacity or openness of the creature to being filled with the divine *dynameis*'.[220] It is an 'infinite ascent ... our true "correspondence" to the divine infinity'.[221] Vanneste argues that the triad *aphairesis-agnousia-henousis* (negation-unknowing-union) dominates the *Mystical Theology*.[222]

Theosis

Theousis[223], also *theosis* and *theôsis*, is translated variously as deification, divinization or becoming godlike. The One 'is the source of all divinization (*theouseous*)'.[224] According to Dionysius, 'divinization (*theousis*) consists of being as much as possible like and in union with God'.[225] The One has provided the 'symbolic mode (*symbolikous paradedotai*) ... because he wanted us to be godlike (*analogou theouseous*)'.[226]

In enumerating the attributes of the first order of angels, the seraphim, cherubim and thrones, in the *Celestial Hierarchy*, Dionysius observes:

> They are 'perfect,' then, not because of an enlightened understanding which enables them to analyze the many sacred things, but rather because of a primary and supreme deification (*hyperechoyses theouseous*), a transcendent and angelic understanding of God's work.[227]

The most frequent references to *theousis* are in the *Ecclesiastical Hierarchy*, where he describes 'our hierarchy' as a means of deification. 'We see our human hierarchy, on the other hand, as our nature allows, pluralized in a great variety of perceptible symbols lifting us upward hierarchically until we are brought as far as we can be into the unity of divinization (*theousin*).'[228]

Participation in the human hierarchy 'consists of a feast upon that sacred vision which nourishes the intellect and divinizes everything (*theousa panta*) rising up to it'.[229] The generosity of the One 'has bestowed hierarchy as a gift to ensure the salvation and divinization (*theousei*) on every being endowed with reason and intelligence'.[230] This divine generosity is mirrored in the generosity of the leaders of the human hierarchy who 'made human what was divine'. 'Like gods, they had a burning and generous urge to secure uplifting and divinization (*theouseous*) for their subordinates.'[231] The leaders explain that 'like a fire, [the One] has made one with himself all those capable of being divinized (*theousin*)'.[232]

In his discussion of baptism, 'the rite of illumination' and 'the divine birth', in the *Ecclesiastical Hierarchy*, Dionysius uses the imagery of an athletic contest to describe the process of deification. The reader is exhorted to 'do battle with every activity and with every being which stand in the way of his divinization (*theousin*)'.[233]

The synaxis, or communion rite, 'draws our fragmented lives together into a one-like divinization (*theousin*). It forges a divine unity out of the divisions within us.'[234] Through participation in the synaxis some humans are lifted up to 'perfecting divinization (*theousesin*)' and 'arrive at the highest possible measure of divinization (*theousei*) and will be both the temple and the companion of the Spirit of the Deity'.[235] During the communion there are hymns of praise to 'that source ... who has established for us those saving sacraments by means of which the participants are divinized (*theousin*)'.[236] In his discussion of the consecration of 'therapeutae' or monks, Dionysius notes that the monastic initiation is followed by communion. The monk is 'uplifted and are more or less made godlike (*theouseous*)'[237] through his/her monastic profession, but participation in the synaxis brings that vocation into fuller union with the community and with God.

In his argument about unity and differentiation in the *Divine Names*, Dionysius states that when the mind struggles to comprehend the hiddenness of the One, 'we find ourselves witnessing no divinization (*theousin*), no life, no being which bears any real likeness to the absolutely transcendent Cause of all things'.[238] Any understanding of God, that is achieved by the mind, is the work of the spirit, 'which is located beyond all conceptual immateriality and all divinization (*theousin*)'.[239] The fact, however, that many are uplifted 'to divinization (*theousei*) … [shows] that there is not only differentiation but actual replication of the one God'.[240]

In Chapter Eight of the *Divine Names*, on divine power, Dionysius states that the divinizing power of the One is transmitted throughout the hierarchies. 'To those made godlike it grants the power for deification itself (*theousin auten*).'[241]

Gross identifies two distinct approaches to divinization in the *Corpus Dionysiacum*. On the one hand there is direct contact between the One and the soul. This contact is made possible by a particular faculty of the soul, the one (*hen*) of the soul. This is reminiscent of Proclus' 'flower of the soul'. Gross characterizes this form of *theousis* as mystical:

> Unlike the great majority of the fathers, our mystic does not seem to place the principal element of deification in the immortalization of humankind. For him, as we have seen, it is above all the unification of the soul, its reduction to the hen that is in it, which renders it like the divine Hen and thereby deiform.[242]

On the other hand the liturgical, ecclesiastical path to *theousis* described in the *Ecclesiastical Hierarchy* represents for Gross a less problematic approach. He says that Dionysius does not make any effort to reconcile these two approaches. Gross does not appear to appreciate Dionysius' view that beings are simultaneously embedded within a context and in contact with the One. As Spearritt notes, 'in creation God gives himself, there being nothing else he could give … all recipients who share in the gift must share in the whole gift'.[243]

Hudson observes that, according to Maximus the Confessor, one of the first commentators on the *Corpus Dionysiacum*, *theousis* is 'not a retrieval of a state that should never have been lost, but the fulfillment of a process that originated in God',[244] and that 'there is no gap between the God of creation and the God of redemption'.[245] In *Letter Four* Dionysius refers to 'the new theandric energy' or 'the activity of the God-man':[246]

> Theandricity is precipitated by the tension between the divine immanence in creation and the divine transcendence above it and is expressed in cataphatic and apophatic theology. The theandric aspect of the divine-human relation is fulfilled through the link established between these two movements by theosis.[247]

Here Hudson identifies immanence with *kataphasis*, transcendence with *apophasis* and the link between the two as *theousis*. This view would reflect the triad, *kataphasis-apophasis-ekstasis*. She might however to be at odds with Sells' contention that 'apophatic intensity' is the result of the simultaneity of immanence and transcendence.

In this chapter I have unearthed from the *Corpus Dionysiacum* a wide range of concepts that contribute to the apophatic intensity of Dionysius' work. This is evidence that *apophasis* is deployed to a variety of purposes and acts in a number of directions within his thought and imagination. It would suggest that if we are to locate apophatic elements in the work of Jung that we should expect to find a similarly dynamic kaleidoscope of concepts and images.

Notes

1   See, Stephen Gersh (1978), *From Iamblichus to Eriugena: An Investigation of the Prehistory and Evolution of the Pseudo-Dionysisan Tradition*. Leiden: Brill; Lisa Marie Esposito (1997), *Pseudo-Dionysius: A Philosophical Study of Certain Hellenic Sources*. PhD thesis, University of Toronto; Henri-Dominique Saffrey (1982), 'New Objective Links Between the Pseudo-Dionysius and Proclus', in *Neoplatonism and Christian Thought*, E. J. O'Meara (ed.). Albany, NY: SUNY Press; Wayne J. Hankey (1997), '"Ad intellectum rationcinatio": Three Procline Logics, *The Divine Names* of Pseudo-Dionysius, Eriugena's *Periphyseon* and Boethius' *Consolatio philosophiae'*, *Patristic Studies*, 24.
2   'The Eastern and especially Syrian ascetico-mystical tradition offers us a kind of royal path to the comprehension of the Areopagitica as a coherent and even emphatically Christian vision.' Golitzin, Alexander (2003), '"Suddenly, Christ": The Place of Negative Theology in the Mystagogy of Dionysius Areopagites', in *Mystics: Presence and Aporia*, Michael Kessler and Christian Sheppard (eds). Chicago: University of Chicago Press, p. 8; also, 'The holy men who minted the ideal of the saint in society came from Syria'. Brown, Peter (1982), 'The Rise and Function of the Holy Man in Late Antiquity', in *Society and the Holy in Late Antiquity*. London: Faber and Faber, p. 109; see also, Barnard, Leslie W. (1991), 'Asceticism in Early Syriac Christianity', *Monastic Studies II: The Continuity of Tradition*, Judith Loades (ed.). Bangor: Headstart History; and Beggiani, Chorbishop Seely (1991), *Introduction to Eastern Christian Spirituality: The Syriac Tradition*. London: University of Scranton Press.
3   Proclus (1963) *The Elements of Theology*, E. R. Dodds (trans.). Oxford: Oxford University Press, p. 38. According to Peters, 'The "return" of the Platonic tradition is distinct from, but connected with, the epistemological problem of knowing God (for the connection, see Proclus, *Elem. theol.*, prop. 39). It differs in that it is a function of desire (*orexis*). Its ontological ground is the identification of the transcendent One with the Good (Plato, *Rep.* 509b, *Phil.* 20d; Plotinus, *Enn.* V, 5, 13; Proclus, *Elem. theol.*, prop.8) that is necessarily an object of desire, and the identity of the efficient and final cause, the effect, in Middle Platonism, of combining Plato's *demiourgos* with Aristotle's *nous*. The dialectic of the *epistrophe* is the reverse of that of procession (*proodos*), and is worked out in Proclus, *Elem theol.*, props. 31-39.' Peters, F. E. (1967), *Greek Philosophical Terms: A Historical Lexicon*. New York: New York University Press, pp. 60–1; According to Mortley, 'This is the Greek view of the generation of reality which underpins the development of negative theology. Material reality is an accumulation of characteristics, attached like barnacles to the hull of essential reality … The "descent" of essence into material reality eventually leads to its concealment: the knowledge of essence, whether it be the one or substance, thus becomes a matter of difficulty. Reality could be said to be conceived by addition and it follows that essence could be said to be discovered by subtraction.' Mortley, R. (1982), 'The Fundamentals of the Via Negativa", *American Journal of Philology*, 103(4): 436.

4 'Emanation in general is expressed mainly by the Greek verb *hrein* ("flow" or "stream") ... ideas of "pouring" ... Closely connected with these terms are others expressing "boiling" or "seething" ... Ps. Dionysius uses "bubbling over" and "bubbling forth" (*ekblurein*) extensively in a Christianized version of the same theory.' Gersh (1978), pp. 18–19. The theme of emanation and return is described in the CD in the following passages: CH120B-121C, CH141B, CH260B, EH428D-429C, DN712A, MT1033C.

5 Rorem, Paul (1987), 'note 266, p. 130', in *Pseudo-Dionysius: The Complete Works*, C. Luibheid (trans.). Mahwah, NJ: Paulist Press.

6 DN708C-716A. In this lengthy passage Dionysius argues that *eros*, or 'yearning' as it is translated by Luibheid, is as legitimate a term for divine love as *agape*. See also Lisa Marie Esposito Buckley, 'Ecstatic and Emanating, Providential and Unifying: A Study of Pseudo-Dionysian and Plotinian Concepts of Eros', *Journal of Neoplatonic Studies*, Vol. I, No. 1, Fall 1992; Eric D. Perl, 'The Metaphysics of Love in Dionysius the Areopagite', *Journal of Neoplatonic Studies*, Vol VI, No. 1, Fall 1997. There is a discussion of *eros* and hierarchy in Ronald F. Hathaway (1969), *Hierarchy and the Definitions of Order in the Letters of Pseudo-Dionysius*. The Hague: Martinus, Nijhoff, pp. 51–60. For the relationship between *eros* and *agape*, see John M. Rist (1966), 'A note on Eros and Agape in Pseudo-Dionysius', *Virgiliae Christianae*, 20, Amsterdam. See also Hathaway, p. 51, 'Each member of the hierarchy, as shown above, has an inherent *logos* which is the same as some higher *logos*. What makes a thing beautiful, for example, is the agreement between its *logos* and the *logos* of Beauty itself. Ps.-Dionysius therefore often speaks as if each member of the hierarchy contained within itself this analogical relation to higher principles. But this "symmetry" or "proportion" would not exist if they did not "share" it or "participate" in it. *Eros* is the pervasive force or motion which provides this rapport with higher principles in Ps.-Dionysius.'

7 Golitzin, Alexander (1994), *Et Introibo Ad Altare Dei: The Mystagogy of Dionysius Areopagita, with Special Reference to its Predecessors in the Eastern Christian Tradtion*. Thessaloniki: Analecta Vlatadon, p. 66.

8 Sells, Michael (1994), *Mystical Languages of Unsaying*. Chicago: University of Chicago Press, p. 6.

9 'While *theoria* is a concept of philosophical origin, keeping a certain ambiguous ground between theology and philosophy, *contemplatio* is a concept bound to Latin Christian theology and, more specifically, to one of its subdivisions, spiritual theology. From Augustine to Teresa of Avila, by way of Bernard of Clairvaux and the Carthusian Spiritual School, the concept of *contemplatio* historically underwent a gradual deviation toward psychology, drawing on Augustinianism, where it had already come to designate a "spiritual state of mind".' Nef, Frederic (2005), 'Contemplation', in *Encyclopedia of Christian Theology*, Jean-Yves Lacoste (ed.). London: Routledge, p. 353.

10 Tomasic, Thomas Michael (1969), 'Negative Theology and Subjectivity: An Approach to the Tradition of the Pseudo-Dionysius', *International Philosophical Quarterly*, Vol. IX; (1988), 'The Logical Function of Metaphor and Oppositional Coincidence in the Pseudo-Dionysius and Johannes Scottus Eriugena', *Journal of Religion*, 68(3).

11 Mortley, Raoul (1986), *From Word to Silence II: The Way of Negation, Christian and Greek*. Bonn: Hanstein.

12 Gersh, Stephen (1978).

13 Blum, Richard and Alexander Golitzin (1991), *The Sacred Athlete: On the Mystical Experience and Dionysios, its Westernworld Fountainhead*. London: University Press of America.

14 Counet, Jean-Michel, (2004), 'The Meaning of Apology and Reconciliation for an Apophatic Theology', in *Conflict and Reconciliation: Perspectives on Nicholas of Cusa*, Inigo Bocken (ed.). Leiden: Brill, p. 198.

15 Yannaras, Christos (2005), *On the Absence and Unknowability of God: Heidegger and the Areopagite*. Edinburgh: T&T Clark.

16 Aberth, John (1996), 'Pseudo-Dionysius as Liberator: The Influence of the Negative Tradition on Late Medieval Female Mystics', *Downside Review*, 114(395).

17 Turner, Denys (1995), *The Darkness of God: Negativity in Christian Mysticism*. Cambridge: Cambridge University Press, p. 20.

18 EP9 1105B-C.

19 Fisher, Jeffrey (2001), 'The Theology of Dis/similarity: Negation in Pseudo-Dionysius', *Journal of Religion*, 81(4): 532.

20 Rorem, Paul (1986), 'The Uplifting Spirituality of Pseudo-Dionysius', in *Christian Spirituality: Origins to the Twelfth Century*, B. McGinn and J. Meyendorff (eds). London: Routledge, p. 147.

21 'In rough and over-simplified fashion one may say that all the commentators, and even some of the translators, take Dionysius out of his own context and place him within a medieval philosophy of being, whether Augustinian or Aristotelian.' F. Edward Cranz (2000), 'The (Concept of the) Beyond in Proclus, Pseudo-Dionysius, and Cusanus', in *Nicholas of Cusa and the Renaissance*, T. Izbici and G. Christianson (eds). Aldershot: Ashgate, pp. 102–3.

22 Aristotle, *On Interpretation* 17a 31–33, in *Pseudo-Dionysius: The Complete Works*, Colm Luibheid (trans.), 1987, New York: Paulist Press, p. 136, note 6.

23 MT1000B.

24 DN916A.

25 DN913C; see Proclus, *Elements of Theology*, prop. 32.

26 There are some evocative uses of the term in ancient Greek. 'I. Lead up from a lower place to a higher place. 2. Lead up to the high sea, carry by sea. 3. Take up from the coast into the interior. 4. Bring up, esp. from the dead. 5. Conduct the choir. 6. Lift up, raise. 7. Lift up a paean, a song of lamentation. 8. Raise to honour. 9. Cut teeth, bring up blood, chew the cud, draw a line, erect as an ordinate, carry a line of works to a point. 10. Paid them into a treasury. 11 Bring up a prisoner for examination. 12. Train, rear, i.e. plants. II bring back. 2 carry back, refer to its principles. 3 refer him to a contract. 4. Reduce syllogism to another figure, reduce and argument to syllogism. 5. Return a slave sold with an undisclosed defect. 6. Refer a claimant. 7. Rebuild. 8. Restore to its original shape. 9. Reckon, calculate. 10. Withdraw, retreat, put back again. B. put out to sea, set sail, put to sea, make ready, prepare oneself. 3. In thought ascend to higher unity.' Liddell, H. G. and Scott, R. (1940), *Greek–English Lexicon*, Oxford: Clarendon, p. 102.

27 'Leading up, esp. taking a ship into the high sea, putting to sea, bringing up-stream of a ship. 2. Bringing up from the stomach or lungs, vomiting. 3. Bringing up, rearing. 4. Lifting up of the soul to God, Iamb. Myst. 3.7. 5. Evocation. 6. Sublimation. 7. Distillation. II referring to a principle. 2. Resolution of definitions into syllogisms. 3. Reference to a principle. 4 Return of a defective slave to a vendor. 5. Reference of a claimant or a third party. 6. Delivery, payment. 7. Offerings made on embarkation, a feast of Aphrodite at Eryx.' Liddell and Scott, p. 102.

28 Rorem, Paul (1986), p. 134.

29 Iamblichus, *On the Mysteries*, X.VI, Thomas Taylor (trans.). Frome: Prometheus Trust, p. 152.

30 Rorem, Paul (1982), 'Iamblichus and the Anagogical Method in Pseudo-Dionysian Liturgical Theology', in *Studia Patristica*, Vol. XVII, Part One, Elizabeth A. Livingstone (ed.). Oxford: Pergamon Press, p. 455.

31 MT1033C.

32 See Fisher for a discussion of dis/similarity in Dionysius. 'Precisely the dissimilarity of everything to God enables everything to be similar to God.' p. 536.

33 CH121C-D.

34 DN593C.

35 DN640B Rolt.

36 DN641A.

37 Golitzin, Alexander (1994), *Et Introibo Ad Altare Dei: The Mystagogy of Dionysius Areopagita, with Special Reference to its Predecessors in the Eastern Christian Tradition*. Thessaloniki: Analecta Vlatadon, p. 112.

38 DN697A Rolt.

39 DN704B.

40 DN872A. See also Rolt: 'advancing through the Negation (*aphairesei*) and Transcendence of all things.'

41 MT1025A.

42 Kenny, John Peter (1993), 'The Critical Value of Negative Theology', *Harvard Theological Review*, 86(4): 448.

43 MT1048B; Rolt's translation conveys the order of the Greek text more plainly. '... nor can any affirmation or negation apply to it; for while applying affirmations or negations to those orders of being that come next to It, we apply not unto It either affirmation or negation, inasmuch as It transcends all affirmation by being the perfect and unique Cause of all things, and transcends all negation by the pre-eminence of Its simple and absolute nature – free from every limitation and beyond them all.' (p. 201).

44 'Apophasis refers to an investigation into serious threats to the Athenian democracy, especially treason and bribery ... This procedure, an innovation of the later fourth century BCE, began with an investigation conducted by the Areopagus, which would issue a report. This report was called an apophasis. Eventually, the whole procedure – investigation, report, prosecution – came to be known by this term.' Blackwell, Christopher (2000), 'Apophasis', in *Demos: Classical Athenian Democracy*, R. Scaife and A. M. Mahoney (eds), The Stoa: a Consortium for Electronic Publication in the Humanities, available at: http://www.stoa.org/projects/demos/home. See also Cartledge, Paul, Paul Millett and Stephen Todd (2002), *Nomos: Essays in Athenian Law, Politics and Society*, Cambridge: Cambridge University Press, p. 217. Some patristic writers use the word in the sense of a decree, judgement (i.e. of God) or opinion (i.e. of another). See G. W. H. Lampe (1961), *Patristic Greek Lexicon*, Oxford: Clarendon, p. 219. See also Liddell and Scott, p. 226.

45 'Demosthenes uses the term several times, but in each case he seems to use the word generically, "an account", such as someone might give when returning from a voyage, or (often) when itemizing an estate so the inheritance can be settled.' Blackwell.

46 Carabine, Deirdre (1995), *The Unknown God: Negative Theology in the Platonic Tradition: Plato to Eriugena*. Louvain: Peeters Press, p. 184.

47 'The rejection of several reasons why a thing should or should not be done and affirming a single one, considered most valid', Richard Sherry (1550), *A Treatise of Schemes and Tropes*. London: John Day. See Warren Taylor (1938), 'A Note on English Figures of Speech', *Modern Language Notes*, 53(7): 514; see also http://humanities.byu.edu/rhetoric/silva.htm

48 1657 J. Smith *Myst. Rhet.* 164 'Apophasis: a kind of an Irony, whereby we deny that we say or doe that which we especially say or doe.' 1753 *Chambers Cycl. Supp.*, 'Apophasis: whereby we really say or advise; a thing under a feigned show of passing over, or dissuading it.' *OED*.

49 'Mary Matlin, the Bush campaign's political director, made the point with ruthless venom at a press briefing in Washington, saying, "The larger issue is that Clinton is evasive and slick. We have never said to the press that he is a philandering, pot-smoking, draft-dodger. There's nothing nefarious or subliminal going on."'(*Manchester Guardian*, 1992) http://grammar.about.com/od/ab/g/apophasis.htm

50 'Some useful phrases for apophasis: nothing need be said about, I pass over, it need not be said (or mentioned), I will not mention (or dwell on or bring up), we will overlook, I do not mean to suggest (or imply), you need not be reminded, it is unnecessary to bring up, we can forget about, no one would suggest.' http://web.cn.edu/kwheeler/lit_terms_A.html

51 http://ai.stanford.edu/~csewell/culture/litterms.htm

52   'The phrases "not to mention such and such" and "to make a long story short" are apophases.' faculty.ksu.edu.sa/25299/DocLib5/Aحرف.doc

53   http://www.talktalk.co.uk/reference/dictionaries/difficultwords/data/d0001290.html

54   *American Heritage Dictionary of the English Language*, Fourth Edition, 2000, Houghton Mifflin Company, p. 84.

55   *OED*.

56   Sells, p. 3.

57   Sells, p. 6.

58   McGinn, Bernard (1992), *The Foundations of Mysticism*, London: SCM, p. 31.

59   Duclow, Donald (1994), 'Isaiah Meets the Seraph: Breaking Ranks in Dionysius and Eriugena?', in *Eriugena: East and West*, Bernard McGinn and Willemien Otten (eds). Notre Dame, IN: University of Notre Dame Press.

60   Gregory of Nyssa (1965), 'On the Making of Man', *Gregory of Nyssa: Dogmatic Treatises, etc.*, W. Moore and H. A. Wilson (trans.), in *Nicene and Post-Nicene Fathers of the Christian Church*, Vol. 5 Series II, P. Schaff and H. Wace (eds). Grand Rapids, MI: Eerdmans, p. 397.

61   Marion, Jean-Luc (2005), '*Mihi magna quaestio factus sum:* The Privilege of Unknowing', *Journal of Religion*, 85(1): 1.

62   DN981B.

63   Marion, p. 18.

64   MT1000B.

65   EP4 1072B.

66   Sells, pp. 16–17. *Hoios*, is '*such as, of what sort ... what* a man for valour ... *hois* is an independent sentence as an exclam. of astonishment ... *hoios, hoia, hoion* freq. introduce an "indirect exclamation", giving the reason for what precedes ... *hoion, as for instance ... as for example* ... in numerical estimates, *about ... as it were, so to speak ... that is to say.*' Liddell and Scott, p. 1209.

67   Rorem, Paul in *Pseudo-Dionysius: The Complete Works*, C. Luibheid (trans.), p. 61. The term appears in DN641A, 645B, 648B and 697B.

68   DN641A.

69   DN645B.

70   DN648B.

71   DN697B.

72   Van Den Daele, Albert (1941), *Indices Pseudo-Dionysiani*. Louvain: Bibliothèque de l'Université, pp. 138–41.

73   69 times in the DN; 23 in CH; 8 in MT; 6 in EH; and 10 in the Letters.

74   Lampe, pp. 1436–43.

75   Mortley (1982), p. 438; 'Negative theology is rendered more or less radical a method depending on whether God is said to be within being or outside being. The way of abstraction is already an instrument of metaphysics in Aristotle, but it becomes an instrument of transcendental theology in Clement.' p. 439.

76   '*Remove*; pass., *be removed from*; hence *transcend; ... transcendent ... transcendence ... detachment*; from things of this life ... *set free, deliver*, from eternal punishment', Lampe, p. 491.

77   CH165C, 205D, 237C, 293B, 301A2, 304C2, 305BD, 329A, 332D/ EH481B/ DN588C, 592D, 593AC, 597C, 645BC3, 648C, 649C, 649B, 712BC, 720B, 721B, 825AB, 869A, 889C2, 972A, 981AB/ MT1025B/ EP8 1088D/ EP9 1109C, 1112C, 1113B.

78   CH165C.

79   DN712BC.

80   EP9 1113B; Liddell and Scott offer '*profound* sleep' as an example for *apeiron*, p. 184.

81   DN889C.

82   DN592D.

83   DN593AC.

84   DN721B.

85   EH481B.

86   MT1025B.

87   EP8 1088D.

88   'On yonder side, beyond ... farther than ... the part beyond, the far side ... beyond it ... the times beyond or before, earlier times ... henceforth.' Liddell and Scott, p. 616.

89   DN588B, 593A, 641A2, 697C, 713C, 716C, 865C, 869D, 913A, 949B, 956B. Also in EH373D; MT1000C, 1001A, 1048B; EP2 1068A, 1069A; EP4 1072AC; EP5 1076A; EP9 1112C.

90   DN588B.

91   DN641A.

92   DN869D.

93   DN593A.

94   DN949B.

95   Cranz, p. 97.

96   Proclus, *Parmenides*, 1073, 11.

97   Cranz, p. 96.

98   'On a sudden ... the moment that he is dead; at first hearing ... the instantaneous, that which is between motion and rest, and not in the time-series.' Liddell and Scott, p. 582.

99   See Plato, *Parmendes* 156de; *Epistle VII* 341cd; *Symposium* 210c; and Plotinus, *Enneads* V.3.17; 5.7; VI.7.36. See Beierwaltes, W. (1966), 'Exaiphnes oder die Paradoxie des Augenblicks', *Philosophisches Jahrbuch* 74: 272–82; Stang, Colin (1974), 'Plato and the Instant', *Proceedings of the Aristotelian Society*, Suppli.Vol. 48, pp. 63–79; Bostock, David (1978), 'Plato on Change and Time in the "Parmenides"', *Phronesis*, 23: 229–242. For a comprehensive treatment see Niko Stobach (1998), *The Moment of Change: A Systematic History in the Philosophy of Space and Time*. Dordrecht: Kluwer.

100 Malachi 3:1; Luke 2:13; Mark 13:36; Acts 9:3; 22:6.

101 'The earliest example comes from the Syriac work of the third century, the Acts of Judas Thomas, where, in the "Hymn of the Pearl", the Apostle "suddenly" encounters the "robe of glory" woven for him in heaven ... In Athanasius' Life of Anthony, the father of monks is rescued from demonic assault by the "sudden" beam of light from heaven which then comforts him with the voice of Christ. In Ephrem Syrus, the "sudden" occurs at least three times. In his Hymns on Nature, Christ is the "star of light Who shone forth suddenly" at the Incarnation, while in the Hymns on Paradise, the "sudden" is linked, first, with the trisagion of the Seraphim breaking the silence before the Presence in Eden and, second, with the recognition of the Risen Christ at the clearly eucharistic "breaking of the bread" in the Emmaus story of Luke 24: "Bread was the key", says Ephrem, "whereby their eyes were opened ... darkened eyes beheld a vision of joy and were suddenly [*men shelya*] filled with happiness". Thus, again, we find the term linked with the mystical vision, Christ, light, and the liturgies of both heaven and earth ... The *men* of the Syriac translation of *exaiphnes* is merely the equivalent of the Greek *ek*, "from", "out of". *Shelya*, however, denotes "rest", "silence", and "stillness", and in Christian Syriac is usually connected with eremetic ascetics, as is *hesychia* in Christian Greek.' Golitzin (2003), pp. 23–5.

102 Mortley (1986), p. 237.

103 CH329C.

104 EP3 1069B.

105 EP3 1069B.

106 Hathaway, p. 80.

107 Golitzin, Alexander (2001), 'Revisiting the "Sudden": Epistle III in the *Corpus Dionysiacum*', *Studia Patristica* 37: 491.

108 'Displacement ... change ... movement outwards ... differentiation ... standing aside ... distraction of mind, from terror, astonishment, anger ... entrancement, astonishment ... ecstasy ... drunken excitement.' Liddell and Scott, p. 520.

109 'Inclined to depart from ... excitable ... out of one's senses ...able to displace or remove ... causing mental derangement.' Liddell and Scott, p. 520.

110 EP112C.
111 DN712AB.
112 DN865D.
113 DN865CD.
114 MT1000A.
115 Jones, MT1000A.
116 Rist, pp. 235–43.
117 Perczel, Istvan (2000), 'Pseudo-Dionysius and the Platonic Theology: A Preliminary Study', in *Proclus et la Theologie Platonicienne*, Segonds and Steel (eds). Leuven: University Press, p. 525.
118 Golitzin (1994), p. 47.
119 Golitzin, p. 48.
120 Golitzin, p. 67.
121 Louth, Andrew (1992), *The Origins of the Christian Mystical Tradition from Plato to Denys*. Oxford: Oxford University Press, p. 51.
122 Corrrigan, Kevin (1996), '"Solitary" Mysticism in Plotinus, Proclus, Gregory of Nyssa, and Pseudo-Dionysius', *Journal of Religion*, 76(1): 41–2.
123 Esposito Buckley, Lisa Marie (1992), p. 55.
124 '*Infinity, infinitude … eternity*. See also *apeiritos, boundless, immense*.' Liddell and Scott, p. 184.
125 '*Boundless, endless … countless* people … *profound* sleep … *vast* concourse … *without end or escape* … of persons standing in *a circle*.' Liddell and Scott, p. 184.
126 DN593C. See DN980C.
127 Lilla, Salvatore R. C. (1980), 'The Notion of Infinitude in Ps.-Dionysius Areopagita', *Journal of Theological Studies*, 31(1): 98.
128 DN680B.
129 DN825AB. Also used in the same sense in DN705C, 909C and 912B.
130 DN889D-892A.
131 Lilla cites Gregory, *Contra Eunom*. II (I 246); *Contra Eunom*. III (II 58); *Quod non sit tres dii* (52); and Aristotle, *Phys*. I 187b 7; *Phys*. III 207a 25-6; *Rhet*. III 1048b 27-8. Lilla, pp. 102–3.
132 DN588B.
133 See DN588C.
134 Hager, F. -P. (1993), 'Infinity and Simplicity of God in Plotinus, Proclus and Pseudo-Dionysius', *Journal of Neoplatonic Studies*, 2(1), pp. 68–9. See DN588C.
135 Hager, pp. 67–8.
136 '*Ignorance … lack of acquaintance … being unknown, obscurity*'. Liddell and Scott, p. 12; see also Lampe, '*Ignorance* … ordinary state of man in this life … special feature of paganism … moral evil … caused by sin … liable to punishment … healed by Christ … destroyed by H. Ghost … suprarational, mystical, knowledge of God, if compared with rational knowledge, being and "unknowing",' Lampe, p. 22.
137 '*Unknown …. unheard of, forgotten … unfamiliar … most unintelligible …. Not an object of knowledge, unknowable … harder to know … not knowing, ignorant of*.' Liddell and Scott, p. 12; see also Lampe, '*unknown … unknowable … ineffable … unintelligible … ignorant*.' Lampe, p. 22.
138 '*Without the knowledge of other, secretly … in a marvellous manner … without using the normal means to knowledge, i.e. without discursive reasoning*.' Lampe, p. 22.
139 EP1 1065AB.
140 EP3 1069B.
141 EH393D.
142 EH400C.
143 '*Unknown … obscure, unintelligible … dark, vague … obscure, ignoble … unknown to fame … ignorant*." Liddell and Scott, p. 12.

144 EH445B.
145 CH137B.
146 CH329A.
147 CH336A.
148 CH305B.
149 In a discussion about Gregory of Nyssa, Saward argues that 'corresponding to *Deus absconditus* there is *homo absconditus*.' Saward, John (1974), 'Towards an Apophatic Anthropology', *Irish Theological Quarterly*, 41: 229.
150 DN585B; for a clearer translation see Jones, 'Hereby, will you be ineffably and unknowingly joined to what is ineffable and unknowable', and Rolt, 'in a manner surpassing speech and knowledge, we embrace those truths which in like manner, surpass them'.
151 DN588A.
152 DN592C; see Jones, 'We shall share in the unity beyond intellect in the unknown and blessed radiations.'
153 DN592C.
154 DN592D Jones.
155 DN872A.
156 DN593B Jones. Also 'more than unknowable (*hyperagnoustou*)' in DN640D.
157 DN648A.
158 DN892A.
159 DN913B.
160 DN949B.
161 DN641A, 708D, 816B, 869C, 949C.
162 MT997A.
163 MT997B.
164 MT1001A.
165 MT1025A.
166 MT1025B.
167 Acts 17:23–32.
168 Hathaway, p. 70.
169 Rolt, p. 33.
170 Rolt, p. 32; for discussions of Spencer see, Jordan, Elijah (1911), 'The Unknowable of Herbert Spencer', *Philosophical Review*, 20(3); and Swenson, David F. (1905), 'The Category of the Unknowable', *Journal of Philosophy, Psychology and Scientific Methods*, 2(19).
171 '*Combination into one, union … compression.*' Liddell and Scott, p. 579; also, '*Union, unity … simplicity*', Lampe, pp. 486–9; see also *henoou*, Lampe pp. 479–81.
172 CH121B.
173 DN916A.
174 DN589D.
175 DN712C.
176 DN816B; also DN593C.
177 MT997B.
178 CH165A.
179 CH293B.
180 EH376A, 392A.
181 EH393A.
182 DN592C.
183 CH260B.
184 EH444C.
185 EH424D.
186 EH400C.
187 DN680B.
188 DN593C.

189 DN708D.
190 DN865C.
191 DN648B.
192 DN588A.
193 DN872B.
194 DN640D.
195 DN641A.
196 DN640D.
197 DN641A.
198 DN696A.
199 DN641B.
200 DN641C.
201 *Henouseoun*, appears once in the Greek. Luibheid repeats it again for effect by translating, 'not only the union of things corporeal, but also the union of souls.'
202 DN641C.
203 DN644A; 821A.
204 DN644AB.
205 DN652A.
206 In Jones, 'their unities and their differences, their identities and their otherness.'
207 DN704B.
208 DN705C.
209 DN720B.
210 DN949A.
211 DN821B.
212 DN824C.
213 DN825A.
214 DN913C.
215 DN916A.
216 DN949B.
217 DN949C.
218 DN949C.
219 DN949D.
220 Golitzin, Alexander (1994), *Et Introibo Ad Altare Dei: The Mystagogy of Dionysius Areopagita, with Special Reference to its Predecessors in the Eastern Christian Tradition*. Thessaloniki: Analecta Vlatadon, p. 115.
221 Goltizin, p. 116.
222 Goltizin, pp. 109. *Henousis* appears only once in the MT.
223 'Deification, divinization ... of Christ's body, of angelic hierarchies, of man', Lampe, pp. 649–50.
224 EH376B.
225 EH373D. According to Finlan and Kharlamov, Dionysius offers 'the first theological definition of theosis'. Finlan, S. and V. Kharlamov (eds) (2006), *Theosis: Deification in Christian Theology*. (Princeton Theological Monograph Series), Eugene, OR: Pickwick Publications, p. 5.
226 CH124A.
227 CH208C.
228 EH373A.
229 EH376A.
230 EH376B.
231 EH376D.
232 EH393A.
233 EH404A.
234 EH424C.

235 EH433C.
236 EH436C.
237 EH536C.
238 DN645A.
239 DN645C.
240 DN649C.
241 DN893A.
242 Gross, Jules (2002), *The Divinization of the Christian According to the Greek Fathers.* Anaheim, CA: A & C Press, p. 247.
243 Spearritt, Placid (1970), 'The Soul's Participation in God According to Pseudo-Dionysius', *The Downside Review*, 88(293): 384–5.
244 Hudson, Nancy Joyce (1999), *Theosis in the Thought of Nicholas of Cusa: Origin, Goal, and Realized Destiny of Creation.* PhD thesis, Yale University, p. 34.
245 Hudson, p. 37.
246 EP4 1072C.
247 Hudson, p. 28.

Chapter 4

Jung, Neoplatonism and Dionysius

From an early age Jung read widely in philosophy and theology. He 'was fascinated by all forms of Platonism and neo-Platonism'.[1] 'Between the ages of sixteen and nineteen, he began to read both early Greek philosophy – Heraclitus, Pythagoras, and Empedocles, as well as Plato – and such medieval thinkers as Thomas Aquinas and Meister Eckhart.'[2]

The problem of *apophasis* is central to this tradition. The persistence of Jung's preoccupation with the problem of unknowing is evident from two statements written forty years apart. In 1912, in a comparison of symbolic thinking and directed thinking in *Symbols of Transformation*, he observed:

> The fact that these problems could be posed at all – the stock metaphysical problem of how to know the unknowable comes into this category – proves how peculiar the medieval mind must have been, that it could contrive questions which for us are the height of absurdity.[3]

The final sentence of *Answer to Job*, published in 1952, reads:

> That is to say even the enlightened person remains what he is, and is never more than his own limited ego before the One who dwells within him, whose form has no knowable boundaries, who encompasses him on all sides, fathomless as the abysms of the earth and as vast as the sky.[4]

Ultimately, the question of influence in Jung's thought is difficult to decide. What is not in doubt is that Jung plundered the religious and philosophical literatures of the world to find the language with which to express his thoughts and intuitions:

> From Jung's point of view, to say he borrowed ideas from other philosophers in the sense that his ideas originated in the study of philosophy would be a mistake. Instead, Jung's inner experiences, his dreams, his intuitions, and his reflections were the ultimate sources of his thought. However in his study of philosophy, as he tells us in his autobiography, he found the confirmation of his intuitions and, one might add, the verbal structures through which he gave them form.[5]

The issue of how one is to understand Jung's adoption of any particular religious and philosophical concept for his psychological thought must be faced anew in each instance.

Given the importance of the Platonic strain in Jung's thought it is surprising that there are only just over 120 citations of Plato and his writings, ten references to Plotinus, six to Proclus, three to Iamblichus, and a mere sixteen to Neoplatonism/ists. (Aristotle merits twenty-one mentions.) Many of these are embedded in quotations from other writers, as well as in Jung's own words, in which a Neoplatonic philosopher, text or theme is mentioned in passing. For example, 'Thomas Tyler, who was strongly influenced by Proclus, says …'[6] This compares with a special section in the index to the *Collected Works* of 27 pages, containing many hundreds of references to alchemy and alchemical writings.

Jung held some aspects of the Platonic tradition to be potential remedies for what he considered to be the cultural malaise of modern man:

> The development of Western philosophy during the last two centuries has succeeded in isolating the mind in its own sphere and in severing it from its primordial oneness with the universe. Man himself has ceased to be the microcosm and eidolon of the cosmos, and his 'anima' is no longer the consubstantial *scintilla,* or spark of the *Anima Mundi,* the World Soul.[7]

The concept of the macrocosm/microcosm is fundamental to Jung's concept of the self and his cultural project of the recovery of meaning. In his view, Western man had become disconnected from nature. He argued that the self was a part of nature, while the Western ego had developed into an alienated, unrooted construct. In his view the collective unconscious, of which the self is a part, is natural. The individual is linked to the cosmos through his inner experience because the experience of the unconscious is an experience of the microcosm which reflects and is reflected by the macrocosm.

Jung felt that he had discovered a liberating truth in the fact, as he saw it, that the microcosm which was projected at various times in history onto the body or matter, could be observed within human psychology:

> The ancient and long obsolete idea of man as a microcosm contains a supreme psychological truth that has yet to be discovered. In former times this truth was projected upon the body, just as alchemy projected the unconscious psyche upon chemical substances. But it is altogether different when the microcosm is understood as that interior world whose inward nature is fleetingly glimpsed in the unconscious.[8]

The process of the 'birth of the self' which can be empirically observed corresponds to the creation of the world. He claimed that it was possible to know 'what it is in man that corresponds to the cosmos'. He felt there was urgent need for this knowledge because neurosis was produced by lack of meaning:

For the alchemists the process of individuation represented by the *opus* was an analogy of the creation of the world, and the *opus* itself an analogy of God's work of creation. Man was seen as a microcosm, a complete equivalent of the world in miniature. In our picture, we see what it is in man that corresponds to the cosmos, and what kind of evolutionary process is compared with the creation of the world and the heavenly bodies: it is the *birth of the self*, the latter appearing as a microcosm. It is not the empirical man that forms the 'correspondentia' to the world, as the medievalists thought, but rather the indescribable totality of the psychic or spiritual man, who cannot be described because he is compounded of consciousness as well as of the indeterminable extent of the unconscious. The term microcosm proves the existence of a common intuition (also present in my patient) that the 'total' man is as big as the world, like an Anthropos.[9]

The process of individuation is the process of the unfolding of the microcosm. The relationship between this 'objective' unfolding process and the individual ego is complex and the subject of psychopathology and psychoanalysis. Psychotherapy is a form of 'alchemical research':

The alchemist, however, had at the very least an indirect inkling of it: knew definitely that as part of the whole he had an image of the whole in himself, the 'firmament' or 'Olympus,' as Paracelsus calls it. This interior microcosm was the unwitting object of alchemical research. Today we would call it the collective unconscious, and we would describe it as 'objective' because it is identical in all individuals and is therefore one. Out of this universal One there is produced in every individual a subjective consciousness, i.e., the ego. This is roughly, how we today would understand Dorn's 'formerly one' and 'separated by a divine act of creation'.[10]

The motif of the microcosm/macrocosm is widespread in Jung's work and provides him with a useful concept to think about the place of the individual in the cosmos. He insisted throughout that he approached these studies as an empiricist. For the modern reader there is the constant question of his use of metaphysical language to describe psychology. Nagy argues that Jung's theory of archetypes does in the end amount to metaphysics rather than metapsychology:

Jung suggests that while we may never know more than what the psyche itself presents to us, we must assume a transcendental reality – a thing-in-itself – which lies in back of and causes the phenomena which we experience. 'One must assume that the ... ideas ... rest on something actual.' 'The reactions of the psychic system ... [reflect] the behavior of a *metaphysic* reality.' Though he cannot hope to know it, Jung assumes that his dreams and feelings do give evidence of an invisible, that is non-material reality undergirding his subjective experience. Yet he claims not to be a metaphysician.[11]

This tension between metaphysical and psychological language is a recurring issue in Jung's psychological interpretations of religious and philosophical writings. According to Altizer, 'The chief problems posed by Jung's methodology are derived from his ambiguous attempt to bring together the language and method of scientific-rational analysis and the mythical symbolism of the romantics and mystics.'[12] In Altizer's view Jung fails because although his stated intention is to bridge the gaps between conscious and unconscious and between history and nature he cannot reconcile 'the truth which is reached by scientific-objective analysis with the truth that is grasped by unconscious intuition. Jung's thought dwells in two worlds and he has not found a genuine way to bring them together.'[13] Altizer contends that Jung, in his late work in particular, emphasized the unconscious to the detriment of the conscious, thereby in effect collapsing the opposites rather than reconciling them as he claimed to be doing. Jung of course believed that his analytical psychology did in fact provide, for the individual and for culture, genuine theoretical and practical solutions to the problem of opposites.

Barnes, in her essay 'Neo-Platonism and Jung', compares Plotinus and Jung. In spite of their many differences, she finds that there are striking similarities in their interpretation of religious experience and 'in urging the importance of a certain spiritual faculty other than the intellect'. She describes the relationship between the individual and the All-Soul in Plotinus and the relationship between the ego and the collective unconscious in Jung. They both stress the importance of 'the conscious realization of the power of a greater than the conscious psyche'.[14]

She sees important differences between Plotinus and Jung in three areas. Firstly, that while the All-Soul and the collective unconscious can be viewed as analogous, 'the supra-individual, as Plotinus sees it, is not limited to the All-Soul, which is actually but the lowest of the three realms of true being'. Secondly, the collective unconscious has developed and will continue to develop, whereas the All-Soul is unchanging. And, thirdly where Jung asserts the value of the individual and the importance of attaining an embodied balance between consciousness and the collective unconscious, Plotinus argues for 'a flight away from the body':[15]

> Whatever the similarities between the conceptions, it should be evident, I believe, that the individual's hope of salvation or adjustment in this world is the effecting of harmonious contact between his individual psyche and the world of greater scope of which he at best usually only dimly perceives himself to be apart. Plotinus refers to this process as an *ascent* into higher spheres; Jung speaks of it as the *descent* into deeper realms of consciousness. Each expression is, of course, metaphorical and is, I think, substantially the same in meaning. Plotinus' method is primarily intellectual and contemplative in the traditional philosophical sense. Jung's is based on the scientific and intellectual interpretation of dreams. Both involve at the end a power that is non-rational, at least so far as human understanding can at present take us.[16]

In Plotinus' system there are four steps for the soul to take to attain reality: 'the pursuit of the virtues, attainment of self-knowledge, dialectic, and the final vision wherein one passes beyond intellect'.[17] While Jung did not describe his approach in this language, there are, according to Barnes, similar stages in his concept of individuation.

The philosopher's pursuit of virtue is analogous to the psychotherapist's resolution of problems at the level of the personal unconscious. 'The personal unconscious must always be disposed of first, i.e., made conscious; otherwise the entrance to the collective unconscious cannot be opened.'[18] For both, self-knowledge involves loss of self. One's personal sense of individuality is thrown into relief by encounter with the impersonal or the divine. 'The loss of self is really self-expansion … [for Jung] when one encounters the unconscious he becomes the known as opposed to the knower.':[19]

> Self-knowledge with Jung then results in the perception of the divine by a study of oneself, but this realization is not an objective observation of an identifiable part of one's thought and motives but rather a discovery of oneself in relation to a power greater than that of ordinary conscious being. This is exactly the result to be attained in Neo-Platonism.[20]

The next two steps, dialectic and 'the final act of vision', raise the problem of the role of the intellect. 'The One can never be actually grasped by intellect alone nor without intellect.'[21] For Jung, therapy is a dialectical process between two individuals as well as a dialectical process between the conscious and unconscious. 'Jung finds that consciousness may have to rise to higher intellectual levels to keep up with the unconscious.'[22] The final ecstasy in Plotinus or the transformative experience in Jung occur after prolonged and strenuous intellectual effort:

> In the final analysis one is brought by both the system of Plotinus and the interpretation of Jung to the somewhat paradoxical conclusion that the individual receives a mystic or at least non-rational sense of the power and peace, transferable into future living and coming from insight into an abstraction so complete as to have no meaning in terms of any human ethical ideal or divine personality. The One comes close to Nothingness in all save its power over him who experiences it.[23]

Robertson, in his paper 'Stairway to Heaven: Jung and Neoplatonism', includes Iamblichus and Proclus in his reading of Neoplatonism. He sees Proclus as the supreme representative of Neoplatonic philosophy. Perhaps this explains his significantly different representation of the Neoplatonic view of the body, compared with Barnes' account. Robertson points out that the Neoplatonists did not see Plato and Aristotle as representatives of two irreconcilable traditions. 'They didn't see any dramatic split between the ideas of Plato, with his world of ideal forms, and Aristotle, with his emphasis on the actual forms we encounter in nature …[they] were talking about the same thing. It is in the Neoplatonist's ability to see a unity' that they remind us of Jung.[24]

There is a correspondence between the Neoplatonic capacity to hold mind and matter together through the mechanism of emanation and Jung's theory that archetypes have both spiritual and material manifestations. Neoplatonism and Jung's psychology stand out within the Western tradition as the only systems of thought that have successfully resolved the mind/body split. Philosophically, this is achieved in Neoplatonism by the doctrine of emanation. 'Each emanation, since it comes from the One and partakes of the One, must in some way also contain the One. Therefore, the instincts can't be totally evil, since somehow they must also contain the divine.'[25] Robertson highlights the similarity between the Neoplatonic practice of theurgy and Jung's approach to dream interpretation and active imagination. He observes that theurgy means 'god work'. Theurgy enabled the embodied human to participate in the divine energy by opening communication between the human and divine which went beyond thought. The rituals included the body in the relationship with the One. According to Jung, for many people traditional symbols and rituals no longer carry the numinous. Through engaging with material from their unconscious in active imagination and dream interpretation, however, it is possible for these individuals to discover 'living symbols':

> Precisely because the new symbol is born of man's highest spiritual aspirations and must at the same time spring from the deepest roots of his being, it cannot be a one-sided product of the most highly differentiated mental functions, but must derive equally from the lowest and most primitive levels of the psyche.[26]

Robertson also contends that 'Neoplatonism originated the concept of a progressive, evolutionary path' toward union with the One. This is a 'holographic concept that at each step of the journey, we have the potential to experience the One that is the goal of the journey.'[27] This resonates with Jung's concept of individuation in which the path and the goal are both expressions of the archetype of the self.

Robertson discusses, in an earlier book, the fundamental importance of number in Platonic and Neoplatonic concepts of archetypes. Jung did not neglect this aspect of the problem:

> He speculated that number itself – as expressed most basically in the small integers – was *the most primitive archetype of order* … Jung felt that number might be the primary archetype of order in the *unus mundus* itself; i.e., the most basic building blocks of either psyche or matter are the integers.[28]

MacLennan explores the relationship between Neoplatonism, Jungian psychology and evolutionary neuroethology. He argues that the genome is 'the unified archetypal Form or Idea from which all other archetypal Ideas derive, the *eidos eidon* (Form of Forms) in Proclus' terms'.[29] He relates this to the noetic or intelligible order. 'In the genome the archetypal Ideas are "all in all, but each in its own way" (*panta en pasin, oikeious de en ekastou*), which is how Proclus described the Henads (e.g. *Elements of Theology*, proposition 118), which exist in an undifferentiated unity in the One.'[30]

The relationship between the human genome, the gene sequence of a particular individual and the *phenotype*, 'the resulting individual, whose traits have been conditioned, but not determined by the genotype'[31], is described, by MacLennan, as being analogous to the relationship between the collective unconscious, the archetypal image and the individual personality, on the one hand, and the relationship between the Henads, the world soul and the individual soul, on the other.

He discusses the Neoplatonic debate about the complete descent of the soul. Although the 'genome, and even the individual genotype, remains "above" in the noetic sphere … the articulated noeric images of the archetypal Ideas are represented in our brains in the structures subserving the archetypal behavior'.[32] He does not resolve the debate, but shows that it resonates with debates in analytical psychology and neuroethology. He also compares Jung's idea that the collective unconscious develops with the fact that 'the genome is not a fixed essence, but a time-varying form'.[33] 'The human genome at a given time is defined over a population existing at that time … the genome is defined by the set of participated genotypes.'[34] New DNA is created from the DNA of the parents and one manifestation of DNA goes out of existence when someone dies. 'Thus the evolution of the genome, as statistical average, is mediated by processes in the natural world.'[35] Similarly, there is an evolution of archetypes that is mediated through the material world.

MacLennan compares a number of theurgical operations with the practice of analysis. Theurgy uses *sunthemata* and *sumbola* (signs and symbols) and practises dream incubation. *Telestike* is the process of ensouling or animating a statue 'by placing in or on the image appropriate *sunthemata*, including stones, plants, animals, scents, and figures'.[36] He compares this to finding the appropriate archetypal image to make the presence of the archetype known. In *desmos* (binding) 'a *kletour* (caller) invokes a god or daimon to possess another person, called the *doxeus* (recipient), *theates* (seer), or *kataxos* (held–down one)'.[37] Although MacLennan does not indicate as much, this is clearly similar to transference/countertransference dynamics. *Eustasis*, 'liaison with a god or daimon in order to establish an alliance with it',[38] he compares with active imagination, a way of dialoguing with aspects of the unconscious. And finally he observes that 'in the preceding, the divinity is experienced as "other," but in the *anagoge* the theurgist ascends so that their soul, so far a possible, unites with the god; that is, they experience deification'.[39] MacLennan associates this with wholeness, 'integrating the conscious, personal unconscious, and collective unconscious minds'.[40]

Dionysius

In his library Jung had two manuscripts of the *Corpus Dionysiacum* – Strassburg (1502–3) and Paris (1644).[41] He cites Dionysius twelve times in the Collected Works,[42] usually referencing the English translations of Rolt and Parker. On one occasion he also quotes a paraphrase of Dionysius in a work by Pachymeres from Migne.[43]

The references to Dionysius fall into two main categories. He cites Dionysius as an important link in the genealogy of the concept of the archetype and Dionysius is among the main targets of his invective against the doctrine of the *privatio boni*. He also mentions Dionysius with reference to statues and to symbolism.

Jung observes, 'the actual term "archetype" … is to be found in Dionysius the Areopagite and in the *Corpus Hermeticum*':[44]

> The term 'archetype' occurs as early as Philo Judaeus, with the reference to the *Imago Dei* (God-image) in man. It can also be found in Irenaeus, who says: 'The creator of the world did not fashion these things directly from himself but copied them from archetypes outside himself.' In the *Corpus Hermeticum*, God is called *to archetypon phoos* (archetypal light). The term occurs several times in Dionysius the Areopagite, as for instance in *De caelesti hierarchia*, II, 4: 'immaterial Archetypes,' and in *De divinis nominibus*, I, 6: 'Archetypal stone.' [Note 6. In Migne, *P.G.*, vol. 3, col. 144. 7. Ibid., col. 595. Cf. *The Divine Names*, (trans. By Rolt), pp. 62, 72.][45]

He enlists the late antique discussion of archetypes to support his theory of the unconscious. In his essay 'On the Psychology of the Unconscious' he writes:

> The primordial images are the most ancient and the most universal 'thought-forms' of humanity. They are as much feelings as thoughts; indeed, they lead their own independent life rather in the manner of part-souls, as can easily be seen in those philosophical or Gnostic systems which rely on perceptions of the unconscious as the source of knowledge. The idea of angels, archangels, 'principalities and powers' in St. Paul, the archons of the Gnostics, the heavenly hierarchy of Dionysius the Areopagite, all come from the perception of the relative autonomy of the archetypes.[46]

In *Psychological Types*, Jung notes that Dionysius, whose 'writings exercised a considerable influence on early medieval philosophy, distinguished the categories *entia rationalia, intellectualia, sensibilia, simpliciter existentia*'.[47] Jung includes Dionysius among those who value the use of symbols:

> The timid defensiveness certain moderns display when it comes to thinking about symbols was certainly not shared by St. Paul or by many of the venerable Church Fathers. [Note 2. Of the older ones I refer chiefly to Clement of Alexandria (d. c. 216), Origen (d. 253) and Pseudo-Dionysius the Areopagite (d. end of 5th cent.).][48]

In *Mysterium Coniunctionis*, Jung describes symbolic thinking in Neoplatonic, hermetic and alchemical ideas about statues:

> The idea of a precious substance in the 'statue' is an old tradition and is particularly true of the statues of Hermes or Mercurius. Pseudo-Dionysius says that the pagans made statues of Mercurius and hid in them a simulacrum of the god. In this way they worshipped not the unseemly herm but the image hidden inside. [Note 60. Dionysius is cited in the alchemical literature. See *Theatr. chem.*, VI, p. 91.] [Note 61. 'They made in them [the statues] both doors and hollows, in which they placed images of the gods they worshipped. And so statues of Mercury after this kind appeared of little worth, but contained within them ornaments of gods' (Pachymeres' paraphrase of Dionysius the Areopagite, *De caelesti hierarchia*, in Migne, *P.G.*, vol. 3, col. 162).][49]

In *Mysterium Coniunctionis* Jung also refers to Dionysius' schema of 'mystical ascent':

> It seems to me that Eleazar's text conveys some idea of this, as the transformation of the black Shulamite take place in three stages, which were mentioned by Dionysius the Areopagite as characterizing the mystical ascent: *emundatio* (*katharsis*, 'purification'), *illuminatio* (*phoutismos*), *perfectio* (*telesmos*). Dionysius refers the purification to Psalm 51:7: 'Wash me, and I shall be whiter than snow'; and the illumination to Psalm 13:3: 'Lighten mine eyes.' (The two heavenly luminaries, sun and moon, correspond on the old view to the two eyes.) The perfection he refers to Matthew 5:48: 'Be ye therefore perfect, even as your Father which is in heaven is perfect.' Here we have one aspect of the approximation to divinity: the other aspect is exemplified by the image of the Apocalyptic Son of Man, described earlier. (354 *The Celestial Hierarchies*, III, 3 [Eng. Trans., p. 18])[50]

The most significant references to Dionysius in Jung's work, however, are in relation to the problem of evil. In Jung's opinion, Dionysius was one of the prime culprits in the development of the concept of the *privatio boni*. This doctrine 'nullifies the reality of evil and can be found as early as Basil the Great (33-79) and Dionysius the Areopagite (2nd half of the 4th century), and is fully developed in Augustine'.[51] Jung explains Dionysius' view of the relationship between good and evil and then supplies a quotation from Parker's translation of the *Divine Names*:

> Dionysius the Areopagite gives a detailed explanation of evil in the fourth chapter of *De divinis nominbus*. Evil, he says, cannot come from good, because if it came from good it would not be evil. But since everything that exists comes from good, everything is in some way good, but 'evil does not exist at all.'

Evil in its nature is neither a thing nor does it bring anything forth.

Evil does not exist at all and is neither good nor productive of good.

All things which are, by the very fact that they are, are good, and come from good; but in so far as they are deprived of good they are neither good nor do they exist.

That which has no existence is not altogether evil, for the absolutely non-existent will be nothing, unless it be thought of as subsisting in the good superessentially. Good, then as absolutely existing and as absolutely non-existing, will stand in the foremost and highest place, while evil is neither in that which exists nor in that which does not exist.[52]

Jung cites references from Augustine and quotes a lengthy commentary from Aquinas on this passage from Dionysius:

These quotations clearly exemplify the standpoint of Dionysius and Augustine: evil has no substance or existence in itself, since it is merely a diminution of good, which alone has substance. Evil is a *vitium*, a bad use of things as a result of erroneous decisions of the will (blindness due to evil desire, etc.).[53]

In a note in 'A Study in the Process of Individuation', Jung says he is 'purposely disregarding ... the heavenly hierarchies of Dionysius the Areopagite', along with a number of other symbolic systems, because 'these all ignore the reality of evil, because they regard it as a mere *privatio boni* and thereby dismiss it with a euphemism'.[54]

In this discussion Jung selects texts which serve his polemical purpose. There is some question in my mind whether he does justice to the complexity of Dionysius' view of evil. This problem however is beyond the scope of this study. In any case, this is one of many instances in Jung's work where there appears to be confusion and lack of clarity in his attempt to move between of the language of metaphysics and the language of psychology.

Jung's reading of Dionysius, as well as other Platonic and Neoplatonic texts, placed him close to the source of important currents of apophatic discourse. It is likely, however, that he was looking for material to bolster his own ideas rather than to study and appropriate the thoughts of these writers on their own terms.

Notes

1 Dourley, John (1995), *Jung and the Religious Alternative: The Rerooting*. Lampeter: Edwin Mellen, p. 28.
2 Bishop, Paul (2000), *Synchronicity and Intellectual Intuition in Kant, Swedenborg, and Jung*. Lampeter: Edwin Mellen, p. 74.
3 CW5 21.
4 CW11 758.

5   Pauson, Marian (1988), *Jung the Philosopher: Essays in Jungian Thought*. New York: Peter Lang, p. 1.
6   CW11 190.
7   CW11 759.
8   CW16 397.
9   CW9i 550.
10 CW9ii 251.
11 Nagy, Marilyn (1991), *Philosophical Issues in the Psychology of C. G. Jung*. Albany, NY: SUNY Press, pp. 149–50.
12 Altizer, Thomas J. J. (1955), *A Critical Analysis of C. G. Jung's Understanding of Religion*. PhD thesis, University of Chicago, p. 248.
13 Altizer, p. 249.
14 Barnes, Hazel E. (1945), 'Neo-Platonism and Analytical Psychology, *Philosophical Review*, 54(6): 565.
15 Barnes, p. 560.
16 Barnes, p. 567.
17 Barnes, p. 567.
18 Jung, C. G. (1939), *The Integration of the Personality*. London: Routledge & Kegan Paul, p. 111.
19 Barnes, p. 570.
20 Barnes, p. 573.
21 Barnes, p. 573.
22 Barnes, p. 574.
23 Barnes, p. 576.
24 Robertson, Robin (2002), 'Stairway to Heaven: Jung and Neoplatonism', http://www.angelfire.com/super/magicrobin/STAIRWAY.htm, p. 5.
25 Robertson, p. 6.
26 CW6 823.
27 Robertson, p. 8.
28 Robertson, Robin (1995), *Jungian Archetypes: Jung, Godel, and the History of Archetypes*. York Beach, ME: Nicholas-Hays, p. 270.
29 MacLennan, Bruce (2003), 'Evolution, Jung, and Theurgy: Their Role in Modern Neoplatonism', http://www.cs.utk.edu/~mclennan, p. 6.
30 MacLennan, p. 6.
31 MacLennan, p. 6.
32 MacLennan, p. 9–10.
33 MacLennan, p. 15.
34 MacLennan, p. 15.
35 MacLennan, p. 15.
36 MacLennan, p. 19.
37 MacLennan, p. 19.
38 MacLennan, p. 20.
39 MacLennan, p. 20.
40 MacLennan, p. 20.
41 *C. G. Jung Bibliothek: Katalog, Kusnacht-Zurich*, 1967.
42 CW6 62; 7 104; 9i 5, 603*n*; 9ii 80, 87, 88, 91; 11 170*n*; 14 564&*n*, 644.
43 Migne, *PG*, vol. 3, col. 162 (CW14:564*n*).
44 CW6 62.
45 CW9i 5.
46 CW7 104.
47 CW6 62.
48 CW11 170*n*.

49   CW14 564&*n*.
50   CW14 644.
51   CW9ii 80.
52   CW9ii 87–8. The quotation from Dionysius is accompanied by the following footnote: Migne, *P.G.*, vol. 3, cols. 716–18. Cf. the *Works of Dionysius the Areopagite*, trans. by John Parker, I, pp. 53*ff*.
53   CW9ii 91.
54   CW9i 603*n*.

Chapter 5

The opposites

The theme of the relations between opposites is central to Jung's thought. Looking back on his life he recalled reading Goethe when he was a teenager. '*Faust* struck a chord in me and pierced me through in a way that I could not but regard as personal. Most of all, it awakened in me the problem of opposites, of good and evil, of mind and matter, of light and darkness.'[1] While initially he experienced this as a personal problem he came to see that it had wider resonances. 'The fact, therefore, that a polarity underlies the dynamics of the psyche means that the whole problem of opposites in its broadest sense, with all its concomitant religious and philosophical aspects, is drawn into the psychological discussion.'[2] As we shall see, however, this theme did not emerge explicitly in his work until well after his break with Freud.

In his writings Jung discusses the union of opposites, the coincidence of opposites (*coincidentia oppositorum*), *complexio oppositorum*, conjunction of opposites (*coniunctio oppositorum*), the tension of opposites, compensation, complimentarity, enantriodromia and psychic balance. Jung is not systematic in his use of these terms. I will discuss in some detail his use of the following concepts: coincidence of opposites, *complexio oppositorum*, *coniunctio oppositorum* and union of opposites.

Coincidence of opposites

The coincidence of opposites (*coincidentia oppositorum*) is one of the fundamental organizing principles in Jung's thought. Key concepts such as the self, the god image, the collective unconscious, wholeness and synchronicity are instances of the coincidence of opposites. In 1931, in his first use of the term, Jung describes the practice of psychology as a kind of performance of the coincidence of opposites:[3]

> The modern psychologist occupies neither the one position nor the other, but finds himself between the two, dangerously committed to 'this as well as that' – situation which seductively opens the way to a shallow opportunism. This is undoubtedly the great danger of the *coincidentia oppositorum* – of intellectual freedom from the opposites. How should anything but a

formless and aimless uncertainty result from giving equal value to two contradictory hypotheses? In contrast to this we can readily appreciate the advantage of an explanatory principle that is unequivocal: it allows of a standpoint that can serve as a point of reference. We must be able to appeal to an explanatory principle founded on reality, and yet it is no longer possible for the modern psychologist to take his stand exclusively on the physical aspect of reality once he has given the spiritual aspect its due.[4]

Here, Jung is holding the physical and spiritual to be a coincidence of opposites and is arguing that a modern psychology must accommodate both. Pietkainen writes:

> Like Cassirer, Jung holds that the conditions of cultural evolution are determined by the 'law' of *coincidentia oppositorum*, which he interprets as the dynamic equilibrium between conscious and the unconscious. The idea of this 'dynamic equilibrium' was one of Jung's most fundamental tenets. With good reason he could be called a *psychologist of coincidentia oppositorum*. He was well aware that this term was devised (or rather reawakened) by Cusanus, and in his psychology it is closely related to his energetic conception of the psyche as a self-regulating system.[5]

As McCort observes:

> [one] peculiarly modern, underground 'hideout' in the West for the *coincidentia* is the psychotherapist's office … [Jung's] entire vast enterprise is a tireless working-out of the idea of *conjunctio*, theoretically in his writings and practically in his efforts to guide his patients toward 'individuation'.[6]

Eliade links Heraclitus, Dionysius, Cusa and Jung, and states that, for Jung, 'the *coincidentia oppositorum* [is] the ultimate aim of the whole psychic activity'.[7]

Coincidence here refers to simultaneity, not to chance or randomness. Two phenomena coincide when they occupy the same space, be it logical, imaginative or material space. In popular usage this notion of coincidence is often missed:

> To call something a coincidence implies that it should not really happen and thus allows us to dismiss the coincidence as an unexpected, unusual anomaly that, according to probability, will not happen again. The history of the word in English, as chronicled in the *Oxford English Dictionary*, reveals that this dismissive meaning gradually creeps in, as the word is linked with 'casual' and 'undesigned.' The root meaning of the Latin word, which was used in the seventeenth century as a verb in English in its Latin form, 'coincidere,' is simply 'to occur together'.[8]

Even as important a commentator on Jung as Bishop misconstrues the true nature of coincidence by settling for the most colloquial usage. He suggests that Jung was 'misleading' when he defined synchronicity as meaningful coincidence. 'This expression is somewhat misleading, for the whole point, as far as Jung was concerned, was that more than mere chance was involved.'[9]

Jung's lifelong preoccupation with the coincidence of opposites is a preoccupation with trying to understand the simultaneous appearance of apparently incompatible phenomena, events or situations. We are reminded here of Sells' description of apophatic discourse:

> Classical Western apophasis shares three key features: (1) the metaphor of overflowing or 'emanation' which is often in creative tension with the language of intentional, demiurgic creation; (2) dis-ontological discursive effort to avoid reifying the transcendent as an 'entity' or 'being' or 'thing'; (3) a distinctive dialectic of transcendence and immanence in which the utterly transcendent is revealed as the utterly immanent.[10]

Sells seems to be describing three instances of the coincidence of opposites: overflowing/intentional (emanation/creation), dis-ontological/reifying, and transcendence/immanence.

This link between the coincidence of opposites and *apophasis* is strengthened by the fact that Jung cites Nicholas of Cusa (1401–1464) as his source for the term.[11] Jung asserts that the often 'tortuous language' associated with the discussion of the union of opposites 'cannot be called abstruse since it has universal validity, from the *tao* of Lao-tzu to the *coincidentia oppositorum* of Cusanus'.[12]

Cusa is a major figure in the tradition of apophatic discourse in the West[13] and Dionysius was an important influence on Cusa.[14] Along with the infinite disproportion between the finite and the infinite, and learned ignorance, the coincidence of opposites is one of the three central doctrines of Cusa's thought.[15] Ideas of the coincidence of opposites predate Cusa, but he is the first to develop the concept systematically and to make it a lynchpin of his philosophy and theology. For Cusa the coincidence of opposites is a methodology:

> At infinity thoroughgoing coincidence occurs ... at true infinity there is one only and all are one. The coincidence of opposites provides a method that resolves contradictions without violating the integrity of the contrary elements and without diminishing the reality or the force of their contradiction. It is not a question of seeing unity where there is no real contrariety, nor is it a question of forcing harmony by synthesizing resistant parties. Coincidence as a method issues from coincidence as a fact or condition of opposition that is resolved in and by infinity.[16]

Cusa used the idea of the coincidence of opposites to accomplish a range of tasks:

In every case by applying the logic of infinitude, coincidence, as Cusa intends it, accomplishes certain common tasks: (1) It unites opposites; (2) it transcends analogy and comparison; (3) it overcomes the limits of discursive reasoning; (4) it exceeds composition and synthesis; (5) it surpasses both affirmative and negative language; (6) it frees the mind from quantitative concepts and enables it to achieve a comparatively pure abstraction; and (7) whether operating from theology, philosophy, mathematics, or geometry, it renders infinite concepts understandable and describable without violating their incomprehensibility or illimitability.[17]

Jung simultaneously appealed to Cusa's thought and denigrated it. He described it as an expression of the influence of the collective unconscious on the development of ideas in the fourteenth century. He claims that Cusa's coincidence of opposites is a staging post on the way to developing a more balanced god image. Under compensatory pressure from the collective unconscious, the idea of the *summum bonum* was being undermined. According to Jung, Cusa did not, and could not, grasp the import of this aspect of his thought, because he did not have the necessary psychological concepts at his disposal. Jung writes, 'It should not be forgotten, however, that the opposites which Nicholas had in mind were very different from the psychological ones.'[18] In fact, Cusa's use of the concept of coincidence of opposites was more complex than Jung appears to acknowledge. Cusa uses it not only as a theological tool but applies it to all aspects of reality, including to the natural world.

Beyond the polemical strategy of playing off psychological language against metaphysical language and his tendency to sometimes pick up concepts and make use of them with minimal attention to how they were used by the author he is citing, the fact that Jung appears to have relied on two very early works by Cusa probably contributes to his narrow understanding of Cusa's use of the coincidence of opposites. For the purposes of this discussion I suggest that there are three distinct phases of Cusa's thought about the coincidence of opposites. The first occurs in the two works cited by Jung, *On Learned Ignorance* (1440) and *De Coniectruis* (1442). The second phase in *On the Vision of God* (1453) and the third in *On the Summit of Contemplation* (1464), completed shortly before Cusa's death. Cusa's understanding of the coincidence of opposites continued to develop after the versions that Jung cites.

In *On Learned Ignorance* the coincidence of opposites is described as one type of union of opposites. It is a 'unity in convergence, that is, a "falling together" … a unity geometrically conceived, but without quantity … It is a unity of substance without mingling and without obliteration of either party or substance.'[19] Other types of union of opposites include instances where one opposite supersedes the other, where the two opposites are superseded by creation of a third, and where the elements of the opposites are mingled. The coincidence of opposites is beyond the reach of discursive reasoning. The coincidence of opposites is a 'unity to which neither otherness nor plurality nor multiplicity is opposed'.[20]

Moving beyond the discussion in *On Learned Ignorance*, in *On the Vision of God* 'Cusa takes the notion of coincidence to its limits, beyond itself'.[21] In *On the Vision of God*, which Jung does not cite, the term *coincidence* occurs forty-six times. It is:

> the device by which finite knowing and saying can grasp the incomprehensible and speak the ineffable ... It is a fact or principle and therefore discoverable, but no merely invented or contrived as we might use comparisons, metaphors, or analogies in ordinary language ... it sets forth the way God works, the order of things in relation to God and to each other, and the manner by which humans may approach and abide in God.[22]

The idea that coincidence is discoverable would chime with Jung's assertion that his psychology is empirical. The fact that it applies to relations in nature as well as those between nature and God and beyond nature, contradicts Jung's assertion that Cusa's coincidence of opposites is a purely metaphysical idea.

In *On the Vision of God* Cusa describes the coincidence of opposites as the wall of paradise, beyond which is God:

> God is beyond the realm of contradictories ... there exists an impenetrable barrier to human vision and reason ... he intends that the reader understand not so much that God is the coincidence of opposites, but rather that opposites coincide in God ... the notion of opposites coinciding requires a transcendent vision – seeing beyond particularity and sensibility, a seeing through and beyond the image or symbol, and an antecedent seeing, considering problems in their infinitely simple principle prior to contradiction.[23]

> To see coincidence is still not to see God. God, the object of human's effort to see, however, acts on our seeing as subject so that the searcher and observer discovers oneself searched out, observed, measure, defined. This is one of the more interesting features of Cusa's treatise – the human as *figura*, the theologian discovering oneself as symbol; the searcher after the meaning behind symbols becomes oneself a symbol:[24]

> Mystical theology makes special demands on the theologian, both affective and didactic. The ministry of such a theology requires a coincident method and an iconographic language, acknowledging the utter transcendence and mystery of god and communicating the paradoxical truth that God is known, and seen, as made known ... The coincident method in service to mystical theology, therefore performs both an evocative and a descriptive function.[25]

The idea that 'the searcher after meaning behind symbols becomes oneself a symbol' resonates with Jung's observations at the end of *Memories, Dreams, Reflections*:

When Lao-tzu says: 'All are clear, I alone am clouded,' he is expressing what I now feel in advanced old age. Lao-tzu is the example of a man with superior insight who has seen and experienced worth and worthlessness, and who at the end of his life desires to return into his own being, into the eternal unknowable meaning. The archetype of the old man who has seen enough is eternally true. At every level of intelligence this type appears, and its lineaments are always the same, whether it be an old peasant or a great philosopher like Lao-tzu. This is old age, and a limitation. Yet there is so much that fills me: plants, animals, clouds, day and night, and the eternal in man. The more uncertain I have felt about myself, the more there has grown up in me a feeling of kinship with all things. In fact it seems to me as if that alienation which so long separated me from the world has become transferred into my own inner world, and has revealed to me an unexpected unfamiliarity with myself.[26]

There are some parallels between Jung's late reflections and Cusa's last work, *On the Summit of Contemplation*, published in 1464. Earlier, in 1460, Cusa had used the term *possest* to name God. It is 'a play on words, a coincidence of *posse* ('can') and *est* ('is'), the Can, the Possibility that at the same time Is, the Can-Is, which only God can be.'[27] In *On the Summit of Contemplation* Cusa calls God *Posse* Itself. According to Bond, Cusa is 'superseding not only negation and affirmation but also the coincidence of opposites'.[28] This echoes Dionysius' schema of *kataphasis, apophasis, ekstasis. Posse* Itself is:

> that without which nothing whatsoever can be, or live, or understand … without *posse* nothing whatsoever can be or can have, can do or can undergo … if it were not presupposed, nothing whatever could be … In its power are necessarily contained those things that are as well as those that are not.[29]

Seeing the *Posse* Itself involves neither comprehension nor cognition. Cusa 'embraces the negation of knowing and at the same time the affirmation of sight'.[30] The mind's capacity to see *Posse* Itself lies in its own *posse*. In this sense the *posse* of the mind is the image of God, *Posse* Itself:

> This *posse* of the mind to see beyond all comprehensible faculty and power is the mind's supreme *posse*. In it *Posse* Itself manifests itself maximally, and the mind's supreme *posse* is not brought to its limit this side of *Posse* Itself. For the *posse* to see is directed only to *Posse* Itself so that the mind can foresee that toward which it tends, just as a traveller foresees one's journey's end so that one can direct one's steps toward the desired goal … For *Posse* Itself, when it will appear in the glory of majesty, is alone able to satisfy the mind's longing. For it is that *what* which is sought.[31]

Jung and Cusa share a view that there is a bridge between the human and a greater reality. For Jung this bridge is the self and for Cusa it is the *posse* of the mind.

When Herbert links Jung and Cusa, he quotes from *On the Vision of God*, which, as we have seen, Jung does not refer to in his own work and which, I would conjecture, Jung had not read:

> The psychologist C. G. Jung reinforces this linkage in his volume of the collected works entitled *Alchemical Studies* when he asserts that in the first so-called *negredo* stage of alchemical transformation associated with 'the dark Mercury', and the god himself plus the spirit he represents 'is the *uroborus*, the One and All, the union of opposites accomplished during the alchemical process'. Jung's statement here highlights not only the connection between the *ouroboros* and the *Eins und Alles* theme but also 'the union of opposites' each embodies, thereby establishing them as an illustration and a formulation respectively of the idea of universal complementarity enclosed within the unified wholeness of either a circle or a conceptual Oneness (*Eins*). In German terms this is highly expressive of Nikolaus Cusanus's theory and goal of the *coincidentia oppositorum* (the concurrence of opposites) which culminate in an ultimate order that is God, who 'is Himself the Absolute Ground, in which all otherness is unity, and all diversity is identity' (*De Visione Dei*).[32]

McCort has a restricted view of how the coincidence of opposites operates in Jung's thought. He sees the coincidence of opposites as an aspect of the self archetype, as 'an idea embodying man's ineradicable yearning for ultimate reconciliation ... that reveals to us the impossible, yet necessary, congruence of transcendence and immanence ... the metamyth of the overcoming of difference'.[33] He asks whether the coincidence of opposites is an archetype:

> Precisely put, the question would seem to be whether the *coincidentia* is equitable with Jung's self archetype which, as it manifests in myths and certain dreams, is characterized by Jung as 'the *eidos* behind the supreme ideas of unity and totality that are inherent in all monotheistic and monistic systems' [*Aion* 34]. My answer to this is a reluctant yes, reluctant for the following reason. Strictly speaking, the *coincidentia* is prior to all manifestation, being rather the eternal, dynamic threshold of manifestation, while yet comprehending anything through manifestation as an archetypal image, however lofty or powerful, it of necessity takes on a certain kind of bipolarity, becoming, so to speak, one vis-à-vis others (call it the one superior versus the many inferior archetypes) and thus is already less than the pleroma. I know Jung was well aware of this 'paradox of manifestation', yet on occasion he forgets himself and writes carelessly of the self as if it were a *prima causa* and thus merely the *primus inter pares* of a descending order of archetypal causes: 'Wholeness is thus an objective factor that confronts the subject independently of him, like anima or animus; and just as the later have a higher position in the hierarchy [of archetypes] than the

shadow, so wholeness lays claim to a position and a value superior to those of the syzygy … Unity and totality stand at the highest point on the scale of objective values.' [*Aion* 31] … My own sense is that the *coincidentia*, or what Jung calls the self, is not itself a cause, even a first cause, but rather the condition of all causation, as of all other principles of relative existence. It is beyond causation even while comprehending causation – indeed, how else could it be a true *coincidentia oppositorum*? Perhaps calling it a meta-archetype, ontologically beyond the order of archetypes yet remaining 'close' to them, would help to keep this important distinction in mind. In the end, it is the Great Abyss, in whose proximity even poles of archetypal power yearn to lose themselves in one another.[34]

The coincidence of opposites as a limit or door to paradise, described in Cusa's *On the Vision of God*, brings to mind Paper's distinction between functional and non-functional ecstasies.[35] Functional ecstasies include visions, lucid dreams and problem-solving; dreams; shamanism; mediumism; and prophecy. Non-functional ecstasies include: unitive experiences; pure consciousness; and mystic experience. Jung uses coincidence of opposites in a functional way to describe a psychological, therapeutic process. Since Jung's aim is to develop a psychology based on a teleological view of psychic phenomena it is not clear what place he allows for non-functional states. It is unclear whether or not Jung can accommodate 'mystic experience', in Paper's sense, because it goes beyond psychology, much as God is beyond the coincidence of opposites in *On the Vision of God*.

Jung's earliest reference to Cusa is in his paper of 1942, 'A Psychological Approach to the Trinity'. He writes, 'Thus the spirit as a *complexio oppositorum* has the same formula as the "Father," the *auctor rerum*, who is also, according to Nicholas of Cusa, a union of opposites', and adds a footnote: 'It should not be forgotten, however, that the opposites which Nicholas had in mind were very different from the psychological ones.'[36] In 1951 in *Aion* he asserts that *complexio oppositorum* is 'a definition of God in Nicholas of Cusa'.[37]

A major problem arises because Jung repeatedly attributes the term *complexio oppositorum* to Cusa, rather than *coincidentia oppositorum*. In seven places Jung links *complexio oppositorum* with Cusa and in three places he uses *coincidentia oppositorum*. It is not until 1946 in 'The Psychology of the Transference' that Jung links Cusa with the *coincidentia oppositorum*.[38] Jung seems to treat the two terms as interchangeable. In fact *complexio oppositorum* does not appear in Cusa. Perhaps Jung has projected his own concept of the complex onto Cusa's concept of coincidence. Beyond the clear factual error of misattribution, there is the conceptual error of confusing *coincidentia* and *complexio*.

In 'The Psychology of the Transference' Jung references *De Docta Ignorantia*, without citing a particular edition,[39] and a second quotation is presumably from the same source,[40] though this is not clear. A third reference in the same paragraph is attributed to Heron's 1954 English translation of Rotta's 1923 edition of *De Docta Ignorantia*.[41] Koch's 1936/7 edition of Cusa texts is cited in the bibliography of CW16, but does not appear in any footnotes. Jung's text of *De Conjectures Novissimorum Temporum* is from 1565 and presumably in Latin.[42] A further source, cited once in 1946, is Vansteenberghe's 1920 work on Cusa.[43] From this evidence I think that we can assume that Jung became familiar with Cusa after 1920, and most likely not until the 1930s. In any case it is not until the 1940s that Jung begins to use the coincidence of opposites to describe the self and/or God. Most of his references to the coincidence of opposites occur in the 1950s.

Jung uses the term 'coincidence of opposites' on a number of occasions without explicit reference to Cusa.[44] The earliest of these is the one cited above in 'Basic Postulates of Analytical Psychology', published in 1931. The next occurrence of the term in the *Collected Works* is in a quotation from Rudolf Otto in 1939.[45]

In 1943 in 'The Spirit Mercurius', it seems to me that Jung is painting a picture of Mercurius as an apophatic symbol. Mercurius 'consists of the most extreme opposites'.[46] Jung argues that the alchemists understood hell to be 'an internal component of the deity, which must indeed be so if God is held to be a *coincidentia oppositorum*. The concept of an all-encompassing God must necessarily include his opposite.' Jung cautions however, that:

> the *coincidentia* … must not be too radical or too extreme, otherwise God would cancel himself out. The principle of the coincidence of opposites must therefore be completed by that absolute opposition in order to attain full paradoxicality and hence psychological validity.[47]

Full paradoxicality and psychological validity contribute to what Sells calls 'apophatic intensity'. Jung's statement, however, that 'the principle of coincidence of opposites must therefore be completed by that absolute opposition in order to attain full paradoxicality and hence psychological validity', demonstrates that he has not fully grasped Cusa's notion of the coincidence of opposites, because in Cusa coincidence does not abolish absolute opposition.

In his discussion of a dream in *Psychology and Alchemy* (1944), Jung states that conflict is an essential aspect of the self. 'The self is made manifest in the opposites and in the conflict between them; it is a *coincidentia oppositorum*. Hence the way to the self begins with conflict.'[48]

In 'The Psychology of the Transference', published in 1946, Jung describes the alchemical procedure of *mundificatio* (purification) as 'an attempt to discriminate the mixture, to sort out the *coincidentia oppostitorum*'.[49] Here, the coincidence of opposites is presented as a pathological situation in which the patient is stuck. After the *mundificatio* the relationship between conscious and unconscious is 'depicted in the alchemists' Rebis, the symbol of transcendental unity, as a coincidence of opposites'.[50] In a lengthy paragraph on wholeness at the end of this essay, in which he refers to Cusa three times, Jung writes: 'The symbol of this is a *coincidentia oppositorum* which, as we know, Nicholas of Cusa identified with God.'[51] As we have seen this is an oversimplification of Cusa's view.

In 'A Psychological Approach to the Trinity' (1948), a revised and expanded version of a talk given at the Eranos Conference in 1942, Jung wonders 'with what right Christ is presumed to be a symbol of the self, since the self is by definition a *complexio oppositoum*, whereas the Christ figure wholly lacks a dark side?'[52]

In 1951, in *Aion*, his exploration of the relationship between the image of God and the self, Jung asserts:

> The coincidence of opposites is the normal thing in a primitive conception of God, since God not being an object of reflection, is simply taken for granted. At the level of conscious reflection, however, the coincidence of opposites becomes a major problem, which we do everything possible to circumvent.[53]

To the conscious mind the paradoxical nature of the god image, containing good and evil, can be shocking. Further on in a discussion of *agnousia* Jung observes that for Eckhart the Godhead 'represents an absolute coincidence of opposites', which from the standpoint of human logic 'is equivalent to unconsciousness'.[54]

Mysterium Coniunctionis: An Inquiry into the Separation and Synthesis of Psychic Opposites in Alchemy, published in 1955, contains seven references to the coincidence of opposites. Early in the text he has a footnote explaining his concept of the self. 'The concept of the self is essentially intuitive and embraces ego-consciousness, shadow, anima, and collective unconscious in indeterminable extension. As a totality, the self is a coincidentia oppositorum; it is therefore bright and dark and neither.'[55] This description of the self as 'bright and dark and neither', echoes Dionysius' schema of kataphatic, apophatic and ecstatic.

One of the many alchemical images Jung comments on is the dog. 'The ambiguity of this figure is thus stressed: it is at once bright as day and dark as night, a perfect *coincidentia oppositorum* expressing the divine nature of the self.'[56]

The motif of the crossing of the Red Sea is also an image of the coincidence of opposites for the Peratic group of Gnostics. The creative and destructive powers of the unconscious are contained within this image:

> This *coincidentia oppositorum* forms a parallel to the Messianic state of fulfilment described in Isaiah ... though with one important difference: the place of 'genesis outside of generation' − presumably an *opus contra naturam* − is clearly not paradise but *he eremos*, the desert and the wilderness. Everyone who becomes conscious of even a fraction of his unconscious gets outside his own time and social stratum into a kind of solitude.[57]

In another Gnostic source the crossing of the Red Sea involves 'running without running, moving without motion', which Jung characterizes as a coincidence of opposites.[58]

The theme of transformation continues in Jung's discussion of the alchemical symbol of the marriage of the king and queen. 'The coronation, apotheosis, and marriage signalize the equal status of conscious and unconscious that becomes possible at the highest level – a *coincidentia oppositorum* with redeeming effects.'[59]

The last reference to the coincidence of opposites in the Collected Works is in the 1958 essay, 'Flying saucers: a modern myth', Jung observes about the action in a dream he is discussing: 'This shows that it is a sequence and not a *coincidentia oppositorum*.'

Complexio oppositorum

We have seen that in several places Jung uses the term *complexio oppositorum* in a way that would give the impression he was quoting Cusa. There are in addition a number of occasions when he makes use of the term without reference to Cusa. He uses this term almost exclusively from 1950 onwards. The only times the term appears before 1950 are in 'The Spirit Mercurius' (1943), *Psychology and Alchemy* (1944), 'On the Nature of the Psyche' (1947) and 'A Psychological Approach to the Trinity' (1948). 'The paradoxical nature of Mercurius reflects an important aspect of the self – the fact, namely, that it is essentially a *complexio oppositorum*, and indeed can be nothing else if it is to represent any kind of totality.'[60] The unicorn is a common symbol in alchemy. 'Originally a monstrous and fabulous beast, it harbours in itself an inner contradiction, a *complexio oppositorum*, which makes it a singularly appropriate symbol for the *monstrum hermaphroditum* of alchemy.'[61] In discussing the 'chaotic assortment of images' that appear in fantasies, he observes that: 'Triadic formations, apart from the *complexio oppositorum* in a third, were relatively rare and formed notable exceptions.'[62]

In 'A Psychological Approach to the Trinity' Jung makes a statement that might be characterized as a type of apophatic anthropology.

> The unconscious is trying to express certain facts for which there are no conceptual categories in the conscious mind. The contents in question need not be 'metaphysical,' as in the case of the Holy Ghost. Any content that transcends consciousness, and for which the apperceptive apparatus does not exist, can call forth the same kind of paradoxical or antinomial symbolism.[63]

He asserts that 'the Holy Spirit is a *complexio oppositorum*' and supplies a flavour of the qualities that the *complexio oppositorum* symbolizes:

> But the spontaneous symbolism of the *complexio oppositorum* points to the exact opposite of annihilation, since it ascribes to the product of their union either everlasting duration, that is to say incorruptibility and adamantine stability, or supreme and inexhaustible efficacy.[64]

In 1950, in 'A Study in the Process of Individuation', Jung gives us what we might take to be his clearest definition of the *complexio oppositorum*:

> The ancient formula *lithos ou lithos* (the stone that is no stone) expresses this dilemma: we are dealing with a *complexio oppositorum*, with something like the nature of light, which under some conditions behaves like particles and under others like waves, and is obviously in its essence both at once. Something of this kind must be conjectured with regard to these paradoxical and hardly explicable statements of the unconscious. They are not inventions of a conscious mind, but are spontaneous manifestations of a psyche not controlled by consciousness and obviously possessing all the freedom it wants to express views that take no account of our conscious intentions ... One can only conclude that the unconscious tends to regard spirit and matter not merely as equivalent but as actually identical, and this in flagrant contrast to the intellectual one-sidedness of consciousness, which would sometimes like to spiritualize matter and at other times to materialize spirit ... This duality reminds one of the alchemical duality *corpus* and *spiritus*, joined together by a third, the *anima* as the *ligamentum corpus spiritus*.[65]

In the same year, in 'Concerning Rebirth', he describes the legend of Khidr. At the end of the narrative 'the opposites are separated and a timeless state of permanence sets in'. This view of eschatology is 'in contrast to the view that sees the end as a *complexio oppositorum*'.[66]

In *Aion*, published in 1951, in a discussion of the *privatio boni* Jung reiterates his opposition to metaphysics. 'Since psychology is not metaphysics, no metaphysical dualism can be derived from, or imputed to, its statements concerning the equivalence of opposites.' In a footnote to this sentence he refutes Victor White's assertion that Jung has 'a Manichaean streak' and asserts the 'my critic should know how very much I stress the unity of the self, this central archetype which is a *complexio oppositorum* par excellence, and that my leanings are therefore toward the very reverse of dualism'.[67] In the conclusion he argues deductively that we can know that 'the self is a *complexio oppositorum* precisely because there can be no reality without polarity'.[68]

In *Aion*, Jung develops the idea that the fish is an image of the self. 'Silver and gold, in alchemical language, signify feminine and masculine, and the hermaphrodite aspect of the fish, indicating that it is a *complexio oppositorum*.'[69] The self is an archetype and 'all archetypes spontaneously develop favourable and unfavourable, light and dark, good and bad effects'. Therefore, 'in the end we have to acknowledge that the self is a *complexio oppositorum* precisely because there can be no reality without polarity'.[70]

In the Prefatory Note to *Answer to Job* (1952) Jung explains how he came to focus on Job:

Moreover, the study of medieval natural philosophy – of the greatest importance to psychology – made me try to find an answer to the question: what image of God did these philosophers have? Or rather: how should the symbols which supplement their image of God be understood? All this pointed to a *complexio oppositorum* and thus recalled again the story of Job to my mind: Job who expected help from God against God. This most peculiar face presupposes a similar conception of the opposites in God.[71]

In the Book of Revelation, at the opening of the seventh seal the sun-woman gives birth to a son, 'a *complexio oppositorum*, a uniting symbol, a totality of life'.[72] Further along in the same text Jung observes, 'As a totality, the self is by definition always a *complexio oppositorum*, and the more consciousness insists on its own luminous nature and lays claim to moral authority, the more the self will appear as something dark and menacing.'[73] *Answer to Job* is an extended meditation on light and dark, good and evil in the god image.

In 1954, in a discussion about dogma in a letter to Pere Lachat, Jung writes that he prefers to maintain the independence of the Holy Spirit. '[T]he Holy Spirit is *one*, a *complexio oppositorum*, in contrast to YHWH after the separation of the divine opposites symbolized by God's two sons, Christ and Satan.'[74] A year later, in *Mysterium Coniunctionis*, he rehearses the arguments of Koepgen, in *Die Gnosis des Christentums*, that because Christ and the Church are by nature androgynous there is no need for 'the marriage of the Lamb at the end of time, for the androgyne "has everything it needs" and is already a *complexio oppositorum*'.[75]

'Jung and Religious Belief' consists of extracts from *Jung and the Problem of Evil*, H. L. Philp's 1958 volume of correspondence between himself and Jung. It also includes correspondence with David Cox, the author of *Jung and St Paul*. In response to a question from Philp about his concept of the quaternity, Jung argues that the quaternity is a 'natural and spontaneous symbol' while the Trinity is an abstraction. He states that the Star of David is a *complexio oppositorum* which contains triangles within a quaternity.[76]

In 'Two Essays on Analytical Psychology' Jung had stated, in effect, 'that Western culture has no name or concept for the "union of opposites by the middle path" which could be compared to the concept of Tao'.[77] Cox wanted to know whether the doctrine of justification by faith might be such a concept. Jung's response is that 'if you understand Christ by definition as a *complexio oppositorum*, the equation is solved. But you are confronted with a terrific historical counter-position.'[78] The counter-position is that Christ is identified exclusively with light and the good and that darkness and evil are contained in the devil.

A further question concerns Jung's objections to the doctrines of the *summum bonum* and *privatio boni*. Jung dismisses the identification of the good with being and evil with non-being. He also implies that the concept of the Good beyond being and non-being has no psychological meaning. If God is 'a *complexio opposi-torum*, i.e. beyond good and evil, it is possible that he may appear equally well as the source of evil which you believe to be ultimately good for man'.[79] Notions of good and evil can only have meaning as a pair of opposites in relation to human experience. Metaphysical concepts of the Good are meaningless from the point of view of psychology. In a lengthy reply to a letter from Cox, Jung reiterates his view that his own descriptions of Christ and God as instances of *complexio opposi-torum* are at odds with traditional Christian understanding.[80]

Again in 1958, in 'Flying Saucers: A Modern Myth', Jung draws on alchem-ical material to interpret a painting by Jakoby, *The Fire Sower*.[81] The painting is said to depict 'two worlds which interpenetrate yet do not touch'. While this is difficult for the modern viewer of the painting to comprehend, the alchemists' concept Mercurius would have enabled them to reflect on the image:

> Their Mercurius is *hermaphroditus* and *duplex*, a *complexio oppositorum*, the messenger of the gods, the One and the All … He is the panacea itself and the elixir of life, but on the other hand he is a deadly danger for the igno-rant. For the educated person of those days, who studied the philosophy of alchemy as part of his general equipment – it was a real *religio medici* – this figure of the Fire Sower would have been full of allusions, and he would have had no difficulty in assimilating it to his stock of knowledge.[82]

In 1960, a definition of the 'self' was added to the list of definitions at the end of *Psychological Types*. The original version of the text published in 1920 had included a definition of the 'ego'. In the new definition Jung wrote that when the image of the self 'represents a *complexio oppositorum*, a union of oppo-sites, it can also appear as a united duality, in the form, for instance of *tao* as the interplay of *yang* and *yin*'.[83]

Beyond the *Collected Works* there are a number of occasions when the term appears in *Memories, Dreams, Reflections*. They all refer to God as a *complexio opposi-torum*. Through the Holy Spirit, 'the *complexio oppositorum* of the God-image thus enters into man, and not as unity, but as conflict'.[84] The dark side of God is in conflict with the idea that God is light. This places a considerable stress on the individual. In Freud's terms the drive places a demand on the mind for work:

> Room must be made within the system for the philosophical *complexio oppositorum* of Nicholas of Cusa and the moral ambivalence of Jacob Boehme; only thus can the One God be granted the wholeness and syn-thesis of opposites which should be His.[85]

If this conflict, which thrusts itself upon human nature, and in a sense constitutes human nature, can be accommodated life is enriched. 'The Word happens to us; we suffer it, for we are victims of a profound uncertainty: with God as a *complexio oppositorum*, all things are possible, in the fullest meaning of the phrase.'[86] There is a limit to the capacity of language to encompass or illuminate religious experience. 'Whatever the learned interpretation may be of the sentence "God is love," the words affirm the *complexio oppositorum* of the Godhead.'[87] As we have seen, the concept of the *complexio oppositorum* was used by Jung primarily with reference to God.

Coniunctio oppositorum

The term *coniunctio oppositorum* (conjunction of opposites) appears in the *Collected Works* exclusively after 1950, except for once in 1944 in *Psychology and Alchemy*, where incest is described as a *coniunctio oppositorum*[88] and there are two illustrations that depict the *coniunctio*.[89]

Aion, published in 1951, has the most references to the term. The *coniunctio oppositorum* is described as necessary for the achievement of wholeness:

> Therefore, anyone who wants to achieve the difficult feat of realizing something not only intellectually, but also according to its feeling–value, must for better or worse come to grips with the anima/animus problem in order to open the way for a higher union, a *coniunctio oppositorum*. This is an indispensable prerequisite for wholeness.[90]

The doctrine of the marriage of Christ and the Church is an important image of the union of opposites. In alchemical and cabalist texts of the Middle Ages 'the symbolism developed ... into the alchemical conjuction of opposites, or "chymical wedding," thus giving rise on the one hand to the concept of the *lapis philosophorum*, signifying totality, and on the other hand to the concept of chemical combination'.[91]

Numinous images of the self appear spontaneously across cultures. These images are necessarily paradoxical because of the limits of consciousness:

> These naïve and completely uninfluenced pictorial representations of the symbol show that it is given central and supreme importance precisely because it stands for the conjunction of opposites. Naturally the conjunction can only be understood as a paradox, since a union of opposites can be thought of only as their annihilation. Paradox is a characteristic of all transcendental situations because it alone gives adequate expression to their indescribable nature.[92]

Jung describes the view within medieval astrology that Judaism, Christianity, Islam and the Antichrist are all products of a variety of conjunctions of Jupiter (life) and Saturn (death). 'The conjunction of the two therefore signifies the *union of extreme opposites*.'[93]

Jung discusses the crucial role that self-knowledge plays in the development of the self. The alchemist Morienus writes, 'This thing is extracted from thee, for thou art its ore; in thee they find it, and to speak more plainly, from thee they take it; and when thou has experienced this, the love and desire for it will be increase in thee.'[94] The alchemical lapis which emerges in this process is an image of the self. 'The transformation is brought about by the *coniunctio*, which forms the essence of the work.'[95]

In 'Answer to Job' (1952) Jung states that '[a]s a totality, the self is by definition always a *complexio oppositorum*'.[96] The conflicts within the self are compounded by contact with God. 'The paradoxical nature of God has a like effect on man: it tears him asunder into opposites and delivers him over to seemingly insoluble conflict.'[97] Consequently, 'the real subject of Hermetic philosophy is the *coniunction oppositorum*'[98] and in the apocalyptic vision of John there is an attempt to resolve this conflict through 'a divine birth which was characterized by a *coniunction oppositorum* and which anticipated the *filius sapientiae*, the essence of the individuation process'.[99]

In 'Flying Saucers: A Modern Myth' (1958) Jung describes the squaring of the circle as 'another *coniunctio oppositorum*'.[100] Orfeo Angelucci left a record of his experiences while in a lengthy somnambulant state which included 'a *noce celeste* … a mystic union analogous to the *coniunctio oppositorum* in alchemy'.[101]

In 'Jung and Religious Belief' (1958) Jung points again to the idea that *coniunctio oppositorum* is an attempt to resolve internal conflict:

> The 'Will of God' often contradicts conscious principles however good they may seem. Penitence or remorse follows the deviation from the superior will. The result is – if not a chronic conflict – a *coniunctio oppositorum* in the form of the symbol (*symbolum* = two halves of a broken coin), the expression of totality.[102]

In *Memories, Dreams, Reflections* he comments that the image of Aquarius, a figure with personal and collective meaning, 'is a *coniunctio oppositorum* composed of two fishes in reverse',[103] and he returns to the theme of the self and the god image:

> The unavoidable internal contradictions in the image of a Creator-god can be reconciled in the unity and wholeness of the self as the *coniunctio oppositorum* of the alchemists or as a *unio mystica*. In the experience of the self it is no longer the opposites 'God' and 'man' that are reconciled, as it was before, but rather the opposites within the God-image itself.[104]

He is here expressing his view that the conflicts within the god image, and other collective images, should not be placed as burdens on individuals. As we have seen, Jung's use of the term encompasses primitive or unconscious states, such as incest, and differentiated, highly conscious, processes of individuation.

Union of opposites

Jung began to make use of the concept of the union of opposites in *Psychological Types* (CW6) published in 1921. References to the union of opposites in

Symbols of Transformation (CW5) were not included in that text until its revision in 1952. The earlier translation of *Wandlungen und Symbole der Libido* (1912) by Hinkle, published in 1916 as *Psychology of the Unconscious*, speaks of a relationship between opposites but does not go so far as to single out the union of opposites as a crucial feature of psychic processes. In CW5 Jung writes:

> Thus the Mother of Death joins the Mother of Life in lamenting the dying god, and, as an outward token of their union, Mary kisses the cross and is reconciled. In ancient Egypt this union of opposite tendencies was naively preserved in the Isis mother-imago.[105]

In Hinkle the corresponding passage reads:

> In their lament for the dying god, and as outward token of their union, Mary kisses the cross, and is reconciled to it. The naïve Egyptian antiquity has preserved for us the union of the contrasting tendencies in the mother idea of Isis.[106]

'Union of contrasting tendencies' has become 'union of opposites'. This intensification of the relationship of the opposites emerges further in Jung's description of Christ as hero. In 1952 he wrote:

> In the Christ-figure the opposites which are united in the archetype are polarized into the 'light' son of God on the one hand and the devil on the other. The original unity of opposites is still discernible in the original unity of Satan and Yahweh. Christ and the dragon of the Anti-Christ lie very close together so far as their historical development and cosmic significance are concerned. The dragon legend concealed under the myth of the Anti-Christ is an essential part of the hero's life and is therefore immortal. Nowhere in the latter-day myths are the paired opposites so palpably close together as in the figures of Christ and Anti-Christ.[107]

In the earlier text he wrote:

> Christ and the dragon of the Antichrist are in the closest contact in the history of their appearance and their cosmic meaning ... The legend of the dragon concealed in the Antichrist myth belongs to the life of the hero, and, therefore, if immortal. In none of the newer forms of the myth are the pairs of opposites so perceptibly near as in that of Christ and Antichrist.[108]

By the time of the revision, the role of the archetype had become central to Jung's thought and the dynamic of unity and polarization of opposites has achieved the power to explain historical processes.

In his description of the Roman Trivia, which was dedicated to Hecate, Jung's earlier text reads, 'And where roads branch off or unite sacrifices of dogs were brought her; there the bodies of the executed were thrown; the sacrifice occurs at the *point of crossing*.'[109] By 1952 this had become:

> Where the roads branch off or meet, dog-sacrifices were offered to her, and there too were thrown the bodies of the executed: the sacrifice occurs at the point of union. Where the roads *cross* and enter into one another, thereby symbolizing the union of opposites, there is the 'mother,' the object and epitome of all union.[110]

By using the concept of the union of opposites Jung has opened up the meaning of the earlier image, 'point of crossing'. Finally, in 1952, discussing the Mithraic krater, he wrote:

> The combination of the bull's blood and the snake therefore looks like a union of opposites, and the lion and snake fighting for the krater may mean the same thing. This is probably the cause of the miraculous fertility that results from the sacrifice of the bull ... In the act of sacrifice the consciousness gives up its power and possessions in the interests of the unconscious. This makes possible a union of opposites resulting in a release of energy.[111]

In the earlier text he noted 'the mutual relationship between serpent and bull', and observed that 'the sacrifice of the bull to the serpent, therefore, signifies a willing renunciation of life, in order to win it from death. Therefore, after the sacrifice of the bull, wonderful fertility results.'[112] The fertility, which is a result of sacrifice, becomes in the later version a 'release of energy' characteristic of the union of opposites. We can see here how by 1952 the union of opposites came to have a central place in Jung's psychology, which is only hinted in his writing in 1912.

Returning to *Psychological Types* (CW6) we see how the union of opposites begins to appear as an organizing principle in Jung's work. An important aspect of the concept is its capacity to contain or point to psychic processes with are beyond reason:

> Opposites are not to be united rationally: *tertium non datur* – that is precisely why they are called opposites ... In practice, opposites can be united only in the form of compromises, or *irrationally* ... Such an expression cannot be contrived by reason, it can only be created through living.[113]

The conscious will cannot supply convincing symbols, but relies on 'creative fantasy, an irrational, instinctive function which alone has the power to supply the will with a content of such a nature that it can unite the opposites'.[114]

In Indian philosophy the aim is 'to free the individual altogether from the opposites inherent in human nature ... It is an irrational union of opposites, their final overcoming.'[115] 'Brahman is the union and dissolution of all opposites, and at the same time stands outside them as an irrational factor. It is therefore wholly beyond cognition and comprehension.'[116]

Jung compares the concept of *tao* with Bergson's *durée creatrice*:

> Knowledge of *tao* therefore has the same redeeming and uplifting effect as the knowledge of *Brahman*. Man becomes one with *tao*, with the unending *durée creatrice* (if we may compare this concept of Bergson's with its older congener), for *tao* is also the stream of time, It is irrational, inconceivably It is obviously an irrational union of opposites, a symbol of what is and is not.[117]

There is a lengthy discussion of Schiller's thoughts about opposites. For Schiller, the union of opposites is an active achievement. 'Thus it is not to be a detachment or redemption of the inferior function, but an acknowledgement of it, a coming to terms with it, that unites the opposites on the path of nature.'[118] 'The mediating position between the opposites can be reached only by the symbol.'[119]

Jung writes that Synesius 'assigns to the *spiritus phantasticus* practically the same psychological role as Schiller to the play instinct and I to creative fantasy … It unites the opposites in itself.'[120]

In 1928 Jung describes how the analyst, in the transference, 'becomes both father and a kind of lover – in other words, an object of conflict. In him the opposites are united, and for this reason he stands for a quasi-ideal solution of the conflict.'[121] Another aspect of analysis is the 'godlikeness' that can result when 'two spheres have been brought together which before were kept anxiously apart. After considerable resistances have been overcome, the union of opposites is successfully achieved, at least to all appearances.'[122] The new insight inflates the ego. In his discussion of the mana personality he describes what happens when the ego relinquishes its claim to power (mana):

> In this situation the mana must have fallen to something that is both conscious and unconscious, or else neither. This something is the desired 'mid-point' of the personality, that ineffable something betwixt the opposites, or else that which unites them, or the result of conflict, or the product of energetic tension: the coming to birth of personality, a profoundly individual step forward, the next stage.[123]

The relationship between the ego and the unconscious consists of a kaleidoscope of relations between different sets of opposites.

In the Tavistock Lectures of 1935, Jung asserts that in Wagner's *Parsifal* the bowl and the dagger represent 'the male and female principle which form the union of opposites'. In the unconscious the opposites are 'utterly indistinguishable … a complete union of opposites … is the primordial condition of things, and at the same time a most ideal achievement, because it is the union of elements eternally opposed'.[124] The union of opposites is an archetypal image. Jung compares the Mithraic god Aion, who 'represents the union of opposites', with the *duree creatrice* of Bergson.[125]

In the Terry Lectures, published in 1938, Jung argues that 'the unconscious produces a natural symbol, technically a mandala, which has the functional significance of a union of opposites'.[126] He cites the image of Shiva in Shakti's embrace as an example 'of the male-female opposites united in the centre'.[127] The following year, in a discussion of individuation, he states that '[o]ut of this union emerge new situations and new conscious attitudes. I have therefore called the union of opposites the "transcendent function".'[128]

In his 1940 essay on the child archetype, Jung describes the abandoned child as the image of 'a certain psychic experience of a creative nature, whose object is the emergence of a new and as yet unknown content'. Consciousness is only aware of irreconcilable opposites, but 'out of this collision of opposites the unconscious psyche always creates a third thing of an irrational nature, which the conscious mind neither expects nor understands'.[129] The child is the union of opposites, emerging from the unconscious to resolve the clash of opposites in consciousness. The bisexuality or hermaphroditism of the child expresses the fact that it is 'a union of the strongest and most striking opposites'.[130] It is a 'primordial image … instrumental in uniting opposites, even in pathological states'.[131]

From 1942 Jung began to refer increasingly in his writings to alchemy, which 'is concerned with the union of opposites'.[132] In 1944 he published *Psychology and Alchemy*, in which he described alchemy as 'a *longissima via*, not straight but snakelike, a path that unites the opposites'.[133] The self is a more complete union of opposites than the Christ-symbol since it 'represents in every respect thesis and antithesis, and at the same time synthesis'.[134] Experience of the problem of the opposites is essential to gaining a true understanding of religion and the deepest conflict between opposites and the most paradoxical union of opposites is found in 'the antinomial character of the self, which is itself both conflict and unity'.[135] For Jung this is more satisfactory than 'Christian symbolism, which leaves the conflict open'.[136] While consciousness is a result of the discrimination of opposites, in the unconscious 'the opposites seek one another … particularly in the archetype of unity, the self. Here as in the deity the opposites cancel out.'[137] 'The self begins with conflict'[138] because it is made manifest in the conflict of opposites.

In discussing the image of the world clock in a sixteenth-century alchemical text, Jung states that 'our mandala aspires to the most complete union of opposites that is possible'.[139] In the alchemical process sometimes an initial differentiation of the opposites is necessary as 'the separated condition is assumed at the start'. 'Then a union of opposites is performed under the likeness of a union of male and female (called the *coniugium, matrimoniu, coniunctio, coitus*).'[140] The figure of Mercurius is a 'symbol uniting all opposites' in as much as he 'is metallic yet liquid, matter yet spirit, cold yet fiery, poison and yet healing draught'.[141] The 'antithetical nature' of the elements at the beginning of the alchemical process is 'an almost universal idea'. Jung brings as evidence for this the fact that 'in China the opposites are *yang* and *yin*, odd and even numbers, heaven and earth, etc.; there is also a union of them in the hermaphrodite'.[142] According to the alchemist Melchior Cibinensis, the offertory in the Mass is equivalent to 'the union of opposites – mind and body'.[143]

According to Jung, 'owing to the impersonal, purely objective nature of matter, it was the impersonal, collective archetypes that were projected'[144] by the alchemist during their performance of alchemical procedures. These projections, because they contained images of the union of opposites had the power to fascinate:

> Since the psychological condition of any unconscious content is one of potential reality, characterized by the polar opposites of 'being' and 'not-being,' it follows that the union of opposites must play a decisive role in the alchemical process. The result is something in the nature of a 'uniting symbol,' and this usually has a numinous character.[145]

The theme of the union of opposites is taken up again in 'The Psychology of the Transference', published in 1946. In this essay Jung uses alchemical imagery to reflect on the dynamics of the transference. The alchemical concept of the *coniunctio* 'expresses the archetype of the union of opposites'[146] and in his view accounts for the potency of the transference. One of his patients dreams about Noah's dove and Jung identifies this as 'the first, anticipatory stage of an as-yet-unfulfilled programme that culminates in the union of opposites. This union is analogous to the "royal marriage" in alchemy.'[147] In his detailed commentary on illustrations in the *Rosarium Philosophorum*, an alchemical text from the sixteenth century, Jung describes the '*coniunctio Solis et Lunae* as [a] supreme union of hostile opposites'.[148] The union of opposites is not just an intrapsychic experience:

> Thus the underlying idea of the psyche proves it to be a half bodily, half spiritual substance ... an hermaphroditic being capable of uniting the opposites, but who is never complete in the individual unless related to another individual. The unrelated individual being lacks wholeness, for he can achieve wholeness only through the soul, and the soul cannot exist without its other side, which is always found in a 'You.' Wholeness is a combination of I and You, and these show themselves to be parts of a transcendent unity whose nature can only be grasped symbolically.[149]

Images of the alchemical procedure of *coniunctio* in the *Rosarium*, which depict a couple engaged in sexual intercourse, provide a means of transforming instinctive energy into symbolic activity. 'The union of opposites in the royal art [alchemy] is just as real as coitus in the common acceptation of the word.'[150] In the stage of *putrifactio*, 'after the *coniuctio oppositorum*, deathlike stillness reigns. When the opposites unite, all energy ceases: there is no more flow.'[151] This death of the ego allows for birth of the self, which 'is ego and non-ego, subjective and objective, individual and collective. It is the "uniting symbol" which epitomizes the total union of opposites.'[152] When 'the union of opposites reaches the nadir a change sets in ... the ever deeper descent into the unconscious suddenly becomes illumination from above'. The union of opposites brings light out of darkness and 'by this light it will be possible to see what the real meaning of that union was'.[153] An important dimension of the meaning of these images and experiences only became available when Freud brought a psychological perspective to bear on the sexual instinct. 'The problem of the union of opposites had been lying there for centuries in its sexual form, yet it had to wait until scientific enlightenment and objectivity had advanced far enough for people to mention "sexuality" in scientific conversation.'[154] Because it became possible to interpret the sexual element in alchemical images, 'we give ourselves a chance to see that the alluring sexual aspect is but one among many – the very one that deludes our judgement'.[155] At the end of the essay Jung reiterates that these images 'point to the self, the container and organizer of all opposites'[156] and, in the phrase that we cited earlier, he states that whereas the alchemists were 'the empiricists of the great problem of the opposites', Cusa was 'its philosopher'.[157]

Over the next three years Jung made scattered references to the union of opposites. In 'On the Nature of the Psyche', he observed that 'archetype and instinct are the most polar opposites imaginable' yet 'they do show a constant propensity to union'.[158] In a discussion of pre-Christian concepts of the Trinity he observes that 'Plato begins by representing the union of opposites two-dimensionally, as an intellectual problem to be solved by thinking, but then comes to see that its solution does not add up to reality'.[159] The Platonic triad differs from the Christian Trinity because it 'is built on opposition, whereas the Trinity contains no opposition of any kind'.[160] In both cases however Jung looks to alchemy to provide the concept of quaternity which he believes is an image of wholeness. The uroboros is an image of 'the union of opposites accomplished during the alchemical process'.[161] In a painting by one of his patients Jung sees ' a union of opposites within the irrational life process'[162] which reminds him of the I Ching. Commenting on a mandala painting by another patient Jung felt that it expressed 'the painful experience of the union of opposites'.[163]

In 'The Psychology of the Child Archetype', published in 1951, Jung writes that the child 'unites the opposites'[164] and anticipates the future. The bisexuality of the child expressed in images of the hermaphrodite is 'a *symbol of the creative union of opposites*, a "uniting symbol" in a literal sense'. The energetic influence of archetypal ideas 'unites opposites, mediates between the unconscious substratum and the conscious mind'.[165]

In the same year Jung published *Aion*, his study of the phenomenology of the self. His contention is that in the West Christ represents the self. With the development of modern psychology the understanding of the Christ image has changed as its one-sidedness has become clear. It is simultaneously 'the apotheosis of individuality' and 'a transcendent concept'. As such 'it can only be described in antinomial terms'.[166] It bears the apophatic intensity described by Sells.

The phenomenology of the self has been projected into astrology and alchemy. The conjunction of Jupiter and Saturn in Iranian astrology 'signifies the *union of extreme opposites*'.[167] He conjectures that the coming age of Aquarius 'will constellate the problem of the union of opposites'.[168] The alchemical lapis expresses the self. 'The union of opposites in the stone is possible only when the adept has become One himself. The unity of the stone is the equivalent of individuation, by which man is made one; we would say that the stone is a projection of the unified self.'[169]

One of the characteristics of the 'supraordinate "third"' or symbol, in which the opposites are united is that it can reconcile 'their conceptual polarity through its form and their emotional polarity through its numinosity'.[170] In psychotherapy it is crucial to give due attention to both the conceptual and the emotional elements in the client's personality, while being open to further development. 'Similarly, modern psychotherapy knows that, though there are many interim solutions, there is, at the bottom of every neurosis, a moral problem of opposites that cannot be solved rationally, and can be answered only by a suprordinate third, by a symbol which expresses both sides.'[171]

Jung's discussion of Eckhart's idea of the Godhead includes a psychological interpretation of unknowing. Jung equates unknowing with unconsciousness. He argues that consciousness is the product of difference and that difference does not exist in the coincidence of opposites.

> Union of opposites is equivalent to unconsciousness, so far as human logic goes, for consciousness presupposes a differentiation into subject and object and a relation between them. Where there is no 'other,' or it does not yet exist, all possibility of consciousness ceases.[172]

Psychology cannot comment on the metaphysical status of the idea of the Godhead but it can confirm that phenomena, such as those discussed by Eckhart, produce symbols of wholeness. 'As a rule they are "uniting" symbols, representing the conjunction of a single or double pair of opposites … They arise from the collision between the conscious and the unconscious.'[173]

Jung provides diagrams to illustrate his discussion of the self. One diagram 'emphasized the point of greatest tension between the opposites' and demonstated that 'in the *lapis*, the counterpart of man, the opposites are so to speak united'.[174] A footnote to this paragraph provides a succinct summary of Jung's views on the dynamics of suggestion:

> Most people do not have sufficient range of consciousness to become aware of the opposites inherent in human nature. The tensions they generate remain for the most part unconscious, but can appear in dreams …

The greatest danger about unconsciousness is proneness to suggestion. The effect of suggestion is due to the release of an unconscious dynamic, and the more unconscious this is, the more effective it will be. Hence the ever-widening split between conscious and unconscious increases the danger of psychic infection and mass psychosis. With the loss of symbolic ideas the bridge to the unconscious has broken down. Instinct no longer affords protection against unsound ideas and empty slogans. Rationality without tradition and without a basis in instinct is proof against no absurdity.[175]

In alchemy the development of consciousness, which is a circular process, is represented by the uroboros. It is 'a magic circle consisting of the union of opposites'.[176] The lapis is 'born of the alchemical union of opposites ... Psychologically the self is a union of conscious (masculine) and unconscious (feminine). It stands for the psychic totality.'[177] In *Aion*, Jung argues that the alchemists unwittingly describe in their texts and drawings the process by which an individual might attain a 'sufficient range of consciousness to become aware of the opposites inherent in human nature'.[178]

In 1952 Jung published *Symbols of Transformation*, an expanded and revised version of *Wandlungen und Symbole der Libido*, published in 1912, which was translated into English by Hinkle in 1917 as *Psychology of the Unconscious*. By analysing the revisions to the text made between 1912 and 1952, we get some sense of the development of Jung's ideas about the union of opposites.

In his description of Isis, 'the union of contrasting tendencies'[179] had become 'this union of opposite tendencies'.[180] In 1912 he writes, 'In none of the newer forms of myth are the pairs of opposites so perceptibly near as in that of Christ and Antichrist.'[181] By 1952 this has become 'palpably close together', but more significant is what has been added:

> Christ, as a hero and god-man, signifies psychologically the self; that is, he represents the projection of this most important and central of archetypes. The archetype of the self has, functionally, the significance of a ruler of the inner world, i.e., of the collective unconscious. The self, as a sym-bol of wholeness, is a *coincidentia oppositorum*, and therefore contains light and darkness simultaneously. In the Christ-figure the opposites which are united in the archetype are polarized in the 'light' son of God on the one hand and the devil on the other. The original unity of opposites is still dis-cernible in the original unity of Satan and Yahweh, Christ and the dragon of the Anti-Christ lie very close together so far as their historical develop-ment and cosmic significance are concerned.[182]

His concept of the self had become fully developed, including the idea of 'the original unity of opposites' within the unconscious, which are differenti-ated, in this case as Satan and Yahweh, and then reunited in a more conscious union of opposites.

In an extended passage Jung describes the sacrifice of dogs at a crossroads to the goddess, Hecate. In the 1912 text 'the sacrifice occurs at the *point of crossing*'.[183] In the later text 'the sacrifice occurs at the point of union':

> Where the roads *cross* and enter into one another, thereby symbolizing the union of opposites, there is the 'mother,' the object and epitome of all union. Where the roads *divide*, where there is parting, separation, splitting, there we find the 'division,' the cleft – the symbol of the mother and at the same time the essence of what the mother means for us, namely cleavage and farewell.[184]

The imagery have become enriched and nuanced over the years. In his description of Mithraic sacrifice, Jung writes in the earlier text:

> 'Previously we have pointed out the mutual relationship between serpent and bull, and found there that the bull symbolizes the living hero, the shining sun, but that the serpent symbolizes the dead, buried or chthonic hero, the invisible sun.

The rest of the passage describes the sacrifice in a fairly linear fashion. By 1952 the ideas have become more complex.

> We have already pointed out the reciprocal relationship between bull and snake, and we saw that the bull symbolizes the living hero, whereas the snake symbolizes the dead, buried, chthonic hero ... The combination of the bull's blood and the snake therefore looks like a union of opposites ... In the act of sacrifice the consciousness gives up its power and possession in the interests of the unconscious. This makes possible a union of opposites resulting in a release of energy.[185]

The union of opposites has emerged in Jung's work as a dynamic locus of potency.

In *Answer to Job*, Christ is said to occupy a 'position midway between the two extremes, man and God'. Christ is represented by 'totality symbols' because he is able 'to unite all opposites'.[186] The effect of the 'paradoxical nature of God' on man can be that 'it tears him asunder into opposites and delivers him over to a seemingly insoluble conflict'. In analysis, a patient may find a solution to this conflict by having a dream 'of the child-hero and the squaring of the circle, signifying the union of opposite'.[187] It is necessary to take cognisance of the confrontation of opposites depicted in dreams, and of 'the images of the goal [that] represent their successful reconciliation'.[188] Because a resolution of conflict between conscious and unconscious 'is not possible through logic, one is dependent on *symbols* which make the irrational union of opposites possible'.[189] The relationship between the opposites involves mutual influence.

Images of the union of opposites are simultaneously expressions and catalysts of that union. The apophatic dimension of the individuation process can be seen in the namelessness and ineffability of its origin and goal:

> The encounter between conscious and unconscious has to ensure that the light which shines in the darkness is not only comprehended by the darkness, but comprehends it. The *filius solis et lunae* is the symbol of the union of opposites as well as the catalyst of their union. It is the alpha and omega of the process, the mediator and intermedius. 'It has a thousand names,' say the alchemists, meaning that the source from which the individuation process rises and the goal toward with it aims is nameless, ineffable.[190]

In 1953 there is a single mention of the union of opposites in Jung's work,[191] but in 1954 Jung returns to the theme across a wide range of essays. In a discussion of the role of dogma he observes that along with elements of Christianity and Gnosticism 'it was undoubtedly alchemy, long brewing the union of opposites in secret that came to … [the] aid'[192] of Jakob Bohme. Again we can track the development of Jung's dependence on the concept of the union of opposites, because we do not find this passage in an earlier version of this essay published in 1934.[193] In his clinical work Jung observed a 'chaotic assortment' of archetypal images including 'the union of opposites in a third'.[194] Among these images is the alchemical symbol of the cosmic tree, 'which springs from the union of opposites and, by its eternal presence, also makes that union possible'.[195]

In his discussion of the Mass, Jung makes the interesting observation that 'so long as the self is unconscious, it corresponds to Freud's superego and is a source of perpetual moral conflict'. A transformation occurs, however, if the projection of the self can be withdrawn and it 'is no longer identical with public opinion'. 'The self then functions as a union of opposites and thus constitutes the most immediate experience of the Divine which it is psychologically possible to imagine.'[196]

In the same text Jung comments on the *Acts of Peter*, an apocryphal work from the second century. Peter's speech while hanging upside down on the cross expresses the union of opposites:

> In this passage, too, the symbolical interpretation of the cross is coupled with the problem of the opposites, first in the unusual idea that the creation of the first man caused everything to be turn upside down, and then in the attempt to unite the opposites by identifying them with one another.[197]

The fact that Peter is crucified upside down is an image of birth. It symbolizes the union of creation and death.

Jung criticizes the author of the *Acts of John*, a text from the same period, for losing sight of darkness with an overemphasis on the light. 'He forgets that light only has a meaning when it illuminates something dark and that his enlightenment is no good to him unless it helps him to recognize his own darkness.'[198] 'Opposites unite in new energy potential: the "third" that arises out of their union is a figure "free from the opposites," beyond all moral categories. This conclusion would have been too advanced for the Gnostics.'[199] Jung claims that the 'concretism' of the Church balanced the 'irrealism' of the Gnostics. This conflict festered in the European unconscious until the advent of depth psychology.

In 'Psychological Commentary on *The Tibetan Book of the Great Liberation*' Jung castigates Westerners who immerse themselves in Eastern meditation practices. Their efforts have no effect. 'For this the union of opposites is necessary, and in particular the difficult task of reconciling extraversion and introversion by means of the transcendent function.'[200] The transcendent function underlies rebirth symbolism which 'describes the union of opposites – conscious and unconscious – by means of concretistic analogies'.[201]

In 'The Visions of Zosimos' Jung discusses stone symbolism in a number of mythological stories, including those in which 'the anima contains the secret of the precious stone … the mediator which is the union of opposites'.[202]

In the first half of 'The Philosophical Tree' Jung comments on twenty-three pictures. Several of the paintings express instances of the union of opposites.[203] In the second half of the essay he explores other aspects of tree symbolism. In the alchemical text 'Aquarium Sapientum' there is a connection made between the philosophical stone and Christ. The alchemists did not intentionally 'exalt their stone into a world saviour':

> They simply found these qualities in their idea of a body composed of the four elements and capable of uniting all opposites, and were just as amazed at this discovery as anyone would be who had a singularly impressive dream and then came across an unknown myth with fitted it exactly.[204]

The philosophical tree requires a particular habitat and it 'has a special connection with water, salt, and sea-water, thus with the *aqua permanens*'. The tree is both nourished and destroyed by this water:

> The water that makes the tree grow but also consumes it is Mercurius, who is called 'duplex' because he unites the opposites in himself, being both a metal and a liquid. Hence he is called both water and fire. As the sap of the tree he is therefore also fiery, that is to say the tree is of a watery and a fiery nature.[205]

The tree is a symbol of transformation and transformation involves the suffering brought about by the discrimination of opposites out of an original unity to be followed by a new union of opposites which expresses a sense of wholeness. 'It is still the case today that discrimination and differentiation mean more to the rationalistic intellect than wholeness through the union of opposites.

That is why it is the unconscious which produces the symbols of wholeness.'[206] The symbolism found in the material of analytic patients resonates with the imagery found in alchemy and shamanism. This demonstrates the historical persistence of the theme of the union of opposites:

> The process usually consists in the union of two pairs of opposites, a lower (waster, blackness, animal, snake, etc.) with an upper (bird, light, head, etc.), and a left (feminine) with a right (masculine). The union of opposites, which plays such a great and indeed decisive role in alchemy, is of equal significance in the psychic process initiated by the confrontation with the unconscious, so the occurrence of similar or even identical symbols is not surprising.[207]

Jung returns to the symbol of the tree at the end of 'Psychological Aspects of the Mother Archetype'. The alchemists recognized 'the union of opposites under the symbol of the tree ... which springs from the union of opposites and, by its eternal presence, also makes that union possible'.[208]

In a letter to William Lachat, a priest, Jung discusses his understanding of the role of the Holy Spirit. Its work is 'to reconcile and reunite the opposites in the individual through a special development of the human soul ... [it] progressively unites the opposite'.[209] In Jung's formulation, Christ and Satan represent a split of good and evil, light and dark, emerging for YHWH. The Holy Spirit plays a part in overcoming this split, analogous to the transcendent function:

> In the circumstances the Holy Spirit, the third form of God, becomes of extreme importance, for it is thanks to him that the man of good will is drawn towards the divine drama and mingles in it, and the Spirit is *one*. In him the opposites are separated no longer.[210]

In 1955 there is a passing reference to the union of opposites in *Synchronicity*.[211] In the following year, however, in *Mysterium Coniunctionis*, there are more than twenty references to the union of opposites, plus a twelve-page section entitled, 'The Alchemical View of the Union of Opposites'. After a mention of the union of opposites in Dorn,[212] Jung discusses the place of paradox in alchemy:

> The tremendous role which the opposites and their union play in alchemy helps us to understand why the alchemists were so fond of paradoxes. In order to attain this union, they tried not only to visualize the opposites together but to express them in the same breath. Characteristically, the paradoxes cluster most thickly round the arcane substance, which was believed to contain the opposites in uncombined form as the prima materia, and to amalgamate them as the lapis Philosophorum.[213]

We see here again the idea that there is an original union of opposites, which undergoes a process of differentiation and then reunification. There is an extended footnote at this point in the essay with a long list of opposites, from a text by the alchemist Petrus Bonus, which demonstrates the paradoxical nature of the lapis. Bonus' description of the lapis has an apophatic intensity. He asserts that 'those things that are and those that are not, those which may be spoken of and those which may not be spoken of, all these things they are able of say of this worshipful stone'.[214]

After the differentiation of opposites, 'the alchemist's endeavours to unite the opposites culminate in the "chymical marriage," the supreme act of union in which the work reaches its consummation'.[215]

Christianity and alchemy attempt to find a solution to 'the conflict between worldliness and spirituality' through quite different means. Christianity sees the relationship between the sexes as a spiritual allegory:

> Alchemy, on the other hand, exalted the most heinous transgression of the law, namely incest, into a symbol of the union of opposites, hoping in this way to bring back the golden age. For both trends the solution lay in extrapolating the union of sexes into another medium: the one projected into the spirit, the other into matter. But neither of them located the problem in the place where it arose – the soul of man.[216]
>
> Incest is 'a preliminary form of the unio oppositorum'.[217]

In a further play on the trope of pre-existent opposites that can be differentiated Jung identifies the ego and shadow as two halves of the self. 'If we hypostatize the self and derive from it (as from a kind of pre-existent personality) the ego and the shadow, then these would appear as the empirical aspects of the opposites that are preformed in the self.'[218] In alchemy the dragon's head represents consciousness. It is 'the symbolic image of the self, and just as the lapis unites the opposites so the self assimilates contents of conscious and the unconscious'.[219]

A feature of intense religious feeling is the image of the royal marriage. An apocryphal saying of Jesus, 'the two shall be one, and the outside as the inside, and the male with the female neither male nor female', points to the 'coniunctio, in which the extreme opposites unite' and serves as a 'paradigm for the alchemical union of opposites'.[220] Jung insists that he is merely describing the phenomenology of the imagery, because 'what the union of opposites really "mean" transcends human imagination'.[221] This imagery has had a quality of revelation for previous generations, however, because modern man has some psychological insight, 'we could set out on the road to the union of opposites and … come to the place where the "gods of destruction and the god of salvation are together"'.[222] This might result in the constellation of the transcendent function, 'the psychic process of assimilation and integration … [which] unites the pairs of opposites'.[223]

The alchemist, Michael Maier, wrote an account of his journey through America, Europe and Asia. Each of these was associated with one of the cardinal directions. When he journeyed south, to Africa, he discovered a statue of Mercury 'made of silver with a golden head', which he took to be a good omen. The astrological conjunction of the sun in Leo and the moon in Cancer, when he reached Africa, indicated 'a *coniunctio Solis et Lunae*, the union of supreme opposites, and this is the crowning of the opus and the goal of the per-igrination'.[224] Jung associates Maier's success in reaching Africa with attaining access to the fourth, or the inferior, function. Maier's description of his journey into Africa follows the alchemical pattern of ascent followed by descent, rather than the Gnostic and Christian pattern of descent followed by ascent. 'The arcane substance ... rises from the earth, unites the opposites, and then returns to earth, thereby achieving its own transformation into the elixir ... Here the union of opposites consists in an ascent to heaven and a descent to earth in the bath of the tincture.'[225] This can be taken as an example of how alchemy acted as a compensation to the conscious Christian imagery.

Jung was insistent in his assertion that his work was an empirical description of psychic processes as depicted in alchemical texts:

> The psychological union of opposites is an intuitive idea which covers the phenomenology of this process. It is not an 'explanatory' hypothesis for something that, by definition, transcends our powers of conception. For, when we say that conscious and unconscious unite, we are saying in effect that this process is inconceivable. The unconscious is unconscious and therefore can neither be grasped not conceived. The union of opposites is a transconscious process and, in principle, not amenable to scientific explanation.[226]

This inconceivable process is depicted in the book of Job in a verse that resonates with the alchemists' image of the union of earth and fire. 'As for the earth, out of it cometh bread: and under it is turned up as it were fire.'[227] Jung calls this 'an image of the supreme opposites'.[228]

At this point in the text there is a section entitled 'The Alchemical View of the Union of Opposites'. According to Jung, the 'union of the substances' described in alchemical texts was more than a primitive form of chemistry:

> The union of the 'natures' which 'embrace one another' was not physical and concrete, for they were 'celestial natures' which multiplied 'by the command of God' ... the conjunction they strove for was a philosophical operation, namely the union of form and matter.[229]

These 'natures' had a numinous quality because they were unknown. This numinosity generated a seeming endless stream of images of pairs of opposites.

The initial stage of alchemy is the recognition that the four elements, and the opposites which arise from them, coexist in an undifferentiated state in the original state or prima material:

The alchemical description of the beginning corresponds psychologically to a primitive consciousness which is constantly liable to break up into individual affective processes – to fall apart, as it were, in four directions. As the four elements represent the whole physical world, their falling apart means dissolution into the constituents of the world, that is, into a purely inorganic and hence unconscious state. Conversely, the combination of the elements and the final synthesis of male and female is an achievement of the art and a product of conscious endeavour. The result of the synthesis was consequently conceived by the adept as self-knowledge, which, like the knowledge of God, is need for the preparation of the Philosphers' Stone. Piety is needed for the work, and this is nothing but knowledge of oneself.[230]

The differentiation of the opposites brings 'the "one" world out of the state of potentiality into reality. Reality consists of a multiplicity of things.'[231] The subsequent reunion of opposites is not usually a 'direct union'. It normally requires a medium, often symbolized in alchemy as Mercurius, 'the spiritual water … [which] mitigates and unites the opposites'.[232] Mercurius has the paradoxical quality of being 'not just the medium of conjunction but also that which is to be united'.[233] Jung identifies Mercurius with 'the original, non-differentiated unity of the world or of Being'[234] and the collective unconscious.

According to the alchemist Dorn, 'a mental union was not the culminating point but merely the first stage of the procedure. The second stage is reached when the mental union, that is, the unity of spirit and soul, is conjoined with the body. But a consummation of the *mysterium coniunctionis* can be expected only when the unity of spirit, soul, and body is made one with the original *unus mundus*.'[235] Jung sees the Assumption of Mary, where Mary represents the body, as a Christian version of this cosmic reunion. It is an instance of the motif of incest, where 'the supreme union of opposites expressed a combination of things which are related but of unlike nature'.[236]

Through their successive procedures of separation and reunification, the alchemists 'strove for a *total* union of opposites in symbolic form … Hence they sought to produce that substance in which all opposites were united … It had to be created by man, and at the same time, since it was an "increatum," by God himself.'[237] The gulf between opposites cannot be bridged by logic. Therefore the alchemists sought to follow nature, which 'consists entirely of such "thirds," since she is represented by effects which resolve an opposition – just as a waterfall mediates between "above" and "below"'.[238] This reconciliation of opposites was only possible with the assistance of 'a certain heavenly substance hidden in the human body'. This 'truth' was 'the *imago Dei* imprinted in man'.[239]

Jung finds the procedures of the alchemists echoed in the analytic process:

This is a method which is used spontaneously by nature herself or can be taught to the patient by the analyst. As a rule it occurs when the analysis has constellated the opposites so powerfully that union or synthesis of the personality becomes an imperative necessity … It requires a real solution and necessitates a third thing in which the opposites unite. Here the logic of the intellect usually fails, for in a logical antithesis there is no third. The 'solvent' can only be of an irrational nature. In nature the resolution of opposites is always an energic process: she acts *symbolically* in the truest sense of the word, doing something that expresses both sides, just as a waterfall visibly mediates between above and below. The waterfall itself is then the incommensurable third. In an open and unresolved conflict dreams and fantasies occur which, like the waterfall, illustrate the tension and nature of the opposites, and thus prepare the synthesis.[240]

The uroboros as a 'symbol of the union of opposites'[241] is an image of the goal of the process, not of its beginning in which the elements are in conflict. The union 'between opposites like spirit and matter, conscious and unconscious … will happen in a third thing, which represents not a compromise but something new … a transcendental entity that could be described only in paradoxes'.[242] The archetype of the self provides a unifying structure for the contents of the psyche, which revolve around a numinous centre. 'Co-ordinated with this are all kinds of secondary symbols, most of them expressing the nature of opposites to be united.'[243]

As we have seen, *Mysterium Coniunctionis* contains Jung's most sustained use of the concept of the union of opposites. The book ends with Jung's negative anthropology and reflections on the boundaries of knowledge:

if a union is to take place between opposites like spirit and matter, conscious and unconscious, bright and dark, and so on, it will happen in a third thing, which represents not a compromise but something new, just as for the alchemists the cosmic strife of the elements was composed by the *lithos ou lithos* (stone that is no stone), by a transcendental entity that could be described only in paradoxes … For the psychologist it the self – man as he is, and the indescribable and super-empirical totality of that same man. This totality is a mere postulate, but a necessary one, because no one can assert that he has complete knowledge of man as he is. Not only in the psychic man is there something unknown, but also in the physical … he too is a *lithos ou lithos*.[244]

In the same year Jung commented on the union of opposites in two letters. In response to a question from H. L. Philp about enantiodromia, Jung states, 'Of course it does not lead to the union of opposites.'[245] In reply to D. Cox, he writes that the necessity of 'symbolic death':

> Through his further incarnation God becomes a fearful task for man, who must now find ways and means to unite the divine opposites in himself ... Christ has shown how everybody will be crucified upon his destiny, i.e., upon his self, as he was ... If God incarnates in the empirical man, man is confronted with the divine problem ... Christ is the model for the human answers and his symbol is the *cross*, the union of opposites.[246]

This is of a piece with his explanation of alchemy in *Mysterium Coniunctionis*. In the following year there are two references to the union of opposites. The transcendent function is described as 'conjoined opposites'[247] and, in the 'Commentary on *The Secret of the Golden Flower*', Jung states that 'the union of opposites on a higher level of consciousness is not a rational thing ... [but] a process of psychic development that expresses itself in symbols'.[248]

The 1958 essay in which Jung argues that flying saucers are a modern myth contains a number of references to the union of opposites. Flying saucers are images of 'totality whose simple, round form portrays the archetype of the self', which unites 'apparently irreconcilable opposites'[249] and is 'a combination of opposites'.[250] In his analysis of a woman's dream, he suggests that 'the festive white robes of the crew suggest the idea of a marital union of opposites'.[251] In his discussion of a print from a broadsheet of 1561, which depicts a 'very frightful spectacle', Jung identifies crosses in the sky which signify the 'union of opposites ... a crossing'.[252] In the summary of the essay, Jung enumerates a series of antitheses which might represent and which give rise to 'the mediating or "uniting" symbol which necessarily proceeds from a sufficiently great tension of opposites'.[253] One aspect of the meaning of UFOs which he offers 'with all due reserve' is that there might be some actual physical objects in the sky, but that 'the meaningful connection is the product on the one hand of projection and on the other of round and cylindrical forms which embody the projected meaning and have always symbolize the union of opposite'.[254] In an aside, he observes that the aircraft of the Soviet Union have red stars and those of the United States have white stars, and that the alchemists considered that the copulation of the *servus rubeus* (red slave) and the *femina candida* (white woman) 'produced the supreme union of opposites'.[255]

The final reference to the union of opposites in the *Collected Works* is in the essay, 'Symbols and the Interpretation of Dreams', which was written in English in 1961 and was included, in a slightly revised version, as 'Approaching the Unconscious', in *Man and His Symbols*. It refers to the paradoxical nature of symbols, which hold together unity and difference. The sentence demonstrates Jung's attempt to hold together the practice of psychotherapy and the theory of the unconscious, as well as finding the proper balance between nature and interpretation. 'In this part of the individuation process the interpretation of symbols plays an important practical role; for the symbols are natural attempts to reconcile and reunite often widely separated opposites, as is apparent from the contradictory nature of many symbols.'[256]

The theme of opposites is integral to the theory and practice of analytical psychology. The hermeneutic utility of what we might call Jung's discourse on opposites emerges more and more clearly in his writings over time. As this chapter demonstrates the problem of opposites constitutes a site within Jung's work which is saturated with apophatic intensity.

Notes

1 Jung, C. G. (1963), *Memories, Dreams, Reflections*, Aniela Jaffe (ed.), R. and C. Winston (trans.). New York: Random House, p. 235.
2 *Memories, Dreams, Reflections*, p. 350.
3 The version of *Symbols of Transformation* published in the *Collected Works* (CW5) contains the following: 'The self, as a symbol of wholeness, is a *coincidentia oppositorum*, and therefore contains light and darkness simultaneously.' (p. 576) This might give the impression that Jung had begun to use the notion of the coincidence of opposites as early as 1912, the date when this text was first published in German. However the version of this work translated by Hinkle and published in six printings between 1916 and 1951, as *Psychology of the Unconscious*, does not contain this term. The revision, which appears in the *Collected Works* as *Symbols of Transformation*, was published in 1952. The paragraphs where this phrase was added are on pages 402–3 of the original 1916 translation and page 222 of the sixth printing in 1951. [*Psychology of the Unconscious* (1916), Beatrice Hinkle (trans.). New York: Moffat, Yard and Company and (1951), London: Routledge & Kegan Paul.] Consequently, the argument that Jung acquired the concept from his reading Cusa in the 1920s is not undermined.
4 CW8 679.
5 Pietkainen, Petteri (1999), *C. G. Jung and the Psychology of Symbolic Forms*. Helsinki: Academia Scientiarum Fennica, p. 239.
6 McCort, Dennis (2001), *Going Beyond the Pairs: The Coincidence of Opposites in German Romanticism, Zen and Deconstruction*. Albany, NY: SUNY Press, pp. 7–8.
7 Eliade, Mircea (1965), 'Mephistopheles and the Androgyne', in *The Two and the One*. London: Harvill, p. 81.
8 Smith, Mark Trevor (1993), *'All Nature is but Art': The Coincidence of Opposites in English Romantic Literature*. West Cornwall, CT: Locust Hill Press, p. xii.
9 Bishop, Paul (2000), *Synchronicity and Intellectual Intuition in Kant, Swedenborg, and Jung*. Lampeter: Edwin Mellen, p. 17. See also p. 15 and p. 119.
10 Sells, Michael A. (1994), *Mystical Languages of Unsaying*. Chicago: University of Chicago Press, p. 6.
11 There are seventeen references to Cusa and his writings in the *Collected Works*: CW8 406; 9i 18, 9ii 355*n*; 10 766, 806; 11 279; 14 124, 200; 16 409&*n*, 485, 486, 527*n*, 537&*n*; 18 1537, 1637.
12 CW14 200.
13 See Peter J. Casarella (ed.) (2006), *Cusanus: The Legacy of Learned Ignorance*. Washington, DC: Catholic University of America Press; G. Christianson and T. Izbicki (eds) (1996), *Nicholas of Cusa on Christ and the Church*. Leiden: Brill; Donald F. Duclow (1974), 'Gregory of Nyssa and Nicholas of Cusa: Infinity, Anthropology and the *Via Negativa*', *The Downside Review*, 92(309); Karsten Harries (2001), *Infinity and Perspective*. Cambridge, MA: MIT Press; Jasper Hopkins (1983), *Nicholas of Cusa's Metaphysic of Contraction*. Minneapolis, MN: Arthur J. Banning Press; (1985), *Nicholas of Cusa's Dialectical Mysticism*, Minneapolis, MN: Arthur J. Banning Press; Nancy Hudson (2005), 'Divine Immanence: Nicholas of Cusa's Understanding of Theophany and the Retrieval of a "New" Model of God', *Journal of Theological Studies*, 56(2); Clyde Lee Miller (2003), *Reading Cusanus:*

Metaphor and Dialectic in a Conjectural Universe. Washington, DC: Catholic University of America Press.

14 In a letter Cusa wrote, 'Dionysius, almost everywhere, conveyed a disjunctive theology … he leaps through the disjunction to copulation and coincidence, that is to say, to a perfectly simple union, which is not at all indirect but goes directly above all absence and all presence, to where absence coincides with presence, and negation with affirmation. Such is the most secret theology, to which none of the philosophers has arrived nor could arrive if he maintains the accepted principle of all philosophy, according to which two contradictories do not coincide at all. That is why it is necessary that anyone who does theology in the mystical mode, above all reason and all intelligence, going so far as to abandon himself, must penetrate into the shadows; and he will discover how to know that what reason judges impossible – that a thing can be and not be at the same time – is necessity itself. Let us say more: if such shadowy and thick impossibility does not appear, then the supreme necessity does not exist at all, which is not in contradiction with that impossibility, because the impossibility is the true necessity itself.' Smith, p. 31. See also F. Edward Cranz (2000), 'The (Concept of the) Beyond in Proclus, Pseudo-Dionysius, and Cusanus', 'Nicolaus Cusanus and Dionysius Areopagita' and 'Cusanus' Use of Pseudo-Dionysius' all in *Nicholas of Cusa and the Renaissance*, T. M. Izbicki and G. Christianson (eds). Aldershot, UK: Ashgate; Donald F. Duclow (1972), 'Pseudo-Dionysius, John Scotus Eriugena, Nicholas of Cusa: An Approach to the Hermeneutic of the Divine Names', *International Philosophical Quarterly*, Vol. XII; Pauline Moffitt Watts (1987), 'Pseudo-Dionysius the Areopagite and Three Renaissance Neoplatonists: Cusanus, Ficino, and Pico on Mind and Cosmos', in *Supplementum Festivum: Studies in Honor of Paul Oskar Kristeller*, J. Hankins, J. Monfasani and F. Purnell, Jr. (eds). Binghamton: Medieval and Renaissance Texts and Studies.

15 Hopkins, Jasper (2006), 'Nicholas of Cusa's Intellectual Relationship to Anselm of Canterbury', in *Cusanus: The Legacy of Learned Ignorance*. Washington, DC: The Catholic University of America Press, p. 55.

16 Bond, H. Lawrence (1997), 'Introduction', *Nicholas of Cusa: Selected Spiritual Writings*. New York: Paulist, p. 22.

17 Bond, p. 23.

18 CW11 279n10.

19 Bond, p. 28.

20 Nicholas of Cusa, *On Learned Ignorance*, DDI I.24.76 (h. I.49).

21 Bond, p. 46.

22 Bond, pp. 44–5.

23 Bond, p. 46.

24 Bond, pp. 46–7.

25 Bond, 48–9.

26 MDR, p. 359.

27 Bond, p. 58.

28 Bond, p. 59.

29 Nicholas of Cusa, *On the Summit of Contemplation* paras 5, 6 and 8, in Bond, pp. 294–6.

30 Bond, p. 62.

31 Nicholas of Cusa, *On the Summit of Contemplation*, para. 11, in Bond, pp. 297–8.

32 Herbert, Jack (2001), *The German Tradition: Uniting the Opposites: Goethe, Jung and Rilke*. London: Temenos Academy, p. 27.

33 McCort, p. 3.

34 McCort, p. 8–9.

35 Paper, Jordan (2004), *The Mystic Experience: A Descriptive and Comparative Analysis*, Albany, NY: SUNY Press.

36 CW11 279.

37 CW9ii 355n.

38 CW16 537.
39 CW16 537 *n*27.
40 CW16 537 *n*28.
41 CW16 537 *n*30. The bibliography to CW16 has the following: *De docta ignorantia.* Edited by Paolog Rotta. Bari, 1923. For translation, see: *Of Learned Ignorance.* Translated by Germain Heron. London, 1954.
42 CW16 p. 352. '*De conjectures novissimorum temporum.* In: *Opera.* Basel, 1565.'
43 Vansteenberghe, Edmond (1920), *Le Cardinal Nicolas de Cues*, Paris: H. Champion.
44 CW8 679; 9ii 191, 301; 10 674; 11 881; 12 259; 13 256; 14 258, 274, 540; 16 502, 522.
45 CW11 881.
46 CW13 269.
47 CW13 256.
48 CW12 259.
49 CW16 502.
50 CW16 522.
51 CW16 537.
52 CW11 283.
53 CW9ii 191.
54 CW9ii 301.
55 CW12 129*n*.
56 CW14 176.
57 CW14 258.
58 CW14 274.
59 CW14 540.
60 CW13 289.
61 CW12 526.
62 CW8 401.
63 CW11 277.
64 CW11 277-8.
65 CW9i 555. An earlier version of this essay was published in 1934 as 'The Integration of the Personality', but it does not contain the term *complexio oppositorum.*
66 CW9i 257.
67 CW9ii 112 & 112*n*.
68 CW9ii 423.
69 CW9ii 237.
70 CW9ii 423.
71 CW11 p. 358.
72 CW11 712.
73 CW11 716.
74 CW18 1553.
75 CW14 528.
76 CW18 1617.
77 CW18 1624.
78 CW18 1632.
79 CW18 1640.
80 CW18 1650, 1668.
81 CW10 Plate II.
82 CW10 727.
83 CW6 790.
84 MDR, p. 334.
85 MDR, p. 338.
86 MDR, p. 341.
87 MDR, p. 353.

88 CW12 436.
89 CW12, figs 167 and 226.
90 CW9ii 58.
91 CW9ii 72, 425.
92 CW9ii 124.
93 CW9ii 130.
94 CW9ii 256.
95 CW9ii 256.
96 CW11 716.
97 CW11 738.
98 CW11 738.
99 CW11 739.
100 CW10 767.
101 CW10 801.
102 CW18 1627.
103 MDR, p. 339.
104 MDR, p. 338.
105 CW5 415.
106 Jung (1916) p. 417.
107 CW5 576.
108 Jung (1916) p. 585.
109 Jung (1916) p. 587.
110 CW5 577.
111 CW5 671.
112 Jung (1916) p. 692.
113 CW6 169.
114 CW6 185.
115 CW6 329.
116 CW6 330.
117 CW6 362.
118 CW6 115.
119 CW6 178.
120 CW6 174.
121 CW7 206.
122 CW7 224.
123 CW7 382.
124 CW18 261-2.
125 CW 18 266.
126 CW11 150.
127 CW11 152.
128 CW9i 524.
129 CW9i 285.
130 CW9i 292.
131 CW9i 295.
132 CW13 187n; 199.
133 CW12 6.
134 CW12 22.
135 CW12 24-5.
136 CW12 25.
137 CW12 30.
138 CW12 259.
139 CW12 311; the union of opposites is also depicted in images 12 *Figs*. 113 and 12 *Figs*. 167.

140 CW12 334.
141 CW12 404.
142 CW12 436n.
143 CW12 450.
144 CW12 557.
145 CW12 557.
146 CW16 354.
147 CW16 381.
148 CW16 410.
149 CW16 454.
150 CW16 460.
151 CW16 467.
152 CW16 474.
153 CW16 493.
154 CW16 533.
155 CW16 534.
156 CW16 536.
157 CW16 537.
158 CW8 406.
159 CW11 184.
160 CW11 196.
161 CW13 279.
162 CW9i 603, published 1950; this wording does not appear in the earlier version of this paper published in 1934.
163 CW9i 705.
164 CW9i 278.
165 CW9i 293.
166 CW9ii 115.
167 CW9ii 130.
168 CW9ii 142.
169 CW9ii 264.
170 CW9ii 280.
171 CW9ii 281.
172 CW9ii 301.
173 CW9ii 304.
174 CW9ii 390.
175 CW9ii 390n.
176 CW9ii 418.
177 CW9ii 426.
178 CW9ii 390n79.
179 Jung (1916) p. 263; 'The naïve Egyptian antiquity has preserved for us the union of contrasting tendencies in the mother idea of Isis.'
180 CW5 415; 'In ancient Egypt this union of opposite tendencies was naïvely preserved in the Isis mother-imago.'
181 Jung (1916) p. 344.
182 CW5 576.
183 Jung (1916) p. 347.
184 CW5 577.
185 CW5 671.
186 CW11 690.
187 CW11 738.
188 CW11 746.
189 CW11 755.

190 CW11 756.
191 CW7 368.
192 CW9i 20.
193 See 'Archetypes of the Collective Unconscious', in Jung (1939), *The Integration of Personality*. London: Routledge & Kegan Paul, p. 59.
194 CW8 401.
195 CW9i 198.
196 CW11 396.
197 CW11 437.
198 CW11 438.
199 CW11 438.
200 CW11 803.
201 CW11 828.
202 CW13 131.
203 CW13 307, 310, 315, 331.
204 CW13 385.
205 CW13 408.
206 CW13 456.
207 CW13 462.
208 CW9i 198.
209 CW18 1553, 1554.
210 CW18 1556.
211 CW8 899–900.
212 CW14 35.
213 CW14 36.
214 CW14 36n.
215 CW14 104.
216 CW14 106.
217 CW14 188.
218 CW14 129n.
219 CW14 141.
220 CW14 200.
221 CW14 201.
222 CW14 258.
223 CW14 261.
224 CW14 276.
225 CW14 291; 292.
226 CW14 542.
227 Job 28:5, King James Version.
228 CW14 633.
229 CW14 654.
230 CW14 657.
231 CW14 659.
232 CW14 658.
233 CW14 659.
234 CW14 660.
235 CW14 664.
236 CW14 664.
237 CW14 676.
238 CW14 674.
239 CW14 681.
240 CW14 705.

241 CW14 718.
242 CW14 765.
243 CW14 776.
244 CW14 765.
245 CW18 1597.
246 CW18 1661.
247 CW8 189.
248 CW13 31.
249 CW10 622.
250 CW10 640.
251 CW10 698.
252 CW10 762.
253 CW10 779.
254 CW10 789.
255 CW10 790.
256 CW18 595.

Chapter 6

The transcendent function

In 1916 Jung wrote a manuscript entitled 'Die Transzendente Funktion', which lay in his files until 1953. It was translated into English by A. R. Pope and published by the student association of the C. G. Jung Institute in Zurich in 1957. Jung's revised version of the original German paper was published in 1958. 'The Transcendent Function', in CW8, is based on the revised German essay and the Pope translation. In a short 'Prefatory Note' Jung states:

> After forty-two years, the problem has lost nothing of its topicality ... The essay may therefore stand, with all its imperfections, as an historical document ... (the) problem is identical with the universal question: How does one come to terms in practice with the unconscious? ... For the unconscious is not this thing or that; it is the Unknown as it immediately affects us.[1]

The relationship between the conscious and the unconscious, the known and the unknown, can only be resolved by an irrational factor:

> In practice, opposites can be united only in the form of a compromise, or *irrationally*, some new thing arising between them which, although different from both, yet has the power to take up their energies in equal measure as an expression of both and of neither. Such an expression cannot be contrived by reason, it can only be created through living.[2]

Jung states with regard to the transcendent function that 'there is nothing mysterious or metaphysical about the term ... it means a psychological function comparable in its way to a mathematical function of the same name, which is a function of real and imaginary numbers.'[3] A 'transcendental function' in mathematics is:

> A function which is not an algebraic function, i.e., a function whose action on its argument(s) cannot be represented by the arithmetic and algebraic operations: addition and subtraction, multiplication and division, raising to a power, or extraction of roots. The exponential function, the logarithm function, and the trigonometric functions are all transcendental.[4]

Jung does not go further in developing this analogy with mathematics. Perhaps there would have been scope for him to expand the comparison by drawing on Cantor's concepts of transcendental function, infinite sets and infinite (or transfinite) numbers.[5]

The 1916 manuscript was written during that crucial point in Jung's personal and intellectual development referred to as 'the confrontation with the unconscious'. This period included the pivotal instance on December 12, 1913 when he let himself 'drop' and experienced a series of emotionally charged images. The *Septem Sermones ad Mortuos* was written in 1916 and he was working on the essays that would become *Two Essays in Analytical Psychology*. It is argued by Homans[6] and Chodorow[7] that the concept of the transcendent function articulated here is the precursor to his concepts of the self, individuation and synchronicity. A link can also be made retrospectively with his earlier work on spiritualism.[8]

The transcendent function makes 'the transition from one attitude to another organically possible, without loss of the unconscious'. One could argue that the act of writing the essay was a way for Jung to make the transition to a future independent of Freud and psychoanalysis. A strong element in the piece is his defence of 'constructive treatment'. 'Constructive treatment of the unconscious, that is, the question of meaning and purpose, paves the way for the patient's insight into that process which I call the transcendent function.'[9]

The transference is an expression of the transcendent function at work in the relationship between analyst and patient:

> The suitably trained analyst mediates the transcendent function for the patient, i.e., helps him to bring conscious and unconscious together and so arrive at a new attitude. In this function of the analyst lies one of the many important meanings of the *transference*. The patient clings by means of the transference to the person who seems to promise him a renewal of attitude; through it he seeks this change, which is vital to him, even though he may not be conscious of doing so.[10]

This state of dependency can lead to 'bitter hatred', 'monotony', and 'poverty of ideas' if the analyst understands the fantasies of the patient 'merely in a concretistic-reductive sense'. Jung maintains that his own approach is not 'suggestion':

> The method is based, rather on evaluating the symbol (i.e., dream-image or fantasy) not *semiotically*, as a sign for elementary instinctual processes, but symbolically in the true sense, the word 'symbol' being taken to mean the best possible expression for a complex fact not yet clearly apprehended by consciousness.[11]

Active imagination is described here as a new and valuable method for 'synthesizing the conscious and unconscious'. It a development of his experience of December 1913 and has roots in his own childhood visions and studies of mediums. The patient allows affect-laden images into consciousness and enters into a form of dialogue with the images while maintaining a secure conscious position. According to Jung this gap between conscious attitude and unconscious affect mediated by an image allowed for emergence of the transcendent function.

In the 1916 paper he presents a woman's dream and offers 'Associations', 'Analytical Interpretations' and 'Constructive Interpretations'. Since dream imagery can be 'unsuitable or difficult' to use, he recommends 'spontaneous fantasies' as material for active imagination to 'produce the transcendent function'. He maintains that:

> The transcendent function not only forms a valuable addition to psycho-therapeutic treatment, but gives the patient the inestimable advantage of assisting the analyst on his own resources and of breaking a dependence which is often felt as humiliating. It is a way of attaining liberation by one's own effort and of finding the courage to be oneself.[12]

Aside from the 1916 essay that we have been considering, there a very few instances of Jung's use of the term. According to Dehing:

> Jung's use of the expression 'transcendent function' is surprisingly infrequent ... Curiously enough, in spite of its obvious relevance to the analytic process, no explicit mention of the concept is to found in Jung's main writings on psychotherapeutic practice (CW16), although we find it in seven articles or books, three of the published seminars and four letters.[13]

Dehing observes that Jung used the term to refer to a function, a method, a process or the outcome of these dynamics.[14] Despite its sparse and varied use by Jung (or perhaps because of this fact) the notion, variously conceived, has become an important part of the Jungian and post-Jungian lexicon and a political marker within analytical psychology.

In 1992 the Twelfth International Congress for Analytical Psychology was held in Chicago on the theme 'The Transcendent Function: Individual and Collective Aspects'. In his presentation, 'The Transcendent Function: A Critical Re-Evaluation', from which I have already quoted above, Dehing uses Winnicott's description of Jung's 'madness' and 'divided self' to illuminate the issues that Jung was grappling with when he was writing the 1916 paper:

> Clearly Jung found no solace in classical psychoanalysis; his problem was not one of repressed personal material, but overcoming a dissociation – a divided self. We are not faced with a horizontal division here, such as Freud presented between conscious and personal unconscious; the split is vertical and leaves no room for Freud's unconscious. ... Jung found

himself forced to devise a new approach which was remarkable in more than one respect. It took intuition and an uncommon courage to bring this attempt to a favorable conclusion.[15]

For Dehing this period 'most certainly had a psychotic structure'. This position draws a sharp reply from Sandner:

> I do not for a moment agree with Winnicott's (1964) diagnosis of Jung as a case of recovered childhood schizophrenia ... I think that Jung, like many other people – some of them Jungians – was not schizophrenic, psychotic or mad, but suffered a childhood wound which resulted in an initiatory illness ... The content of the psyche in initiatory illness is much better organized, with coherent imagery and overall conscious purpose, than in any sort of psychotic state.[16]

The situation is paradoxical. You would expect Dehing, a developmental Jungian, to be sceptical about the efficacy of active imagination, as portrayed in 'The Transcendent Function', to address psychotic states. And you would expect Sandler, a classical Jungian, to be eager to embrace the notion that active imagination can heal psychosis. The fight is about which image of Jung will prevail as much as it is about the concept of the transcendent function.

One debate about the transcendent function is the question as to whether the transcendent function is a clinical concept or a spiritual concept. There is also a question about whether the transcendent function operates only between conscious and unconscious. This would limit the concept unnecessarily and would contradict Jung's own observation that '[i]n normal people, the transcendent function works only in the unconscious, which is continually tending to maintain the psychic balance'.[17]

Solomon claims that 'Jung's concept of the transcendent function derives its philosophical basis from the notion of dialectical change, first expounded by the German Romantic philosopher, Friedrich Hegel'.[18] It is difficult to assess the merits of this claim. She says that while references to Hegel in the *Collected Works* are 'quite scathing', there was one instance when Jung called Hegel 'that great psychologist in philosopher's garb'.[19] She also says, 'We know, however from the libraries of each, that both Freud and Jung read and carefully annotated Hegel's work ... My contention is that the dialectical vision can be seen as the essence of Jung's concept of the transcendent function.'[20]

She goes on to compare diagramatically the transcendent function, the dialectical model and Fordham's description of the self process. In each case she identifies two terms that stand in tension and that give rise to a third. With the transcendent function the dynamic opposition between conscious and unconscious produces a creative synthesis; in the dialectical model the dynamic opposition between thesis and antithesis also produces a creative synthesis; and, in Fordham's model, deintegration breaches the gap between the primary self and the not-self and the process of integration produces the integrate.

In explaining the motivation for her comparison of Jung and Hegel, Solomon writes:

> Although I am concentrating on the relationship between Jung's model of the transcendent function and Hegel's dialectical model, there is a deeper implication. An understanding of the dialectical model contributes to a broader recognition of the philosophical bedrock which underpins the ways of thinking about human nature and development that we call analytic and psychoanalytic theory. It is able to contribute to an understanding of the differential roles of inner and outer influences in the development of personality. Thus it contributes conceptually to a central debate in current depth psychology: whether a primary self or a primary instinct for relatedness forms the basis of personality structure.[21]

Here we can see Solomon using the concept of the transcendent function to support an object-relations, and possibly biological, view of analytical psychology. Salman takes issue with Solomon by pointing out that:

> Although the transcendent function has a dialectical motion, it is an 'opus contra naturam' (work against nature), involving qualities of ego participation that separate it from instinctual developmental and dialectical processes ... the transcendent function goes beyond dialectics into conscious dialogue by introducing creativity, suffering and ethical integrity to the interaction of opposites. These additions act as the alchemical *ferment* which transforms the dialectical process.[22]

For Salman the transcendent function is a gnostic process. 'By this I mean a psychological process which has as its goal immediate, direct, and personal understanding of one's experience.'[23]

Solomon, a developmental Jungian, is espousing a fairly impersonal, archetypal perspective of the transcendent function to support her object-relations position and Salman, a classical Jungian, is taking an existential position to support an archetypal reading of the transcendent function.

Hillman's concept of soul-making could be seen as his version of the transcendent function. For Hillman, images are to be met as wholly other. He objects to a view that sees images as a 'part of myself'. He advocates an encounter with the image, not in expectation for a third or synthetic position, but because the meeting is a good in itself:

> By *soul* I mean, first of all a perspective rather than a substance, a viewpoint toward things rather than a thing itself. This perspective is reflective; it mediates events and makes differences between ourselves and everything that happens. Between us and events, between the doer and the deed, there is a reflective moment – and soul-making means differentiating this middle ground ... In another attempt upon the idea of *soul* I suggested

that the word refers to that unknown component which makes meaning possible, turns events into experiences, is communicated in love, and has a religious concern. These four qualifications I had already put forth some years ago. I had begun to use the term freely, usually interchangeably with *psyche* (from Greek) and *anima* (from Latin). Now I am adding three necessary modifications. First, *soul* refers to the *deepening* of events into experiences; second, the significance *soul* makes possible, whether in love or in religious concern, derives from its special *relation with death*. And third, by *soul* I mean the imaginative possibility in our natures, the experiencing through reflective speculation, dream, image and *fantasy* – that mode which recognizes all realities as primarily symbolic or metaphorical.[24]

It might be said that Hillman starts from the transcendent function, the soul, and imagines the opposites afterward, so to speak; like Plotinus who starts with the One which overflows to produce the *nous*, which contains opposites. He wants to describe the emanation of the soul, rather than the contemplative return to the soul:

Here I am working toward a psychology of soul that is based in a psychology of image. Here I am suggesting both a *poetic basis of mind* and a psychology that starts neither in the physiology of the brain, the structure of language, the organization of society, nor the analysis of behavior, but in the processes of imagination.[25]

Jung's essay is comparatively short and somewhat thin from a scholarly point of view, without his usual armoury of references. Considering the fact that it was unknown until close to the end of his life it is surprising how much currency the idea has had. Miller, who has identified the career of the concept in Jung's essays, letters and seminars between 1916 and 1958, argues that 'the transcendent function is linked with virtually all the concepts that are at the core of Jung's psychology'.[26] He makes the further claim that the transcendent function is the heart of Jung's method:

beyond its stated role in uniting the opposites, the transcendent function is Jung's root metaphor for psyche itself or for becoming psychological and is the well spring from whence flowed much of the rest of Jung's imaginal, depth psychology. Put another way, the transcendent function is Jung's attempt to describe the most fundamental depth psychological activity, the interchange of information and images between consciousness and the unconscious, and everything else that Jung proposed represented merely a refinement or differentiation of that phenomenon. Enunciated immediately after Jung emerged from his own confrontation with the unconscious, the writing of the transcendent function in 1916 was an attempt to give voice to his own indescribable experience of coming to terms with the unknown in the unconscious.[27]

Following on from Miller's view, we could understand the transcendent function as an apophatic methodology at the core of Jung's theory and practice. It is a very precise discipline of unknowing. It is predicated on an apophatic anthropology, which accepts that I do not understand myself:

> The secret participation of the unconscious is everywhere present without our having to search for it, but as it remains unconscious we never really know what is going on or what to expect. What we are searching for is a way to make conscious those contents which are about to influence our actions, so that the secret interference of the unconscious and it unpleasant consequences can be avoided.[28]

The first stage of the discipline involves alert receptivity to the contents of the unconscious. These contents are recorded in writing, drawing, sculpting or movement. 'In giving the content form, the lead must be left as far as possible to the chance ideas and associations thrown up by the unconscious.'[29] The second stage involves the ego's engagement with the material from the unconscious. Humbert identifies three typical activities of the ego in Jung's work as *geschehenlassen* (to let happen), *betrachten* (to consider, to impregnate) and *sich auseinandersetzen* (to confront oneself with). They 'together define conscious activity in its confrontation with the unconscious'.[30] They are verbs that emphasize openness and relationship. In the transcendent function reciprocity is established between conscious and unconscious:

> The shuttling to and fro of arguments and affects represents the transcendent function of opposites. The confrontation of the two positions generates a tension charged with energy and creates a living, third thing – not a logical stillbirth in accordance with the principle *tertium non datur* but a movement out of the suspension between opposites, a living birth that leads to a new level of being, a new situation. The transcendent function manifests itself as a quality of conjoined opposites.[31]

We can hear echoes here of Dionysius' *kataphasis, apophasis, exstasis*. *Kataphasis* corresponds to the given unconscious contents and conscious attitudes. *Apophasis* corresponds to the suspension of judgement and the stance of openness on the part of the ego. *Exstasis* corresponds to appearance of a new symbol or attitude, which is not merely a compromise or combination of the original opposites.

Notes

1 CW8, pp. 67–8.
2 CW6 169.
3 CW8 131.

4 http://www.mathacademy.com.
5 'Cantor's theory became a whole new subject of research concerning the mathematics of the infinite ... In thus developing new ways of asking questions concerning continuity and infinity, Cantor quickly became controversial. When he argued that infinite numbers have an actual existence, he drew on an ancient and medieval philosophy concerning the "actual" and "potential" infinite and also on the early religious training given him by his parents ... Cantor in 1883 allied his theory with Platonic metaphysics.' http://www.britannica.com
6 Homans, Peter (1995), *Jung in Context: Modernity and the Making of Psychology*. Chicago: University of Chicago Press.
7 Chodorow, Joan (ed.) (1997), *Jung on Active Imagination*. London: Routledge.
8 Henderson, David (1999), 'The Medium is the Message', unpublished paper.
9 CW8 147.
10 CW8 146.
11 CW8 148.
12 CW8 193.
13 Dehing, Jef (1993), 'The Transcendent Function: A Critical Re-Evaluation', in *The Transcendent Function: Individual and Collective Aspects: Proceedings of the Twelfth International Congress for Analytical Psychology*, Mary Ann Mattoon (ed.). Einsiedeln, Switzerland: Daimon Verlag, p. 15.
14 Dehing, p. 15.
15 Dehing, p. 22.
16 Sandler, Donald F. (1993), 'Response', in *The Transcendent Function: Individual and Collective Aspects: Proceedings of the Twelfth International Congress for Analytical Psychology*, Mary Ann Mattoon (ed.). Einsiedeln, Switzerland: Daimon Verlag, pp. 31–2.
17 Jung, Let-1, p. 269.
18 Solomon, Hester McFarland (1993), 'Hegel's Dialectical Vision and the Transcendent Function', in *The Transcendent Function: Individual and Collective Aspects: Proceedings of the Twelfth International Congress for Analytical Psychology*, Mary Ann Mattoon (ed.). Einsiedeln, Switzerland: Daimon Verlag, p. 123.
19 Solomon, p. 125.
20 Solomon, p. 125.
21 Solomon, p. 124.
22 Salman, Sherry (1993), 'Response: Fermenting the Dialectic into Psychological Process', in *The Transcendent Function: Individual and Collective Aspects: Proceedings of the Twelfth International Congress for Analytical Psychology*, Mary Ann Mattoon (ed.). Einsiedeln, Switzerland: Daimon Verlag, p. 143.
23 Salman, p. 144.
24 Hillman, James (1975), *Re-Visioning Psychology*. New York: Harper & Row, p. x.
25 Hillman, p. xi.
26 Miller, Jeffery C. (2004), *The Transcendent Function: Jung's Model of Psychological Growth through Dialogue with the Unconscious*, Albany, NY: SUNY Press, p. 77.
27 Miller, p. 78.
28 CW8 158.
29 CW8 178.
30 Humbert, Ellie (1988), *C. G. Jung: The Fundaments of Theory and Practice*. Wilmette, IL: Chiron, p. 13.
31 CW8 189.

Chapter 7

Jung and contemporary theories of *apophasis*

In this chapter I use the work of contemporary writers to explore further apophatic themes in Jung. As I noted in the Introduction, the question of the nature and role of *apophasis* has been a lively topic in philosophy, theology and cultural studies in the past two decades. Of particular interest here is the attention given to the work of Dionysius.

Jung's thought is saturated with apophatic resonance. He is often characterized as having regressed to premodern preoccupations and perspectives. By bringing some of these contemporary writers into contact with him we can see that this is not entirely the case. His attempts to conceptualize the presence and effects of the unknown and unknowable within the psyche can have a very contemporary feel about them.

The writers I am citing fall into three groups. The first are analysing and theorizing the apophatic tradition. Much of their work involves reframing and contextualizing apophatic texts. The writers in this group that I will be considering here are Sells, Milem and Rorem.[1] They have each contributed a distinctive perspective on *apophasis* and negative theology. The second set of writers I will be considering are of interest because their views on negation resonate in some way with Jung's work. Deleuze engaged with Jung in his own work and Derrida has been made use of by a number of post-Jungians. Finally, I look at the work of Tacey and Dourley, two post-Jungians who have commented on aspects of negative theology in relation to Jung's work.

One way this theme is often taken up in psychoanalytic writing is through the use of Keats' concept of 'negative capability'. 'Negative capability' made a sudden appearance in the analytic literature in 1969, in papers in three different journals, and has been in regular use since then.[2] While Jung himself makes no reference to Keats or to 'negative capability', the term begins to appear in the *Journal of Analytical Psychology* from 1972, in reviews by Lambert and Plaut.[3] In the thirty-eight papers in the journal that mention 'negative capability' between 1972 and 2007 the overwhelming number are in book reviews and literature reviews. Mentions in articles are often linked with Bion. On this evidence, in Jungian circles the term did not have as much currency as in other psychoanalytic publications during that period. Does this reflect more acceptance of unknowing and the existence of a broader palette of language and images for the discussion of the paradoxical or ineffable within analytical psychology?

However one might answer this question, the frequency with which Keats' phrase is used within the wider psychoanalytic literature demonstrates the need for ways to think about not knowing. It also demonstrates the scarcity of ways of thinking about not knowing within psychoanalytic discourse. There clearly is an interest in finding language from outside of psychoanalytic discourse to think about not knowing, but the net has not been cast very widely.

Sells

The work of Sells is among the most significant contemporary attempts to understand the language of *apophasis*. A chapter of his book, *Mystical Languages of Unsaying*, is devoted to Eriugena, an early commentator on Dionysius and a key conduit for his influence in Western Europe. Sells claims that:

> Classical Western *apophasis* shares three key features: (1) the metaphor of overflowing or 'emanation' which is often in creative tension with the language of intentional, demiurgic creation; (2) dis-ontological discursive effort to avoid reifying the transcendent as an 'entity' or 'being' or 'thing'; (3) a distinctive dialectic of transcendence and immanence in which the utterly transcendent is revealed as the utterly immanent.[4]

It is possible to identify elements of Jung's work that reflect the features described by Sells.

One of the main ways in which Jung distinguishes his own theory of the unconscious from that of Freud is to question the ubiquity of repression. He states repeatedly that there are contents of the unconscious that appear, as it were, spontaneously. They are not repressed and have no antecedents in consciousness. This can be observed most clearly in psychosis, but the principle applies to all psychic life:

> Since it is highly probable that we are still a long way from the summit of absolute consciousness, presumably everyone is capable of wider consciousness, and we may assume accordingly that the unconscious processes are constantly supplying us with contents which, if consciously recognized, would extend the range of consciousness. Looked at in this way, the unconscious appears as a field of experience of unlimited extent. If it were merely reactive to the conscious mind, we might aptly call it a psychic mirror-world. In that case, the real source of all contents and activities would lie in the conscious mind, and there would be absolutely nothing in the unconscious except the distorted reflections of conscious contents. The creative process would be shut up in the conscious mind,

and anything new would be nothing but conscious invention or clever-
ness. The empirical facts give lie to this. Every creative man knows that
spontaneity is the every essence of creative thought. Because the unconscious is not just a reactive mirror-reflection, but an independent, productive activity, its realm of experience is a self-contained world, having its
own reality – precisely what we say about our experience of the outer
world. And just as material objects are the constituent elements of the
world, so psychic factors constitute the objects of that other world.[5]

Sells argues that within apophatic discourse emanation leads to paradox.

> The dualisms upon which the language of 'flowing out' is based, such as
> the distinction between the vessel that receives the flow and the content it
> receives, are ultimately fused into paradoxes (the vessel is the content) as
> the apophasis unravels its initial premise about the source of emanation.[6]

Within Jung's work the theme of paradox is ubiquitous, in particular in his
discussion of opposites. 'Naturally the conjunction can only be understood as a
paradox, since a union of opposites can be thought of only as their annihilation.
Paradox is a characteristic of all transcendental situations because it alone give
adequate expression to their indescribable nature.'[7]

Another analogy to the metaphor of overflowing in Jung's work is in his discussion of spirit. For Jung 'spirit is the dynamic principle'.[8] 'The hallmarks of spirit are,
firstly, the principle of spontaneous movement and activity; secondly, the spontaneous capacity to produce images independently of sense perception; and thirdly,
the autonomous and sovereign manipulation of these images.'[9] For Jung, the action
of spirit 'consists not only of uprushes of life but of formal products too'.[10]

In a discussion of a patient's material Jung argues that the fantasy 'is surely
a compensatory or complementary formation … [and yet] It is a spontaneous
manifestation of the unconscious, based on contents which are not to be found
in consciousness.'[11] The unconscious phenomenon 'overflows' the limits of
conscious understanding.

Sells' second sign of *apophasis* consists in the 'dis-ontological discursive effort to
avoid reifying the transcendent as an "entity" or "being" or "thing"'. One could
understand the whole of Jung's method to consist of a type of 'dis-ontological discursive effort'. His emphasis on dialectic ensures that no content of the psyche can
be understood on its own – in its own right. Everything must be viewed through
its relationship with an other or a difference. Consciousness must be experienced
as dependent on the unconscious, the unknown. Complexes and archetypes are
illuminated by their relationships with other complexes and archetypes.

This method is at play in the dialect between psychological and historical
knowledge. Jung asserts that 'just as psychological knowledge furthers our understanding of the historical material, so, conversely the historical material can throw
new light on individual problems'.[12] It is also a feature of dream interpretation:

I have developed a procedure which I call 'taking up the context' ... although the taking up of the context resulted in an 'unthinkable' meaning and hence in an apparently nonsensical interpretation, it proved correct in the light of facts which were subsequently disclosed.[13]

Taking up the context of psychic phenomena insures that they are not approached too concretely.

Jung wished to maintain a dialectic between past and present. Freud writes about primordial images and the effects of the murder of the father by the primal horde, but he relies on tacit Lamarkian assumptions to bridge the gap between the primordial and the present or the depth and the surface. He does not attempt to develop a theory about the relationship between the primordial images and the present beyond stating as a fact that the guilt of the first murderers is active in our own individual Oedipal guilts. We can understand Jung's theory of archetypes as an attempt to make good this lacuna in Freud's thought. He tried to think through or imagine the relationship between the archaic and the contemporary. While he may not have been successful or convincing in the detail of his theory, his efforts support my contention that within some areas of his theory he was attempting to clarify our relationship with the unthinkable.

Sells' third feature of apophatic discourse is 'a distinctive dialectic of transcendence and immanence in which the utterly transcendent is revealed as the utterly immanent'. As we saw earlier, this is a theme in Jung's discussion of opposites, such as the statement that the self is bigger than big and smaller than small. In the discussion at the end of *Answer to Job*, Jung argues that the archetype of the self and the god image are empirically indistinguishable. It is possible to 'arbitrarily postulate a difference', but this has risks:

On the contrary, it only helps us to separate man from God, and prevents God from becoming man. Faith is certainly right when it impresses on man's mind and heart how infinitely far away and inaccessible God is; but it also teaches his nearness which has to be empirically real if it is not to lose all significance. Only that which acts upon me do I recognize as real and actual ... The religious need longs for wholeness, and therefore lays hold of the images of wholeness offered by the unconscious, which independently of the conscious mind, rise up from the depths of our psychic nature.[14]

It is necessary for there to be a simultaneous experience which is personal and a meaning that is given from beyond the individual. The 'pleroma' is a notion that carries this sort of apophatic intensity:

the identity of a nontemporal, eternal event with a unique historical occurrence is something that is extremely difficult to conceive ... 'time' is a relative concept and needs to be complemented by that of the 'simultaneous' existence, in Bardo or pleroma, of all historical processes.[15]

We have seen that the three manoeuvres of apophatic discourse described by Sells can be found in Jung's writings.

Milem

I am using the framework provided by Bruce Milem in his paper 'Four Theories of Negative Theology'[16] as a lens to look at the work of Jung. Milem classifies the negative theologies under four headings: metaphysical, desire, experience and renunciation. The metaphysical theory of negative theology 'identifies God as the first cause of the existence of all things and argues that negative theology offers the most appropriate way to talk about this cause'.[17] The desire theory 'describes a desire that only the infinite God can satisfy'.[18] The experience theory understands negative theology as 'an attempt to do justice to a particular experience'.[19] And finally, the renunciation theory states that negative theology is based on an 'ethical imperative to give up positive concepts of God'.[20]

The metaphysical account of negative theology posits the unknowable origin of life. According to a metaphysical perspective:

> although … we cannot help but say that God made or created the world, we also have to admit that we do not understand how. In this way, when it comes to two major theistic beliefs, that God exists and that God created everything, believers have to confess that they do not understand what these beliefs mean.[21]

We see this mirrored in a number of ways in Jung. He acknowledges an unfathomable source:

> We call the unconscious 'nothing,' and yet it is a reality *in potentia*. The thought we shall think, the deed we shall do, even the fate we shall lament tomorrow, all lie unconscious in our today. The unknown in us which the affect uncovers was always there and sooner or later would have presented itself to consciousness. Hence we must always reckon with the presence of things not yet discovered.[22]

Jung describes a psychoid dimension, which is an incomprehensible unity of psyche and matter. The archetypes, with their psychoid foundations, are unknowable in themselves although we can apprehend constellations of archetypal images. Jung argues that only symbols are adequate containers for the multiplicity of meanings and energies which are at play in the psyche, but he is in agreement with the negative theologian in accepting that not only is there an excess that the symbol cannot contain, but that symbols die. The language of symbols breaks down. The life cycle of the symbol is completed in its return to the pleroma.

Jung shares with the metaphysical negative theologian a sensibility that acknowledges the contingency of human nature and language in the face of an incomprehensible origin and destiny.

Milem's second theory of negative theology is based on desire. His describes this approach in the following ways:

> human beings have some desires that no experience, phenomenon, or thing in this world can satisfy.[23]
> ... negative theology expresses the fact that our deepest desires go unsatisfied in this world.[24]
> What we notice in the things around us and in ourselves is God's absence.[25]
> Negative theology is the natural expression of insatiable desire.[26]

For Jung there is no end to individuation. The drive of the self to achieve its own purposes places a continuous pressure on the ego, which must adapt one way or another. The desire of the archetype is endless. In his essay on psychic energy Jung writes:

> The unconscious continues to produce symbols which one could obviously go on reducing to their elements *ad infinitum*. But man can never rest content with the natural course of things because he always has an excess of libido that can be offered a more favourable gradient than the merely natural one. For this reason he will inevitably seek it, no matter how often he may be forced back by reduction to the natural gradient.[27]

Jung agrees with the negative theologian that there is something in human nature that cannot be satisfied.

According to Milem, the experience theory of negative theology is concerned with trying to articulate a particular experience. 'Instead of delivering knowledge about God, it carrries the mind in God's direction and produces reverence and wonder.'[28] Milem uses Jean-Luc Marion as an example of this type of theologian. Marion is interest in 'the saturated phenomenon':

> The mind tries to apply a multitude of concepts to the phenomenon, but none of them is sufficient ... This excess is unknowable by means of any concept and cannot be put into words. Someone encountering this phenomenon does not have an experience of any object. She primarily perceives her own bedazzlement in the face of something that shows itself unconditionally without accommodating itself to the structure of human understanding.[29]

The obvious link here with Jung is in terms of his ideas about the numinous. Numinous experience has a transformative effect. 'This numinous transformation is not the result of conscious intention or intellectual conviction, but is brought about by the impact of overwhelming archetypal impressions.'[30] This impact can be positive or negative. Like a negative theologian the person who is subject to a numinous experience is obliged to make repeated attempts to articulate the content and significance of the experience while acknowledging that in certain important respects it is ineffable. Jung confronts the saturated phenomena brought to him by his patients and pushes language to its limits in his attempts to articulate his own and his patients experiences in the consulting room.

Finally, in the renunciation theory 'negative theology can be interpreted as a project of renunciation motivated by an ethical concern about the possibility of selfishness tainting one's devotion to God'. Milem uses Eckhart as his exemplar for this type of theology.

For Jung the withdrawal of projections is crucial in analysis. As we noted earlier, Humbert highlighted three elements of Jung's practice that contain aspects of renunciation: *geschehenlassen* (to let happen), *betrachten* (to consider, to impregnate) and *sich auseinandersetzen* (to confront oneself with). In the period after his break with Freud, Jung 'gave himself the task of experiencing and learning from his own psyche without relying on any preconceived ideas'.[31] The images that Jung encountered presented an ethical challenge. As Humbert puts it, 'the images that well up from the unconscious call the subject into question.'[32] The ethic of renunciation and sacrifice is a leitmotif in Jung.

Rorem

Rorem identifies three types of negative theologies: progressive apophatic, complete apophatic and incarnational apophatic.[33] It is possible to identify examples of ways in which these three styles resonate in Jung's work.

The progressive apophatic is exemplified by Gregory of Nyssa's *Contemplation on the Life of Moses*. According to Gregory, Moses will never see the face of God – only his back. This is because Moses is following God:

> Gregory charts the Mosaic ascent and ceaseless desire to continue to ascend, culminating in this bold request to behold God ... As high as Moses may climb, 'he is still unsatisfied in his desire for more.' ... 'So Moses, who eagerly seeks to behold God, is now taught *how* to behold Him; to follow God wherever he might lead *is* to behold God.'[34]

This gradual ascent, called *epektasis*, or stretching forward, is a continuous reaching beyond what one has grasped or seen. Rorem points out the connection with Paul's exhortation, 'forgetting what lies behind and straining forward to what lies ahead'. (Philippians 3:13) This type of *apophasis* consists in 'endless desire rather than endless knowledge'.[35] It is a form of apophatic thought that was appreciated by the early Cistercians. In the words of William of St Thierry, 'Always to advance in this way is to arrive.'[36]

Jung describes an analogous process when he argues that the numinous power of the archetype draws libido out of regression:

> When therefore a distressing situation arises, the corresponding archetype will be constellated in the unconscious. Since this archetype is numinous, i.e., possesses a specific energy, it will attract to itself the contents of consciousness – conscious ideas that render it perceptible and hence capable of conscious realization. Its passing over into consciousness if felt as an illumination, a revelation or a 'saving idea'.[37]

Through this dynamic the individual is drawn toward the next step of the individuation process by successive realizations. By following the call of the numinous the patient makes the journey of individuation. 'There is little hope of our ever being able to reach even approximate consciousness of the self, since however much we may make conscious there will always exist an indeterminate and indeterminable amount of unconscious material which belongs to the totality of the self.'[38]

Rorem's exemplars for a complete apophatic are Dionysius, Albert the Great, Aquinas and Eckhart. 'The Dionysian apophatic is not perpetual but completed, in that Moses does arrive, and it is absolute in that by negating and surpassing everything that is not God, Moses ends in God, united with God.'[39] Dionysius describes Moses as 'united to the wholly Unknown':

> [Moses] plunges into the truly mysterious darkness of unknowing. Here, renouncing all that the mind may conceive, wrapped entirely in the intangible and the invisible, he belongs completely to him who is beyond everything. Here, being neither oneself nor someone else, one is supremely united to the wholly Unknown by an inactivity of all knowledge, and knows beyond the mind by knowing nothing.[40]

Dourley doubts that experiences such as this can be accommodated within Jung's theory:

> Eckhart's work seems to point to an experience of so complete a divestiture of individuality in those realms of interiority where humanity and divinity merge, that one is forced to wonder if he did not go deeper into the psyche than its archetypal base, where Jung, at least in his writings, felt he had struck bottom ... one cannot avoid the feeling that Eckhart experienced some void beyond even the archetypal world in that experience he calls breakthrough. Obviously Jung could appreciate and was manifestly aware of this dimension of reality in his linking Eckhart with Zen ... But the experience of so radical a self-loss is only questionably a component of Jung's model of the psyche and its working.[41]

One could argue that Jung's description of the unity of psyche and matter resonates with the type of *apophasis* that Rorem is defining here:

> The deeper 'layers' of the psyche lose their individual uniqueness as they retreat farther and farther into darkness. 'Lower down,' that is to say as they approach the autonomous functional systems, they become increasingly collective until they are universalized and extinguished in the body's materiality, i.e., in chemical substances. The body's carbon is simply carbon. Hence 'at bottom' the psyche is simply 'world'.[42]

Shelburne argues that Jung took the kinds of experiences that Rorem includes in his category of absolute apophatic seriously, but that he disagreed with any interpretation of the experience that implied that personal identity is extinguished in the union:

> However, in spite of the fact that Jung disputes some of the claims that the mystic makes for his experience on psychological grounds, he nonetheless considers the mystic experience as one of considerable value and significance. This is not really surprising since Jung understands mysticism as an experience of the unconscious. Consequently the value of the mystical experience is due to the positive effects of the expansion of consciousness that a direct insight into the unconscious makes possible. The experience affords an opportunity to realize the limitation of the perspective of ego consciousness and thus helps to bring about the process of individuation, the goal of which is an integration of the conscious and unconscious aspects of the personality.[43]

Shelburne states that on the basis of a study of Jung's writings, 'we might feel justified in concluding that Jung had no genuine mystical experiences'.[44] Perhaps Jung comes closest to a notion of the complete apophatic in concepts such as wholeness, synchronicity, the *coniunctio* and the coincidence of opposites, but it is a problem within his thought that is not settled.[45]

Incarnational apophatic is seen by Rorem in the work of Maximus the Confessor and Luther. 'Where Gregory features *epektasis* or endless progress, and Dionysius emphasized *apophasis* or absolute negation, Maximus repeatedly turns to *kenosis*, the idea that the divine Word emptied itself into human likeness to the point of death.'[46]

Luther was dismissive of Dionysius:

> Therefore Dionysius, who wrote about 'negative theology' and 'affirmative theology,' deserves to be ridiculed ... he defines 'affirmative theology' as 'God is being.' 'Negative theology' he defines as 'God is nonbeing.' But, if we wish to give a true definition of 'negative theology,' we should say that is the holy cross and the afflictions [attending it].[47]

Jung understood the centrality of the cross in the Christian imagination as both a kenotic movement by God and a response by humanity:

> God's offering of himself is a voluntary act of love, but the actual sacrifice was an agonizing and bloody death brought about by men ... The terrors of death on the cross are an indispensable condition for the transformation. This is in the first place a bringing to life of substances which are in themselves lifeless, and, in the second, a substantial alteration of them, a spiritualization.[48]

The response in the form of the imitation of Christ is problematic, as it can easily become a substitute for living one's own myth. An authentic imitation of Christ involves enduring the cruciform experience of the tension of opposites. 'It is no easy matter to live a life that is modelled on Christ's, but it is unspeakably harder to live one's own life as truly as Christ lived his.'[49]

Jung was mindful of what we could call the incarnational aspect of individuation with his view that '[i]ndividuation does not shut one out from the world, but gathers the world to oneself'.[50] The destiny of the individual is intimately connected to the destiny of the collective:

> The way of the transcendent function is an individual destiny. But on no account should one imagine that this way is equivalent to the life of a psychic anchorite, to alienation from the world. Quite the contrary, for such a way is possible and profitable only when the specific worldly tasks which these individuals set themselves are carried out in reality. Fantasies are no substitute for living; they are fruits of the spirit which fall to him who pays his tribute to life.[51]

Jung's thought touches on each of the three types of apophatic discourse described by Rorem.

Deleuze

The uncanny experience of being reminded of Jung when one is reading Deleuze is expressed by Zizek in characteristically pithy fashion: 'No wonder, then, that an admiration of Jung is Deleuze's corpse in the closet; the fact that Deleuze borrowed a key term (*rhizome*) from Jung is not a mere insignificant accident – rather, it points toward a deeper link.'[52] This deeper link has been more sympathetically explored by Kerslake[53] and Semetsky.[54] Hallward observes, 'If there is an analogue within the psychoanalytic tradition to Deleuze's conception of the cosmos-brain it is not Lacan's unconscious, but Jung's cosmic consciousness.'[55]

Davis[56] links Deleuze explicitly with the tradition of negative theology, but little has been made of this kind of connection in the secondary literature. For the purposes of this chapter I suggest that it is possible to understand two of Deleuze's key concepts – Body without Organs (BwO) and becoming – as carriers of apophatic intensity. According to de Gaynesford, 'the BwO is defined apophatically, in relation to that which it is not. The same tendency informs the attempts by various theologians to define Christ's incarnation.'[57]

Deleuze borrows the notion of the BwO from the writer Antonin Artaud. The BwO stands in relation to the organism. An organism exists as such because its shape has been externally imposed by God or another powerful agency. 'We come to the gradual realization that the BwO is not at all the opposite of the organs. The organs are not its enemies. The enemy is the organism. The BwO is opposed not to the organs but that organization of the organs called the organism.'[58]

The BwO shares many characteristics of the collective unconscious. In Land's phrase it is a 'swarm'. We might think of it as an archetypal maelstrom:

> The unconscious is not an aspirational unity but an operative swarm, a population of 'preindividual and prepersonal singularities, a pure dispersed and anarchic multiplicity, without unity or totality' … This absence of primordial or privileged relations is the body without organs … Social organization blocks-off the body without organs, substituting a territorial, despotic, or capitalistic socius as an apparent principle of production, separating desire from what it can do.[59]

Deleuze asserts the importance of becoming free from imposed strictures of Oedipal forms. He asks, 'How do you make yourself a Body without Organs?'[60] In some respects it is reminiscent of Jung's pleroma and Bergson's virtual:

> At any rate, you have one (or several). It's not so much that it preexists or comes ready-made, although in certain respects it is pre-existent. At any rate, you make one, you can't desire without making one. And it awaits you; it is an inevitable exercise or experimentation, already accomplished the moment you undertake it, unaccomplished as long as you don't. This is not reassuring, because you can botch it. Or it can be terrifying, and lead you to your death. It is nondesire as well as desire. It is not at all a notion or a concept but a practice, a set of practices. You never reach the Body without Organs, you can't reach it, you are forever attaining it, it is a limit.[61]

Deleuze, like Jung, is interested in the relationship with the impersonal flows of energy. Seem suggests that Laing is involved in a similar project:

> Like Laing, they [Deleuze and Guattari] encourage mankind to take a journey, the journey through *ego-loss*. They go much further than Laing on this point, however. They urge mankind to strip itself of *all* anthropomorphic and anthropological armouring, all myth and tragedy, and all

existentialism, in order to perceive what is nonhuman in man, his will and his forces, his transformations and mutations. The human and social sciences have accustomed us to see the figure of Man behind every social event, just as Christianity taught us to see the Eye of the Lord looking down upon us. Such forms of knowledge project an image of reality, at the expense of reality itself. They talk figures and icons and signs, but fail to perceive forces and flows. They blind us to other realities, and especially the reality of power as it subjugates us. Their function is to tame, and the result is the fabrication of docile and obedient subjects.[62]

One view of analysis is that it undermines 'the fabrication of docile and obedient subjects'. In the archetypal psychology variant of analytical psychology, the process of 'seeing through' brings one to some sort of knowledge or relationship with the otherness of images and fantasies:

> Where psychoanalysis says, 'Stop, find your self again,' we should say instead, 'Let's go further still, we haven't found our BwO yet, we haven't sufficiently dismantled our self.' Substitute forgetting for anamnesis, experimentation for interpretation. Find your body without organs. Find out how to make it. It's a question of life and death, youth and old age, sadness and joy. It is where everything is played out.[63]

The practice of creating the BwO is, like analysis, fraught with dangers. One of the dangers discussed by Deleuze is addiction, when the addict uses drugs to try to create a false BwO. He mentions the hypochondriac body, the paranoid body, the schizo body, the drugged body and the masochist body.[64] In analysis there are dangers of suicide, psychosis, delusional transferences and despair. Deleuze asks, 'What does it mean to disarticulate?' *Apophasis* means 'unsaying'. What does it mean to unsay something; or to disconnect psychic and social structures?:

> What does it mean to disarticulate to cease to be an organism? How can we convey how easy it is, and the extent to which we do it every day? And how necessary caution is, the art of dosages, since overdose is a danger. You don't do it with a sledgehammer, you use a very fine file. You invent self-destructions that have nothing to do with the death drive. Dismantling the organism has never meant killing yourself, but rather opening the body to connections that presuppose an entire assemblage, circuits, conjunctions, levels and thresholds, passages and distribution of intensity, and territories and deterritorializations measured with the craft of a surveyor ... And how can we unhook ourselves from the points of subjectification that secure us, nail us down to a dominant reality?[65]

There are some parallels between the dismantling of the organism to uncover or create the BwO and the process of analysis. Seem compared Deleuze's recommendation to make a BwO to Laing's encouragement to 'mankind to take a journey, the journey through *ego-loss*'.[66] Jung observed:

> The self, in its efforts at self-realization, reaches out beyond the ego-personality on all sides; because of its all-encompassing nature it is brighter and darker than the ego, and accordingly confronts it with problems which it would like to avoid … For this reason *the experience of the self is always a defeat for the ego.*[67]

There are resonances between Deleuze's concept of organism and Jung's concept of possession. The image of possession is used throughout Jung's work to think about the relationship between aspects of the psyche.[68] One can be overwhelmed by any number of psychic forces. Patients are said to suffer from possession by complexes and archetypes, or to be under the influence of ideologies, fantasies, scripts and projections. The psyche is a field with contenting forces.

Possession in Jung's sense could be understood in some circumstances as failed attempts at the creation of a BwO. Jung observes that when a new content emerges from the unconscious it tends to possess the ego. The ego becomes inflated. According to Dionysius:

> the possessed, that is, those who have turned away from a life conforming to divine example and have adopted instead the ideas and character of abominable demons, are exposed to the very worst power. In their extreme folly, so destructive to themselves, they turn away from the truly real.[69]

Jung notes that the alchemists were alert to the dangers that their operations could hold for adepts. 'The difficulties of the art play no small role in alchemy. Generally they are explained as technical difficulties, but often enough … there are remarks about the psychic nature of the dangers and obstacles that complicate the work.'[70]

The creation of the BwO is a practice of unknowing which opens the practitioner to more unrestricted flows of life. Apophatic discourse can move in the direction of origins or in the direction of the future. The emphasis can be on an unknowable beginning or on an unknowable destination. The BwO could be seen as an example of a return to an incomprehensible origin. Becoming, one of the key concepts in Deleuze's work, is concerned to create and accomplish an incomprehensible destiny. 'Deleuze's pragmatic and future-oriented epistemology is oriented toward the creation of concepts "for unknown lands," as well as meanings and values "that are yet to come".'[71]

Deleuze distinguishes between representation and presentation. Stagoll observes that 'becoming is critical, for if the primacy of identity is what defines a world of re-presentation (presenting the same world once again), then becoming (by which Deleuze means "becoming different") defines a world of presentation anew'.[72] The parallels with Jung's concepts of individuation and the transcendent function are immediately evident:

> Becoming is a rhizome, not a classificatory or genealogical tree. Becoming is certainly not imitating, or identifying with something; neither is it regressing-progressing; neither is it corresponding, establishing corresponding relations; neither is it producing, producing a filiation or producing through filiation. Becoming is a verb with a consistency all its own; it does not reduce to, or lead back to, 'appearing,' 'being,' 'equaling,' or 'producing.'[73]

Here, becoming is being defined apophatically by what it is not. Jung describes the necessity for the analyst to follow the lead of the patient; to not intervene with preconceived attitudes and assumptions in the unfolding of the patient's self-discovery or self-creation, 'which sometimes drives him into complete isolation … It is, moreover, only in the state of complete abandonment and loneliness that we experience the helpful powers of our own natures.'[74] The patient is compelled to pursue a perilous course of action:

> And though this desire opens the door to the most dangerous possibilities, we cannot help seeing it as a courageous enterprise and giving it some measure of sympathy. It is no reckless adventure, but an effort inspired by deep spiritual distress to bring meaning once more into life on the basis of fresh and unprejudiced experience. Caution has its place, no doubt, but we cannot refuse our support to a serious venture which challenges the whole of the personality. If we oppose it, we are trying to suppress what is best in man – his daring and his aspirations. And should we succeed, we should only have stood in the way of that invaluable experience which might have given a meaning to life.[75]

Deleuze echoes Jung's call to experience:

> one steps outside what's been thought before, once one ventures outside what's familiar and reassuring, once one has to invent new concepts for unknown lands, then methods and moral systems break down and thinking becomes … a 'perilous act,' a violence, whose first victim is oneself … Thinking is always experiencing, experimenting … and what we experience, experiment with, is … what's coming into being, what's new, what's taking shape.[76]

The transcendent function, which I earlier characterized as an apophatic method at the heart of Jung's work, like becoming, occurs in the between. It is not a repetition but a becoming-other than oneself. The transcendent function produces difference. Differentiation is the engine of individuation:

The subject-in-process, that is, as *becoming*, is always placed between two multiplicities, yet one term does not become the other; the becoming is something *between* the two, this something called by Deleuze a pure *affect*. Therefore *becoming* does not mean becoming the other, but *becoming-other* … The non-place-in-between acts as a gap, or differentiator, introducing an element of discontinuity in the otherwise continuous process of becoming and allowing the difference to actively intervene.[77]

The BwO and becoming operate as sites of *apophasis* with the work of Deleuze, who might be read as the philosopher for analytical psychology. We have seen that the apophatic dynamics of the BwO and becoming have analogies in Jung's thought and practice.

Derrida

Derrida's engagement with apophatic discourse, and in particular with Dionysius, has been widely discussed in continental philosophy of religion. Rayment-Pickard has graphically characterized Derrida's work in this area:

> It is out of his interaction with Husserl and Heidegger that Derrida will step forward beyond negative theology to a new non-real theological understanding in which the old theological concepts and structures are at once negatively deconstructed and yet still glowing with a positive after-life. This theology is able, in Derrida's phrase, 'to put the old names to work' in a non-theological space 'between God and God'.[78]

In the notion of putting 'old names to work' in an unfamiliar context we can recognize Jung's method of putting images and concepts from mythology, alchemy, theology and philosophy to use in a new way in his psychology. His writing is littered with the glow of names which many would consider dead and buried.

In Derrida's early work there were occasional mentions of negative theology, without any discussion of particular writers. In the essay 'Differance' (1967) he acknowledges the resemblance between *differance* and negative theology:

> So much so that the detours, locutions, and syntax in which I will have to take recourse will resemble those of negative theology, occasionally even to the point of being indistinguishable from negative theology … And yet those aspects of *differance* which are thereby delineated are not theological, not even in the order of the most negative of negative theologies, which as one knows are always concerned with disengaging a superessentiality beyond the finite categories of essence and existence, that is, of presence, and always hastening to recall that God is refused the predicate of existence, only in order to acknowledge his superior, inconceivable, and ineffable mode of being.[79]

Twenty years later Derrida returns to the problem of the relationship between deconstruction and negative theology in his essay, 'How to Avoid Speaking: Denegations'. Rubenstein characterized this essay as his 'most thorough (non-)discussion of his own work in relation to Dionysius'.[80] While there is an extensive secondary literature on Derrida, deconstruction and *apophasis*, I am limiting myself here to his direct references to Dionysius.[81]

In this essay he uses the theme of 'place' to organize his thoughts. 'Figuration and the so-called places (*topoi*) of rhetoric constitute the very concern of apophatic procedures.'[82] He develops this thesis in relation to Plato, Dionysius and Heidegger. He does not present these as steps in a dialectic, because 'we are involved in a thinking that is essentially alien to dialectic',[83] but as 'paradigms' or 'signs'. He describes these paradigms in architectural terms as a mode that 'will surround a resonant space of which nothing, almost nothing, will ever be said'.[84] Jung's theory is often described in terms of architectonics. The theme of place also has echoes of Jung's discussion of mandalas. The mandala defines a space – psychic, imaginal, ritual – that provides an orientation toward an ultimately unknowable content:

> All that can be ascertained at present about the symbolism of the mandala is that it portrays an autonomous psychic fact ... It seems to be a sort of atomic nucleus about whose innermost structure and ultimate meaning we know nothing.[85]

The mandala has an apophatic intensity because it performs the coincidence of many archetypes in a single point:

> The mandala symbolizes, by its central point, the ultimate unity of all the archetypes as well as the multiplicity of the phenomenal world, and is therefore the empirical equivalent of the metaphysical concept of a *unus mundus*.[86]

Derrida tells us that there is 'in everything I will say, a certain void, the place of an internal desert'.[87] This also resonates with Dionysius' notion of hierarchy, a word that he coined. 'We have a venerable sacred tradition with asserts that every hierarchy is the complete expression of the sacred elements comprised within it. It is the perfect total of all its sacred constituents.'[88] The hierarchy is a structure – imaginal, linguistic, social, cosmic – which provides access to 'something mysterious or secretly revealed'.[89]

In relation to Plato, Derrida discusses the Good beyond Being from the *Republic* and the *khora* from the *Timaeus*. After a discussion of Dionysius, he reflects on Heidegger's statement to students in Zurich in 1951: 'If I *were* yet to *write* a theology, as I am sometimes tempted to do, the word "being" *ought* not appear there.'

With regard to Dionysius' *apophasis* he claims that it is characterized by the fact that it begins with prayer. In the *Divine Names* Dionysius writes:

> Wherefore, before everything and especially before a discourse about God, it is necessary to begin with a prayer – not so the power present both everywhere and nowhere shall come to us but so that by our divine remembrance and invocations we ourselves shall be guided to it and be united with it.[90]

The prayer functions as an orientation toward the unknown. Derrida observes that the prayer at the beginning of the *Mystical Theology* is addressed simultaneously to God, to Dionysius' disciple Timothy and to the reader:

> The identity of *this* place, and hence of *this* text, and of *its* reader, comes from the future of what is promised by the promise … the *apophasis* is brought into motion – it is *initiated*, in the sense of initiative and initiation – by the event of a revelation which is also a promise … the place that is thus revealed remains the place of waiting, awaiting the realization of the promise. Then it will take place fully. It will be fully a place.[91]

This sense of the revelation that is full of promise can be seen in Jung's attitude toward psychic phenomena. The symbol contains promise of an as yet undisclosed meaning. Jung insisted on the importance of maintaining an open and expectant attitude toward the unconscious – waiting on the images. His texts can be read as addressed simultaneously to the unconscious and to the reader with an expectation of an unknown future.

According to Jung, prayer or invocation directs the libido within:

> the invocation expresses this introversion, and the explicit expectation that God will speak empties the conscious mind of activity and transfers it to the divine being constellated by the invocation, who, from the empirical point of view, must be regarded as a primordial image. It is a fact of experience that all archetypal contents have a certain autonomy, since they appear spontaneously and can often exercise an overwhelming compulsion. There is, therefore, nothing intrinsically absurd about the expectation that 'God' will take over the activity and spontaneity of the conscious mind, for the primordial images are quite capable of doing precisely this.[92]

'I have no idea what this dream means.'[93] 'Even if one has great experience in these matters, one is again and again obliged, before each dream, to admit one's ignorance and renouncing all preconceived ideas, to prepare for something entirely unexpected.'[94]

This is similar to Dionysius' stance of orienting himself in such a way that he is drawn toward the One. The analyst, by accepting his own ignorance, is willing to be moved or illuminated by the dream. The dream provides perspective on the personal unconscious and life circumstances, but because personal complexes have roots in archetypal images dreams are also windows into the collective unconscious. Derrida, reflecting on Eckhart, asserts that apophatic discourse discloses the relationship between being and non-being:

> The place is only a place of passage, and more precisely, a threshold. But a threshold, this time, to give access to what is no longer a place. A subordination, a relativization of the place, and an extraordinary consequence; the place is Being. Being is the place. Solely a threshold, a sacred place, the outer sanctuary of the temple.[95]

In analysis, Jung finds that with some people there comes a time when they have exhausted an exploration of material that is dominated by repetition or family dynamics and the patient is challenged to discover their own individuality in a more radical way. In this situation the analyst must adopt a stance of absolute openness in relation to the patient's individuation:

> A collective attitude enables the individual to fit into society without friction … But the patient's difficulty consists precisely in the fact that his individual problem cannot be fitted without friction into a collective norm; it requires a solution of an individual conflict if the whole of his personality is to remain viable. No rational solution can do justice to this task, and there is absolutely no collective norm that could replace an individual solution without loss.[96]

Derrida's goal is to penetrate the impossible, rather than pointless repetition of a programme:

> Going where it is possible to go would not be a displacement or a decision, it would be the irresponsible unfolding of a program. The sole decision possible passes through the madness of the undecidable and the impossible: to go where it is impossible to go.[97]

The analytic space is a space set apart. The entrance and exit from the space receives a great deal of attention in psychoanalytic technique, as the integrity of the frame of analysis is considered vital in creating the possibility for the kind of openness that Jung is describing. Derrida asserts that in the work of Dionysius, 'It is necessary to stand or step aside, to find the *place* proper to the experience of the secret.'[98] According to Derrida, the practitioners of both deconstruction and negative theology appear suspect to outsiders because they seem to belong to secret societies:

> 'Negative theologies' and everything that resembles a form of esoteric sociality have always been infortuitously associated with phenomena of secret society, as if access to the most rigorous apophatic discourse demanded the sharing of a 'secret' … It is as if divulgence imperilled a revelation promised to *apophasis*.[99]

Mustikos in the *Mystical Theology* is translated by Luibheid as 'mystic' or 'mysterious'. The stain of the secret, real or imagined, casts its aura over the analytic relationship and analytic institutions. The seal of confidentiality breeds both confidence and suspicion. The popular susceptibility to and scepticism of psychobabble seem connected with this point. Beyond this generic analogy with psychoanalysis, we can find some resonances within Jung's work on alchemy. The alchemical vessel must be well sealed. The philosopher's stone is a secret. 'The substance that harbours the divine secret is everywhere, including the human body.'[100]

In this essay Derrida claims that all the forms of negation that he describes 'are always *also* affirmative, either echoing or presupposing the positivities they seek to describe by denials'.[101] When he writes about the trace, it is possible to hear echoes with a possible interpretation of Jung's concept of archetype. 'The most negative discourse, even beyond all nihilisms and negative dialectics, preserves the trace: The trace of an event older than it *or* of a "taking-place" to come, the one *and* the other: there is here neither an alternative nor a contradiction.'[102]

We could read this as a suggestion that one aspect of the apophatic dynamic at play between the ego and the archetype is that for the ego the archetype can represent simultaneously a trace of a primordial event and a trace of an unknown future. This is one way in which the archetype acts as a coincidence of opposites.

The essay, 'Sauf le Nom', published in 1995, is a longer version of a postscript that Derrida wrote for the collection of papers from which the essay we have been discussing was taken. 'Sauf le Nom' is written as a discussion amongst a collection of voices which question, challenge and interrupt each other. Consequently it is difficult to state exactly what the author's argument is. Gersh claims that in this essay Derrida is describing 'negative theology not only as the intersection of two traditions but also through the interaction of two speakers'.[103] On my reading it is not a dialogue but a group discussion.

The point that Derrida is making is that there is not *one* negative theology, but that there are many. His post-script mirrors the conference in having many voices and points of view. 'Are there sure criteria available to decide the belonging, virtual or actual, of a discourse to negative theology?'[104] He maintains that negative theology is not a literary art and that there is no 'classic' negative theology. How can there be? 'If the consequent unfolding of so many discourses (logical, onto-logical, theo-logical or not) inevitably leads to conclusions whose form and content is similar to negative theology, where are the 'classic' frontiers of negative theology?'[105]

This question could be asked of psychoanalysis as well. What criteria are there for determining 'true analysis'? This reflects one of the questions raised here: Do all the forms of analysis 'inevitably lead to a conclusion similar to negative theology'. One way Derrida reflects on the nature of negative theology is to observe that the discourse moves in several directions:

To whom is this discourse addressed? Who is its addressee? Does it exist before this interlocutor, before the discourse, before its actualization [*so passage a l'acte*], before its performative accomplishment? Dionysius the Areopagite, for example, articulates a certain prayer, turned toward God; he links it with an address to the disciple, more precisely to the becoming-disciple of him who is thus call to hear ... The hymn and the didactic become allied ... This conversion turns (itself) toward the other in order to turn (it) toward God, without there being an order to these two movements that are in truth the same.[106]

One can apply this knot of questions to analysis. Does analysis exist in any meaningful sense before it is performed by the analyst, the patient, the unconscious and the analytic community – all of whom are actors, agents and addressees in the analytic encounter. Much as Dionysius is creating his disciple, the analyst is creating a patient. The disciple and the patient are being created within the context of a larger community that authorizes and forms the process through its dogma, theory, institutions and oversight of the encounter. Within a Jungian context the god image, the self, is invoked in the encounter with the other, in the other and through the other. 'The hymn and the didactic become allied.' The invocation of the self and the educative aspect of analysis are 'two movements that are in truth the same'. *Apophasis* and analysis are performances that create new relationships and meaning. They are performances that consist in the endless negation of their own languages.

'God "is" the name of this bottomless collapse, of this endless desertification of language.'[107] The god image for Jung is also endless. 'Likewise the self; as the essence of individuality it is unitemporal and unique; as an archetypal symbol it is a God-image and therefore universal and eternal.'[108]

When Derrida highlights the place of prayer in Dionysius' *apophasis* it is possible to see parallels with repetition, compulsion and individuation. It also resonates with the notions of *Deo consedente* in alchemy[109] and the motto above Jung's front door:

In a moment I will try to show how negative theology at least claims not to be assimilable to a technique that I subject to simulation or parody, to mechanical repetition. It would escape from this by means of the *prayer* that precedes apophatic utterances, and by the address to the other, to you, in a moment that is not only the preamble or the methodological threshold of the experience. Naturally, the prayer, invocation, and apostrophe can also be mimicked, and even give way, as if despite themselves, to repetitive technique.[110]

It is also possible to ask whether Dionysius' prayer, address to the other, can be seen as a form of transference, a transference of the 'originary aporia or trace':

the originary aporia or trace that simultaneously makes identity claims possible whilst at the same time ensuring that they can never be complete …
Derrida's philosophy seeks to articulate an originary point of aporia that precedes and determines the opposition between the transcendental and empirical upon which the metaphysics of presences seeks to institute itself … For Derrida, this (entirely correct) insistence upon the *irreducibility* of this aporia to either the empirical or the transcendental means that deconstruction often turns into a kind of *via negativa*.[111]

Derrida identifies three objections to taking negative theology seriously. One is the accusation of nihilism or obscurantism. The second is that negative theology is a 'simple technique … It comes back to speaking for nothing.' The third objection is of particular interest in this discussion because he touches fleetingly on psychoanalysis:

Here the suspicion takes a form that can reverse the process of the accusation: once the apophatic discourse is analyzed in its logical-grammatical form, if it is not merely sterile, repetitive, obscurantist, mechanical, it perhaps leads us to consider the becoming-theological of all discourse. From the moment a proposition takes a negative form, the negativity that manifests itself need only be pushed to the limit, and it at least resembles an apophatic theology … 'God' would name *that without which* one would not know how to account for any negativity: grammatical or logical negation, illness, evil, and finally neurosis which, far from permitting psychoanalysis to reduce religion to a symptom, would obligate it to recognize in the symptom the negative manifestation of God.[112]

'[…]In itself interminable, the apophatic movement cannot contain within itself the principle of its interruption. It can only indefinitely defer the encounter with its own limit.[113]

Bradley describes Derrida's method as a questioning of binary oppositions:

The binary differences that constitute Western metaphysics are shown to be preceded by a third position that belongs to neither and that allows those differences to appear as oppositional. This unthought space between the transcendental and the empirical is the aporia that – however impossibly – deconstruction attempts to think.[114]

This 'unthought space' is the ground on which deconstruction meets the discourse of negative theology. This potential space between the transcendental and the empirical was also the space that Jung was exploring. His description of the work of the alchemists serves as a description of his own work. In it we can hear echoes of Derrida's discussion of negative theology – 'It situates itself *beyond* all position':[115]

The *imaginatio*, as the alchemists understand it, is in truth a key that opens the door to the secret of the *opus*. We now know that it is a question of representing and realizing those 'greater' things which the soul, on God's behalf, imagines creatively and *extra naturam* – or, to put it in modern language, a question of actualizing those contents of the unconscious which are outside nature, i.e., not a datum of our empirical world, and therefore an *a priori* of archetypal character. The place or the medium of realization in neither mind nor matter, but that intermediate realm of subtle reality which can be adequately only expressed by the symbol. The symbol is neither abstract nor concrete, neither rational nor irrational, neither real nor unreal. It is always both: it is *non vulgi*, the aristocratic preoccupation of one who is set apart (*cuislibet sequestrati*), chosen and predestined by God from the very beginning.[116]

Derrida and Jung are making and unmaking language in order to think about and imagine the space of individuation.

Tacey

We turn now to the work of the post-Jungian writers Tacey and Dourley. Tacey has argued that recent postmodern philosophy and deconstructive critique are suitable partners for Jungian thought. 'But a link with Jung's vision has been established, a bridge has been created between the deconstructionists and Jung's Gnostic spirit. That link is clearly through the *via negativa*.'[117] Tacey is also sensitive to the accusation that Jung is anachronistic:

Jung's non-modernist project seemed *backward* and out of date in his time, but today it can be regarded as offering ground and inspiration for a postmodern recovery of our relationship with the sacred after the collapse of positivistic science and after loss of belief in theistic religion and absolute truth … there is a real possibility of finding common ground between Jung's analytical psychology and postmodern deconstructive philosophy.[118]

Tacey's concern is to rescue transcendence. His argument is broad-brush and has a prophetic urgency. He represents a particular strain of post-Jungian writing that seeks to establish postmodern credentials for Jungian work. It seems to me that *apophasis* offers a greater range of interpretive possibilities than transcendence.

Tacey also privileges experience over interpretation. He claims that Derrida's late work shows that 'he entered a state of mind that could be described as mystical, or at least poetic-lyrical and receptive to mystery'.[119] He claims that deconstruction 'seems to be the "royal road" to the recovery of transcendence in our time'.[120] It is difficult to avoid the conclusion that Tacey has committed the common mistake of misquoting Freud. Freud claimed that 'the interpretation of dreams is the royal road to a knowledge of unconscious activities',[121] but most references to the royal road state implicitly or explicitly that dreams are the royal road to the unconscious. It is the interpretation of dreams, not the dreams themselves that open the way to understanding the unconscious.

Tacey's concern to recover transcendence has quite a concrete, 'substantial' character – more return of the repressed than openness to the unknown. 'Why does the transcendent keep returning in this way? I believe the answer is because it exists and it is real.'[122] This of course echoes the disputes about Dionysius' work. Is it mystical experience or is it philosophy? Tacey sees a preoccupation with the Unknown as the site for the meeting of Freudian and Jungian thought. He claims that psychoanalysts have strayed into 'Jungian territory'.[123]

Dourley

Dourley's work engages in greater depth and specificity than does Tacey's with the place of the apophatic in Jung's psychology. He has written about a variety of themes in Jung's work on religion and mysticism.[124] According to Dourley, 'Jung, in his choice of mystics, would appear to have anticipated the current scholarly renewal of interest in the apophatic.'[125]

Dourley is passionate in his argument that the current condition of humankind requires the emergence of a form of religion based on immanence rather than transcendence. By immanence Dourley means psyche. He opposes any view that there may be something outside of or beyond psyche. Nevertheless, even within this immanent frame there is a drive toward transcendence. As he describes it, the process is reminiscent of Gregory of Nyssa's *epektasis*, a stretching forth beyond what one has grasped or seen. We have seen this type of *apophasis* described by Milem as a negative theology based on desire and by Rorem as progressive *apophasis*:

> Rather in the spirituality emerging in contemporary culture transcendence becomes a function or consequence of a sense of an immanent power native to humanity ... Transcendence becomes a function of immanence in so much as the power native to the human always transcends its realization at any given moment in the individual's development. There is always more to be assimilated ... modern spirituality shares a discernible affinity with Jung's understanding that the self can be only approximated never exhaustively realized.[126]

Dourley places the emphasis on a force from within which propels the mind toward transcendence, rather than on a force from without that draws the mind toward itself. My use of the word 'mind' here is problematic as Dourley's discussion moves, at times seamlessly, between the individual, social, collective and archetypal. 'The process is wholly internal to the psyche as productive of personal unification and universal relatedness. It is one that never ends.'[127]

Dourley argues that apophatic mystics experience a form of passivity that goes 'beyond archetypal urgency'. This decompression, as it were, of the archetypal allows for the assimilation into consciousness of new contents and potentials:

> In fact the Christian mystics to whom Jung turns in his corpus undergo such a loss of distinction in a nothingness in which their personal identity is fused with the divine in an abyss beyond all separation ... the nothingness they undergo carries with it a certain passivity or resignation that moderate the drive of the archetypes to become conscious in human consciousness the unconscious creates for that purpose. Penetration into an area of psyche beyond archetypal urgency, though best described in religious and mystical terms, could be a valuable asset in ushering the archetypes into consciousness, individual and collective, in such a way as to preserve and enhance consciousness in the process. [128]

Dourley contends that Jung's thought opens the way toward a recognition among religions, cultures and political movements 'of their common origin in a psyche preceding their differences whose further reach is a stillness of the nothing prior to all form and drive'.[129] This has strong resonances with Milem's metaphysical theory of negative theology,[130] which 'identifies God as the first cause of the existence of all things and argues that negative theology offers the most appropriate way to talk about this cause'. Dourley's 'stillness of the nothing' echoes as well with Franke's statement that '[w]e begin to perceive the ubiquitous presence of the unsayable in all our saying. All that is said, at least indirectly and implicitly, testifies to something else that is not said and perhaps *cannot* be said.'[131] In Dourley's formulation, however, there is no apophatic movement that can exceed psyche. So psyche is, in effect, the first and the last word:

> The only legitimate sense of the word 'transcendence' in Jungian parlance rests on the fecundity of the archetypal which will always transcend its valuable but ever partial incarnation in historical consciousness ... This is the only legitimate understanding of transcendent divinity in a Jungian universe and its referent is to the commerce between the conscious and unconscious moments of the psychic life in which the latter will always transcend the former.[132]

Dourley cites Jung to the effect that 'everything of a divine or daemonic character outside us must return to the psyche, to the inside of the unknown man, whence it apparently originated.'[133] This appeal to the 'unknown man' resonates with discussions of apophatic anthropology by Saward, Bernauer, Carlson and Otten, cited in the Introduction to this book. The 'unknown man' is an instance of the god image. Carlson, in a more recent work, develops a genealogy of apophatic anthropology that embraces Origin, Gregory of Nyssa, Dionysius, Eriugena and Cusa, among others:

Eriugena's apophatic anthropology complements his apophatic theology: neither God nor the human subject created in his image can comprehend *what* they themselves are – even as they achieve, through their own self-creative self-expression, an awareness *that* they are.[134]

Carlson also observes that Cusa 'marks a crucial link between medieval mysticism and modern conceptions of human creativity'.[135] This is interesting in view of the important use Jung makes of Cusa's coincidence of opposites. However, I suspect that Dourley's thoroughgoing psychic immanence would not sit easily with these earlier writers.

Dourley also constructs a genealogy of mystics that were of interest to Jung. These include Mechthild of Magdeburg, Eckhart and Boehme:

Historically the mystics to whom he is most drawn are mystics whose experience was characterized by an apophatic moment, that is, an immersion in divinity in which all distinction between themselves and the divine was annihilated in a moment of an all consuming nothingness.[136]

He reminds us that for Jung, 'Mystics are people who have a particularly vivid experience of the processes of the collective unconscious. Mystical experience is experience of archetypes.'[137] Dourley discusses the relationship between the 'apophatic moment' and the strengthening of ego consciousness:

What Eckhart and the mystics of the apophatic moment are describing as an immersion in the divine nothingness is a moment of the ego's dissolution in what Jung terms the 'Great Mother' or 'Goddess', who precedes all form and creation and from whom all form and creation derive. In so doing they would seem to go to a moment of total rest or resignation in the source of their being ever present to them in the depths of their personal participation in the universal ground of the psyche … These mystic travellers would seem to go beyond the compulsive creativity of the archetypal to the moment of rest in a fourth, the God beyond the God of Trinity and beyond the Gods of biblical theism, namely, in the Goddess herself.[138]

Hood questions psychoanalytic interpretations of mysticism that rely on the concept of regression, including Jungian formulations. He criticizes Owens' suggestion that 'the mystic is returning to a "pre-infantile" level of existence that is obviously conceptualized in terms of Jung's notion of the collective unconscious'.[139] He argues that it is wrong to characterize mystical experience in terms of states of consciousness. These experiences have to be understood as processes. One crucial element of the process is the awareness of the ego of its own dissolution. This is a capacity which is beyond the scope of infantile consciousness:

Now what is important about this state of consciousness is not simply the state *per se* but rather that the state itself reflects a process of ego loss that is experienced as such. It is this experience as a process, not as a state, that must be adequately grasped before any psychological analysis can be attempted. Not only is the mystical state itself logically one in which the ego is not distinguished from that which it experiences, but mystics themselves affirm the experiential nature of this loss as a process ... not only must the mystical experience of unity logically imply the dissolution of individuality but that *mystics in fact directly experience this dissolution*.[140]

Hood's criticism of Jung, while it is correct in that Jung's view is regressive, is incorrect in overlooking Jung's argument that it is precisely the role of the ego that distinguishes Western from Eastern mysticism. He wishes to safeguard the achievement of the ego and not to lose the dialectical relationship between conscious and unconscious. Jung maintains that '[t]he relation of a psychic content to the ego forms the criterion of its consciousness, for no content can be conscious unless it is represented to a subject'.[141] This is different from the view in the East that consciousness is not dependent on objects or representations. Dourley appears to place greater emphasis on the dissolution of the ego than does Jung. 'Jung understood the process of individuation to entail not only a return to the unconscious as the origin of consciousness but also an immersion of the ego into the unconscious beyond all difference and differentiation.'[142]

Dourley does not explain how this process tallies with the transcendent function, which requires a maintaining rather than a release of tension. In his 2008 book, *Paul Tillich, Carl Jung and the Recovery of Religion*, the transcendent function does not appear in the index. In his 2010 book, *On Behalf of the Mystical Fool: Jung on the Religious Situation*, there are five references to the transcendent function in the index. Only one of those references deals directly with Jung's use of the phrase 'complete abolition' of the ego in the transcendent function and this from a letter to White, not a published essay. This is very thin evidence for Dourley's argument that the abolition of the ego is central to Jung's thought:

Jung's reference to the complete abolition of the ego points to the apophatic dimension of his understanding of the psyche. It aligns his psychology with that strain of mysticism which experiences momentary identity with God in a return to a divine nothingness in which ego consciousness undergoes a moment of obliteration in a state beyond any distinction between itself and the divine.[143]

Dourley repeatedly uses the image of being rooted or becoming rerooted in the maternal nothingness as the agenda of a Jungian spirituality and he uses Jung's description of modern man to validate this agenda:

Indeed, he is completely modern only when he has come to the very edge of the world, leaving behind him all that has been discarded and outgrown, and acknowledging that he stands before the Nothing out of which All may grow.[144]

It seems to me that 'stand[ing] before the Nothing' is different from being rooted in the Nothing and that this difference illustrates the flavour of Dourley's particular take on Jung's work on the mystics.

The whole of Dourley's description of mysticism is framed in terms of a return to the Mother. Dourley wants to go beyond Jung's position that '[m]ysticism is experience of the archetypes'. He appears impatient with what he describes as Jung's fear when confronted by Eckhart's experience of breakthrough. 'The experience of so radical a self-loss is only questionably a component of Jung's model of the psyche and its working.'[145] Dourley suggests that the mystics experience a pre-archetypal level of the psyche, 'beyond archetypal urgency'.[146] 'Such consciousness would be prior to and so transcend any form of archetypal concretion and so stand always in relation to them as the source of their iconoclastic dissolution.'[147] There is here an apophatic dynamic in relation to 'archetypal concretion'; however, having flirted with something beyond the archetypes Dourley reaffirms his faith in the all-embracing nature of psyche:

> The divine nothingness into which the mystics merge is not a power extrinsic to the psyche. It is the primordial level of the psyche itself from which all consciousness, form and culture derive ... Transcendence becomes a wholly intrapsychic reality.[148]

Dourley advances a relentless polemic against monotheism. There is an apophatic twist in his work in that it is human consciousness that transcends God. The human puts God in his/her/its place. He cites Jung's dream in which both Jung and his father are kneeling before the figure of Uriah:

> In the dream Uriah personifies a faith betrayed ... Jung's father kissed the floor before Uriah in submission to Uriah and to his God. Jung bowed to within a millimetre of the floor but did not kiss it. Had he done so he would have capitulated to the pathology of his father's faith ... The millimetre that separated Jung's forehead from the floor before Uriah *is* the 'small but decisive factor' by which the consciousness of the creature surpasses that of the creator.[149]

The millimetre of difference is a small apophatic move that has cosmic consequences for Dourley. While Dourley explores Jung's attraction to and use of a number of apophatic mystics, in this instance Dourley himself is unconsciously performing a rhetorical move of considerable apophatic intensity. Dourley is excoriating about the 'One and Only Gods' of the monotheisms, but there is a risk that his own commitment to a Jungian model of the psyche could be read as being itself a type of monotheism.

In this chapter I have used the work of contemporary writers to explore apophatic elements in Jung's work. This discussion brings to light additional facets of Jung's *apophasis*. Furthermore, it demonstrates that the apophatic problematic in Jung's thought is not regressive but that it is in tune with important currents in contemporary philosophy and theology.

Notes

1 For reasons of space I am not discussing McGinn and Franke. They have both written extensively on *apophasis*, but of particular interest for this chapter see: B. McGinn (2009), 'Three forms of Negativity in Christian Mysticism', in *Knowing the Unknowable: Science and Religions on God and the Universe*, J. Bowker (ed.). London: Tauris; W. Franke (2007), *On What Cannot Be Said: Apophatic Discourses in Philosophy, Religion, Literature and the Arts: Vol. 1 Classic Formulations*, Notre Dame, IN: Notre Dame University Press; (2007), *On What Cannot Be Said: Apophatic Discourses in Philosophy, Religion, Literature and the Arts: Vol. 2, Modern and Contemporary Transformations*, Notre Dame, IN: Notre Dame University Press; (2004), 'A Philosophy of the Unsayable: Apophasis and the Experience of Truth and Totality', *Analecta Husserliana*, 83: 65–83.

2 Grinberg, L. (1969), 'New Ideas: Conflict and Evolution', *International Journal of Psychoanalysis*, 50: 517–28; J.W. Hamilton (1969), 'Object Loss, Dreaming, and Creativity: The Poetry of John Keats', *Psychoanalytic Studies of the Child*, 24: 488–531; P. Withim (1969–70), 'The Psychodynamics of Literature', *Psychoanalytic Review*, 56D: 556–85. The term had appeared once before in a paper by A. H. Williams in 1966, but it was not used with any psychoanalytic content ('Keats' "La Belle Dame Sans Merci": The Bad-Breast Mother', *American Imago*, 23: 63–81).

3 Lambert, Kenneth (1972), 'Books and Journals: Recent Publications in Journals', *Journal of Analytical Psychology*, 17: 77–85; Fred Plaut (1972), 'W.R. Bion: Attention and interpretation. A scientific approach to insight in psychoanalysis and groups. London, Tavistock, 1970. pp. 136. £1.50.' *Journal of Analytical Psychology*, 17: 215–16.

4 Sells, Michael A. (1994), *Mystical Languages of Unsaying*. Chicago: University of Chicago Press, p. 6.

5 CW7 292.

6 Sells, pp. 6–7.

7 CW9ii 124.

8 CW9i 389.

9 CW9i 393.

10 CW9i 390.

11 CW11 35.

12 CW5 5.

13 CW8 542.

14 CW11 757.

15 CW11 629.

16 Bruce Milem (2007), 'Four Theories of Negative Theology', *Heythrop Journal*, 48: 187–204.

17 Milem, p. 188.

18 Milem, p. 192.

19 Milem, p. 194.

20 Milem, p. 197.

21 Milem, p. 190.

22 CW9i 498.

23 Milem, p. 192.
24 Milem, p. 193.
25 Milem, p. 193.
26 Milem, p. 193.
27 CW8 97.
28 Milem, p. 195.
29 Milem, p. 196.
30 CW10 720.
31 Humbert, Elie (1988), *C. G. Jung: The Fundaments of Theory and Practice*. Wilmette, IL: Chiron, p. 9.
32 Humbert, p. 13.
33 Rorem, Paul (2008), 'Negative Theologies and the Cross', *Harvard Theological Review*, 101(3–4): 451–64.
34 Rorem, pp. 452–3.
35 Rorem, p. 454.
36 William of St Thierry (1998), *The Way of Divine Union*, Basil Pennington (trans.). Hyde Park, NY: New City Press, p. 95.
37 CW5 450.
38 CW7 274.
39 Rorem, p. 456.
40 Dionysius, 1.1001A.
41 Dourley, John P. (1992), *A Strategy for a Loss of Faith: Jung's Proposal*. Toronto: Inner City Books., pp. 134–5.
42 CW 9i 291.
43 Shelburne, Walter A. (1988), *Mythos and Logos in the Thought of Carl Jung: The Theory of the Collective Unconscious in Scientific Perspective*. Albany, NY: SUNY Press, p. 94.
44 Shelburne, p. 97.
45 See, for example, the discussion of the 'still point' in Gundry, Mark (2006), *Beyond Psyche: Symbol and Transcendence in C. G. Jung*. New York: Peter Lang; and, of the *unitas indistinctionis* in Herold, Christine (2006), 'One Mind: Jung and Meister Eckhart on God and Mystical Experience', *Journal of Jungian Scholarly Studies*, 2(4).
46 Rorem, p. 460.
47 Luther, Martin, *Luther's Works*, 13: 110-11; WA 40/3: 543, lines 8–13.
48 CW11 338.
49 CW11 522.
50 CW8 432.
51 CW7 369.
52 Zizek, Slavoj (2004), 'Notes on a Debate "From Within the People"', *Criticism*, 46(4): 662.
53 Kerslake, Christian (2002), 'The Vertigo of Philosophy: Deleuze and the Problem of Immanence', *Radical Philosophy*, No. 113; (2004), 'Rebirth Through Incest: On Deleuze's Early Jungianism', *Angelaki: Journal of the Theoretical Humanities*, 9(1); (2006), 'Insects and Incest: From Bergson and Jung to Deleuze', http://multitudes.samizdat.net/Insects-and-Incest-From-Bergson; (2007), *Deleuze and the Unconscious*. London: Continuum; (2009), 'Deleuze and the Meanings of Immanence', http://www.after1968.org/app/webroot/uploads/kerslake-paper(1).pdf
54 Semetsky, Inna (2004), 'The Complexity of Individuation', *International Journal of Applied Psychoanalytic Studies*, 1(4); (2006), *Deleuze, Education and Becoming*. Rotterdam: Sense Publishers; (2009), 'Practical Mysticism and Deleuze's Ontology of the Virtual' (with T. Lovat), *Cosmos and History: The Journal of Natural and Social Philosophy*, 5(2); (2012), 'Deleuze's Philosophy and Jung's Psychology: Learning and the Unconscious' (with Joshua Ramey), in *Jung and Educational Theory*, Inna Semetsky (ed.). Bognor Regis, UK: Wiley-Blackwell.

55 Hallward, Peter (2010), 'You Can't Have It Both Ways: Deleuze or Lacan', *Deleuze and Psychoanalysis: Philosophical Essays on Deleuze's Debate with Psychoanalysis*, Leen de Boole (ed.). Leuven: Leuven University Press.
56 Davies, Oliver (2001), 'Thinking Difference: A Comparative Study of Gilles Deleuze, Plotinus and Meister Eckhart', in *Deleuze and Religion*. London: Routledge.
57 de Gaynesford, Maximilian (2001), 'Bodily Organs and Organisation', *Deleuze and Religion*, Mary Bryden (ed.). London: Routledge, p. 93.
58 Deleuze, Gilles and Felix Guattari (1987), *A Thousand Plateaus: Capitalism and Schizophrenia*. London: Continuum, p. 176.
59 Land, Nick (2011), *Fanged Noumena: Collected Writings 1987–2007*. Falmouth, UK: Urbanomic, p. 304.
60 Deleuze and Guattari, p. 165.
61 Deleuze and Guatarri, p. 166.
62 Seem, Mark (1984), 'Introduction', in *Anti-Oedipus: Capitalism and Schizophrenia*, G. Deleuzes and F. Guattari. London: Continuum, pp. xix–xx.
63 Deleuze and Guattari, p. 167.
64 Deleuze and Guattari, p. 166.
65 Deleuze and Guattari, p. 177.
66 Seem, p. xix.
67 CW14 778.
68 See Craig E. Stephenson (2009), *Possession: Jung's Comparative Anatomy of the Psyche*. London: Routledge.
69 EH 433D.
70 CW13 209.
71 Semetsky and Delpech-Ramey (2010), p. 7.
72 Stagoll, Cliff (2005), 'Becoming', in *The Deleuze Dictionary*, A. Parr (ed.). New York: Columbia University Press, p. 21.
73 Deleuze and Guattari, p. 263.
74 CW11 525.
75 CW11 529.
76 Deleuze, Gilles (1995), *Negotiations, 1972–1990*, Marin Joughin (trans.). New York: Columbia University Press, pp. 103–4.
77 Semetsky (2006), p. 6.
78 Rayment-Pickard, Hugh (2003), *Impossible God: Derrida's Theology*. Aldershot, UK: Ashgate, p. 126.
79 Derrida, Jacques (1967), 'Differance', in *Margins of Philosophy*, (1982), A. Bass (trans.). Chicago: University of Chicago Press, p. 6.
80 Rubenstein, Mary-Jane (2008), 'Dionysius, Derrida, and the Critique of "Ontotheology"', *Modern Theology*, 24(4): 738.
81 See, for example, Kevin Hart (1989), *The Trespass of the Sign: Deconstruction, Theology, and Philosophy*. Cambridge, Cambridge University Press; John Caputo (1997), *The Prayers and Tears of Jacques Derrida*. Bloomington, IN: Indiana University Press; Thomas Carlson (1999), *Indiscretion: Finitude and the Naming of God*. Chicago: University of Chicago Press; Jean-Luc Marion (2001), *The Idol and Distance*. New York: Fordham University Press.
82 Derrida, Jacques (1992), 'How to Avoid Speaking: Denials', in *Derrida and Negative Theology*, H. Coward and T. Foshay (eds). Albany, NY: SUNY Press, p. 97.
83 Derrida (1992), p. 100.
84 Derrida (1992), p. 100.
85 CW12 249.
86 CW14 661.
87 Derrida (1992), p. 100.
88 EH 369.

89   EH 372A – footnote.
90   DN3 680b, Jones' translation.
91   Derrida (1992), pp 117–8.
92   CW5 260.
93   CW8 533.
94   CW8 543.
95   Derrida (1992), p. 121.
96   CW8 142.
97   Derrida, Jacques (1995), *On the Name*. Stanford, CT: Stanford University Press, p. 59.
98   Derrida (1992), p. 89.
99   Derrida (1992), p. 88.
100 CW12 421.
101 Rayment-Pickard, p. 127.
102 Derrida (1992), p. 97.
103 Gersh, Stephen (2006), *Neoplatonism after Derrida*. Leiden: Brill, p. 32.
104 Derrida (1995), p. 41.
105 Derrida (1995), p. 41.
106 Derrida (1995), pp. 37-8.
107 Derrida (1995), p. 55.
108 CW9ii 116.
109 CW9i 277; CW11 448; CW14 86; CW16 385; CW18 1631.
110 Derrida (1992), p. 75.
111 Bradley, Arthur (2006), 'Derrida's God: A Genealogy of the Theological Turn', *Paragraph*,
     29(3): 24–5.
112 Derrida (1992), pp. 76–7.
113 Derrida (1992), p. 81.
114 Bradley, Arthur (2004), *Negative Theology and Modern French Philosophy*. London: Routledge,
     p. 24.
115 Derrida (1992), p. 91.
116 CW8 400.
117 Tacey, David (2008), 'Imagining Transcendence at the End of Modernity: Jung and
     Derrida', in *Dreaming the Myth Onwards: New Directions in Jungian Therapy and Thought*.
     Lucy Huskinson (ed.). London: Routledge, p. 64.
118 Tacey, pp. 65–6.
119 Tacey, p. 62.
120 Tacey, p. 64.
121 Freud, SE IV.
122 Tacey, p. 59.
123 Tacey, David (2007), 'The Gift of the Unknown: Jung(ians) and Freud(ians) at the End
     of Modernity', *European Journal of Psychotherapy and Counselling*, 9(4): 433.
124 Dourley, John (1981), *The Psyche as Sacrament: A Comparative Study of C. G. Jung and
     Paul Tillich*. Toronto: Inner City Books; (1984), *The Illness That We Are: A Jungian
     Critique of Christianity*. Toronto: Inner City Books; (1992), *A Strategy for a Loss of Faith:
     Jung's Proposal*. Toronto: Inner City Books; (1995), *Jung and the Religious Alternative:
     The Rerooting*. Lewiston, NY: Edwin Mellen; (2006), *The Intellectual Autobiography of a
     Jungian Theologian*. Lewiston, NY: Edwin Mellen; (2008), *Paul Tillich, Carl Jung and the
     Recovery of Religion*. London: Routledge; (2010), *On Behalf of the Mystical Fool: Jung on
     the Religious Situation*. London: Routledge.
125 Dourley (2010), p. 131.
126 Dourley (2010), p. 6.
127 Dourley (2010), p. 6.
128 Dourley (2010), p. 8.

129 Dourley (2010), p. 9.
130 Milem, p. 197.
131 Franke, William (2007), *On What Cannot be Said: Apophatic Discourses in Philosophy, Religion, Literature and the Arts: Vol. 1, Classic Formulations*. Notre Dame, IN: Notre Dame University Press, pp. 2–3.
132 Dourley (2010), p. 17.
133 CW11 85.
134 Carlson, Thomas (2008), *The Indiscrete Image: Infinitude and Creation of the Human*. Chicago: Chicago University Press, p. 91.
135 Carlson (2008), p. 114.
136 Dourley (2010), p. 29.
137 CW18 98.
138 Dourley (2010), p. 30.
139 Hood, Ralph W. (1976), 'Conceptual Criticisms of Regressive Explanations of Mysticism', *Review of Religious Research*, 17(3): 184.
140 Hood, p. 181.
141 CW8.
142 Dourley (2008), p. 127.
143 Dourley (2010), p. 118.
144 CW10 75.
145 Dourley (1992), p. 135.
146 Dourley (2010), p. 8.
147 Dourley (2010) p. 226.
148 Dourley (2010), p. 227–8.
149 Dourley (2008), p. 112–3.

Chapter 8

The Ecclesiastical Hierarchy and the psychotherapeutic process

Dionysius' *Ecclesiastical Hierarchy* describes the worshipping community, gathered to grow into conformity with the providential dynamic of the One. There are striking parallels between the metaphors and images used in the *Ecclesiastical Hierarchy* and descriptions of the process of psychoanalytic psychotherapy. Jung describes the Mass as 'the rite of the individuation process'.[1] Hotz argues that 'Denys recognized that the religious subjectivity of Christians is formed in communities through devotional and public worship practices precisely because these practices remap the patterns that make person who they are'.[2]

In this chapter I will weave a tapestry of texts from the *Ecclesiastical Hierarchy* with descriptions of psychoanalytic psychotherapy. In this impressionistic fashion I hope to illuminate the analogies between the symbolic world of Dionysius and contemporary psychoanalytic theory and practice. The liturgy includes the reading of scripture, the chanting of psalmody and the singing of hymns. Dionysius comments that '[i]f one considers these texts with a reverent eye one will see something that both brings about unity and manifests a single empathy'.[3] This chapter aims to inspire in the reader an appreciation of an empathy at work between the imagery and language of the *Ecclesiastical Hierarchy* and the language and practice of psychoanalytic psychotherapy.

This approach differs from the detailed explication of texts and the definition of words and concepts used in previous chapters. While this may result in a loss of conceptual clarity it is intended to highlight the element of process and flow within the *Ecclesiastical Hierarchy* and psychoanalytic psychotherapy. The sources of the quotations and ideas cited in this tapestry are not always identified, perhaps contributing to a sense of a 'harmonious interpenetrating mix-up'.[4] Much of the description of psychoanalytic psychotherapy in this chapter relies on my own experience of the analytic process and can be characterized as common knowledge among psychoanalytic practitioners. It is hoped that this experiential style will illuminate additional facets of the apophatic strain in psychoanalysis.

Chapter One of EH is an introduction to the meaning of the hierarchy. Subsequent chapters deal with different aspects of the liturgy. First there is a description of the rite and this is followed in each case by a 'contemplation', an interpretation of the meaning of the ritual. This structure reflects the theme of emanation and return, the descent into matter and the ascent to mind. Psychoanalytic interpretation is similarly contemplative in its retrospective focus. Events occur within the therapeutic relationship and their meanings are then analysed. Jung observed that 'the alchemical opus consisted of two parts: the work in the laboratory with all its emotional and daemonic hazards, and the *scientia* or *theoria*, the guiding principle of the opus by which its results were interpreted and given their proper place'.[5]

Dionysius refers to the *Ecclesiastical Hierarchy* as 'our human hierarchy', in contrast to the angelic hierarchy described in the *Celestial Hierarchy*. 'A hierarchy is always, simultaneously, order, understanding, and activity.'[6] In the *Ecclesiastical Hierarchy* he sets out to show that 'it is by way of the perceptible images that we are uplifted as far as can be to the contemplation of what is divine'.[7] In an analogous manner the psychotherapist witnesses the gradual revelation of the client's individuality/identity as the transferences and complexes which are constellated in the therapy are gradually analysed and worked through.

The EH is 'the arrangement of all the sacred realities'.[8] The analytic frame and relationship are understood to be the 'space' within which the client's whole personality, history and potential can become manifest. Each session contains the full constellation of the client's psychic situation at that moment. The whole inner world is at play in the transference/countertransference enactment of the session:

> The common goal of every hierarchy consists of the continuous love of God and things divine, a love which is sacredly worked out in an inspired and unique way, and before this, the complete and unswerving avoidance of everything contrary to it. It consists of a knowledge of beings as they really are. It consists of both the seeing and the understanding of sacred truth. It consists of an inspired participation in the one-like perfection and in the one itself, as far as possible. It consists of a feast upon that sacred vision which nourishes the intellect and which divinizes everything rising up to it.[9]

According to Freud, in psychoanalysis, 'Essentially, one might say, the cure is effected by love.'[10] He felt that the capacity to work and to love were the goals of analysis. For Jung the aim of analysis was individuation, which he characterized as the realization of the self. Images of the self appear within the psyche as images of God. In Jung's terms, 'divinization' would consist in attaining wholeness, the appropriate balance between conscious and unconscious aspects of the personality. For Dionysius, Freud and Jung, *eros* plays a crucial role in motivating and energizing the 'human hierarchy'. 'Denys rooted the capacity of the sacramental life of the church to prompt our return to unity in his erotic theological anthropology, sympathetic cosmology and translation of Iamblichan theurgy in to a Christian Incarnational theology.'[11] The process is nourishing for the mind:

> The first leaders of our hierarchy received their fill of the sacred gift from the transcendent Deity. Then divine goodness sent them to lead others to this same gift. Like gods, they had a burning and generous urge to secure uplifting and divinization for their subordinates.[12]

The therapist must first have undertaken their own therapy. The fruits of one's own analysis are available to one's clients. Gratitude to one's analyst enables you to survive the privations of analytic practice. According to Jung, you can only take your clients as far as you have been yourself. A great deal of zeal is required to undertake psychotherapy training and persevere in the development of a psychotherapy practice:

> using images derived from the senses they spoke of the transcendent ... Of necessity they made human what was divine. They put material on what was immaterial. In their written and unwritten initiations, they brought the transcendent down to our level ... In the divine fashion it needs perceptible things to lift us up into the domain of conceptions.[13]

The fashioning and communication of interpretations is a core activity for the psychotherapist. Images from the client's speech are analysed for conceptual content, therefore being 'uplifted' to an intellectual level. The unconscious communication of the client which the therapist experiences in the countertransference is transformed into everyday language. Unconscious meanings are 'materialized' in conscious meaning.

Some clients use abstract language as a defence and need to be encouraged to be more concrete, in Dionysius' terms, to describe the 'perceptible things'. Only if they first of all talk about the detail of their experience can the 'uplifting' action of interpretation be meaningful:

> I am giving you this gift of God, together with other things pertaining to the hierarchs. I do so because of the solemn promises you made, of which I am now reminding you, promises never to pass to anyone except sacred-initiators of your own order the hierarch's superior sacred words.[14]

Psychotherapy occurs within a 'solemn' contract of confidentiality. In Jungian terms, using alchemical imagery, the vessel of the analysis must be well sealed. Clients are encouraged not to allow the intensity of the therapeutic process to lead to leakage. Acting-out is seen by some psychoanalysts as an attack of the therapeutic container. Breaking of confidentiality by the therapist can be a serious ethical breach, which may be grounds for a formal complaint by the client. The imposition of limits on the confidentiality of the therapeutic relationship by the state is a cause of serious concern for some therapists.

One element of the assessment process and of the early stages of psychotherapy is a determination of the client's commitment to the undertaking. Do they have some intuition of the nature of the 'gift' of analysis? Can they tolerate receiving something good; will they feel the urge to reject it or destroy it? Are they frightened or suspicious of the intimacy of the analytic relationship? Is the therapist prepared to be open to this new person; to allow the therapeutic process to evolve and deepen without too much resistance on his/her part? Are both parties respectful of the 'sacred' trust that will arise between them as their relationship grows.

In Chapter Two, Dionysius asks, 'What, then, is the starting point for the sacred enactment of the most revered commandments?'[15] The starting point is baptism, which is described as a 'divine birth' and as 'illumination'. Its purpose is:

> to dispose our souls to hear the sacred words as receptively as possible, to be open to the divine workings of God, to clear an uplifting path toward that inheritance which awaits us in heaven, and to accept our most divine and sacred regeneration.[16]

How does the therapeutic process begin? What stages need to occur to insure solid foundations for its subsequent development? How is the therapeutic alliance formed? First the client will approach the therapist with a desire to move out of his/her present condition of suffering, confusion or contradiction. The approach may be through an intermediary – a general practitioner, a counselling or psychotherapy organization, a friend – or directly to the prospective therapist:

> Someone fired by love of transcendent reality and longing for a sacred share of it comes first to an initiate, asks to be brought to the hierarch, and promises complete obedience to whatever is laid upon him. He asks him to take charge of his training and of everything connected with his future life.[17]

In the initial session or in the assessment, the ground rules of therapy are discussed. Agreement is reached about fees, cancelled sessions and session times and frequency. There may be discussion of how to manage any unexpected meetings on the street, in the supermarket or at social events. Etiquette on use of the phone and holiday dates may be discussed. Some therapists suggest that dreams should be recorded. Freud instructed patients in the basic rule of analysis – free association – and advised them not to make any major life decisions during the course of the analysis:

> When should we start communicating to the analysand? When is the right time to reveal the secret meaning of his associations, to initiate him in to the theory and technical procedures of analysis? The only possible answer is: not until the patient has established a usable transference, a proper rapport. The first objective of the treatment remains to attach him to the therapy and the person of the doctor.[18]

Dionysius' picture of the initiate's anxieties about undertaking the care of the supplicant are similar to a therapist's when beginning an analysis. 'The other is moved by the desire for the man's salvation but when he compares the human situation with the heights confronting the enterprise, fright and uncertainty lay hold of him.'[19] According to Jung:

> It is inevitable that the doctor should be influenced to a certain extent and even that his nervous health should suffer. He quite literally 'takes over' the sufferings of his patient and shares them with him. For this reason he runs a risk — and must run it in the nature of things.[20]

Nevertheless, having overcome these anxieties the sponsor presents the supplicant to the hierarch and through him to the community. When a therapist takes on a new client there is a process of introducing the client to a supervisor, as well as the gradual incorporation of the client into the analytic community and tradition as they exist within the inner world of the therapist. The client becomes aware that 'he must give himself totally'[21] to this new environment.

After his sandals and garments are removed and he has repeated the prescribed declarations and prayers he is covered with oil and immersed three times. This powerful enactment contains elements of conception, life in the womb and birth, all of which can be part of the transference or appear in dreams during early phases of psychotherapy. If someone was an unwanted baby this usually becomes clear very early. It is hard to conceive of the fact that the therapist might want him/her as a client. Some clients treat the consulting room or the couch as a womb. It might be a poisoning womb or the longed-for safe womb. If the mother had tried to abort the child the room is usually experienced initially as dangerous. Difficulties during the birth are symbolized in the relationship with the therapist. If the client was premature and spent time an incubator this will inevitably appear in the transference/ countertransference. Feelings of intense vulnerability and nakedness are often part of the beginning of therapy. The sense of a new beginning or rebirth can be very palpable.

Baptism 'differentiates ... what belongs to the common crowd from the things that bind and unify a hierarchy, and it apportions to each order its due and fitting measure of uplifting'.[22] The sense of relief and excitement at the beginning of therapy can lead to inflation or a flight to health. 'It can happen too that these beings push beyond the reasonable limits set to their vision and that they have the gall to imagine that they can actually gaze upon those beams which transcend their power of sight.'[23] However, the therapist maintains a non-judgemental, even-handed attitude, and 'displays neither a grudge nor profane anger over previous apostasy and transgressions':[24]

> But since God is the source of this sacred arrangement in accordance with which the intelligence of sacred beings acquires self-awareness, anyone

proceeding to examine his own nature will at the start discover his own identity and he will acquire this first sacred gift as a consequence of his looking up toward the light. Having duly examined with unbiased gaze what he himself is he will avoid the dark pits of ignorance. He will not yet be sufficiently initiated into complete union with and participation in God nor will his longing for this come from within himself. Only gradually will he be uplifted to a higher state and this because of the mediation of people more advanced than he.[25]

The client begins to trust that the therapist is reliable and may be of help. A rapport or therapeutic alliance is established. 'For the one truly yearns for the life-giving journey toward the truth ... and the other unerringly guides his follower along the ways handed down by God.'[26] Indeed, the new client will 'quite gladly hurl himself into what he knows to be divine contests and he will follow and scrupulously observe the wise rules of the game'.[27] There is a danger however of acting-out. 'One must fearlessly confront any disastrous backsliding.'[28]

Baptism is a participation in death, as well as a birth. 'Now because of this it is quite appropriate to hide the initiate completely in the water as an image of this death and this burial where form is dissolved.'[29] Images of death abound at the beginning of psychotherapy. Many people start by grieving the deaths of parents, children or other loved ones. Others are very conscious of the death of certain aspects of themselves. There is grief at stillborn aspects of the self, unfulfilled potential. There is anxiety about whether the therapist will survive. Psychic deadness, past and present, threatens the client's sense of coherence and potency. The consulting room and the couch can become a tomb, a coffin or a clostrum. Decay and breakdown threaten:

> To us death is not, as others imagine, a complete dissolution of being. It is rather, the separation of two parts which had been linked together. It brings the soul into what for us is an invisible realm where it, in the loss of the body, becomes formless.[30]

In psychotherapy, psychological mindedness, the capacity to symbolize, and awareness of the unconscious emerge when familiar structures of living and imagining the self dissolve. 'Order descends upon disorder within him. Form takes over from formlessness. Light shines through all his life.'[31]

In Chapter Three, Dionysius describes the initiate's participation in the synaxis (gathering) or communion:

> Every sacredly initiating operation draws our fragmented lives together into a one-like divinization. It forges a unity out of the divisions within us ... the perfection of the other hierarchical symbols is only achieved by way of the divine and perfecting gifts of Communion.[32]

In psychoanalysis the proper engagement with the images of the internal parents and of the mother's breast and the father's penis are considered foundational to the proper development of subsequent psychological capacities. The 'gathering' applies to both internal aspects of the personality and the ordering of interpersonal relationships. Images of feeding and incorporation are ubiquitous in psychoanalysis.

'We, however, when we think of the sacred synaxis must move in from effects to causes ... to glimpse the contemplation of the conceptual things.'[33] The concern of the client moves gradually from a recitation of events to a reflection on motives. The therapist allows this process to unfold at its own pace. According to Freud, we start at the surface and then move to depth. While listening to the ins and outs of the client's story the therapist holds in mind a sense of the person's potential for wholeness:

> In his mind he journeys toward the One. With a clear eye he looks upon the basic unity of those realities underlying the sacred rites. He makes the divine return to the primary things the goal of his procession toward secondary things, which he had undertaken out of love for humanity.[34]
>
> The sacred tablets have a lesson for those capable of being divinized ... They teach that God himself thus gives substance and arrangement to everything that exists ... They lay down the divisions by lot, the distribution and the sharing that have to do with God's people.[35]

The therapist's interventions and interpretations are informed by the collective wisdom of the analytic community. The client begins to sense that there is a logic to what might at first appear to be bizarre, irrational or offensive questions or statements by the therapist. The client comes to see that his/her problems which seemed painful, alienating secrets are part of the human pattern, because:

> these sacred hymns, with their summaries of holy truth, have prepared our spirits to be at one with what we shall shortly celebrate, when they have attuned us to the divine harmony and have brought us into accord not only with divine realities but with our individual selves and with others.[36]

In spite of the plethora of seemingly incompatible schools of psychoanalysis, 'if one considers these texts with a reverent eye one will see something that both brings about unity and manifests a single empathy.'[37]

Nevertheless, some people are unable to appreciate a psychological perspective. 'Those who are stone deaf to what the sacred sacraments teach also have no eye for imagery.'[38] Their sense of reality is very concrete. Unless the therapist has the capacity to establish a relationship with them on their own terms they will end the therapy. 'Shamelessly they have rejected the saving initiation which brings about the divine birth, and ruinously they have echoed the scriptural text, "I do not wish to know your ways".'[39]

The catechumens, the possessed and the penitents may listen to the readings and join in the singing of hymns, but they will not be able to participate in the Eucharist. The catechumens are compared to premature babies who 'have not received an inspired existence in the divine birth, but are yet being incubated by the paternal scriptures'.[40] Many clients will spend an extended time within the containment of the analytic setting without being aware of what is being provided for them by the frame and the therapist. Later, they may be able to enter into a more conscious relationship with the therapist and with themselves:

> It gives them the introductory food of scripture which shapes them and brings them toward life ... it withholds the perfect things from them since it wishes both to safeguard the harmony of these sacred things and to watch over the incubation and life of the catechumens, and it does so in accordance with the divine order laid down by the hierarchy.[41]

The therapist allows for the client's regression or lack of development and avoids premature interpretations or confrontation. The therapist's understanding of the client's needs during this phase is informed by the theory of the particular school of therapy that he/she espouses.

The possessed are at a higher level than the catechumens because they have 'taken part in some of the sacred rites but [are] held fast by opposing charms or by confusion'.[42] They are possessed by 'the illusions and terrors of the adversary' and 'the ideas and character of abominable demons ... In their extreme folly, so destructive to themselves, they turn away from the truly real.'[43] As time goes by the client's resistances, defences, splits and delusions emerge. His/her investment in psychopathology blocks the development of the capacity to symbolize, awareness, insight, or more mature object relations. Jung describes psychosis as possession of the ego by a content from the collective unconscious. Freud's negative therapeutic reaction is like a demonic possession. An hysterical symptom is the result of an inability to be truthful with oneself. For Klein, the baby's envy prevents a satisfactory feed. 'It is wrong for them to be present at any part of the rite other than that scriptural teaching aimed at their return to better things.'[44] The therapist must stay faithful to the frame until the client can participate in the analytic relationship in a more creative manner. He/she tries to avoid being drawn into a pathological collusion with a mad, sadistic or destructive aspect of the client. The client may attack the therapist's sanity and sense of reality.

> Hence, I believe – or, rather, I know for a fact – that the members of the hierarchy, being very wise in their judgement, understand that the possessed, that is, those who have turned away from a life conforming to divine example and have adopted instead the ideas and character of abominable demons, are exposed to the very worst power.[45]

Freud came to feel that many psychological problems are the result of the death instinct. Jung wrote about the power of the collective shadow and considered evil to be an entity.

Also barred from communion are the penitents, who had previously taken part, but 'who are not yet purified of empty imaginings because they have not yet acquired as something permanent the undiluted yearning for God'.[46] Some clients lack ego-strength, object-constancy or self-esteem and they find it difficult to take responsibility for the awareness or insight that they have gained in therapy. As a result they may act-out or their behaviour may be quite erratic. While there may be glimmers of a new sense of identity or direction it lacks potency and definition. The therapist's holding and containment in the countertransference supports the client during periods of lack of integration:

> Then it reminds us that when we had lost the divine gifts because of our own folly, God took the trouble to recall us to our original condition through adventitious gifts, that he gave us a most perfect share of his nature by completely taking on our own.[47]

By his/her capacity to contain the projected anxiety and destructiveness the therapist holds the way open for the client to return to him/herself.

This is a very intimate experience and provides the matter to be digested in future analysis. There is a sense of recognition between client and therapist and a feeling that one is being nourished by real experience. 'The love of the Diety for humanity having been thus reverently celebrated, the covered divine bread is brought forward, together with the cup of blessing. The divine kiss of peace is exchanged.'[48] These experiences of acceptance and recognition become good objects in the client's inner world and contribute to the formation of the ego-ideal. They constellate positive archetypal images:

> The names are announced of those who have lived holy lives and whose consistent efforts earned for them the perfection of a virtuous life. In this way we are enticed and encouraged to follow their example ... For this proclamation announces them as alive, as those who have not died but ... who have passed from death to a more perfectly divine life.[49]

The psyche becomes a living reality for the client, who becomes aware of the transference, dreams, projections and the autonomy of unconscious contents. There is the realization that much of what we experience and of what motivates us is determined by forces outside of consciousness. 'Christ knows all our thoughts, even the most secret of them ... I must now try as best I can to describe those divine workings of which we are the objective.'[50] The client reworks the narrative of his/her life to accommodate the insights gained in therapy. This often involves a journey during which bad choices were made and destructive patterns were established:

From the very beginning human nature has stupidly glided away from those good things bestowed on it by God ... and came at the end to the catastrophe of death. There followed the destructive rejection of what was really good ... down to the deplorable peril of destruction and dissolution of being.[51]

The client's narrative describes how through good fortune and hard work a change occurred. It might be attributed to God, the individual's innate potential or the help of the therapist:

Beneficently it wrought a complete change in our nature. It filled our shadowed and unshaped minds with a kindly, divine light ... It saved our nature from almost complete wreckage and delivered the dwelling place of our soul from the most accursed passion and from destructive defilement.[52]

By working through (Freud) or living one's own myth (Jung) the new psychological situation is established. The client's psychopathology is transformed by being repeatedly constellated, contained and analysed. What was opaque, dense and heavy gradually becomes something that can be thought about and discussed. The client learns that his/her somatic symptoms are symbols of psychological states. 'This imitation of God, how else are we to achieve it if not by endlessly reminding ourselves of God's sacred works.'[53] It is the holding of the tension between past and present (Jung) or recovering the repressed memory (Freud) which opens the possibility for reordering the elements of the psyche. Whether it is the memory of human nature, as in Jung's collective unconscious, or the memory of the individual, as in Freud's unconscious, finding the appropriate relationship with the past is the key to living the present and future. 'Do this in remembrance of me.'

The client now 'beholds with the eyes of the mind this spectacle for conceptual contemplation'.[54] The client can now operate from a new centre. 'Where id was, there ego shall be.' (Freud) For Jung, the appearance of the self reorients and energizes the personality. The elements of the client's life, which previously appeared inert or in opposition to his/her intentions, now carry meaning. 'The bread which had been covered and undivided is now uncovered and divided into many parts. Similarly, he shares the one cup with all, symbolically multiplying and distributing the one in symbolic fashion.'[55] For Jung, differentiation of psychic contents leads to individuation of the personality. The unity of the personality is a result of the clarification of the differences within the psyche and between the individual and others. This is an example of the creative function of negation or *apophasis*. Disparate aspects of the personality find places within a whole. In *Transformation Symbolism in the Mass*, Jung writes:

Without this 'dichotomy of God,' if I may use such a term, the whole act of sacrifice would be inconceivable and would lack actuality ... God in his humanity is presumably so far from himself that he has to seek himself through absolute self-surrender. And where would God's wholeness be if he could not be the 'wholly other'? ... The dichotomy of God into divinity and humanity and his return to himself in the sacrificial act hold out the comforting doctrine that in man's own darkness there is hidden a light that shall once again return to its source, and that this light actually *wanted* to descend into the darkness in order to deliver the Enchained One who languishes there and lead him to light everlasting.[56]

The symptom having been analysed (divided into many parts) releases the energy and meaning which had been bound into its form. For Freud, the repressed wish (desire/eros) is disguised by processes of condensation, displacement etc. which produce a symptom or dream. For Jung, the symptom is a symbol, which has 'an objective and a subjective – or psychic – origin, so that it can be interpreted on the "objective level" as well as on the "subjective level"'.[57]

Psychoanalysis is concerned with both the negative and the positive aspects of communion and 'gathering'. For Freud, symptoms and dreams are products of the fusion of psychic elements in order to disguise the repressed desire. The persistence of the symptom or dream bears witness to the insistence of the desire. The crisis of the Oedipus complex is about whether or not an appropriate communion can be negotiated between parent and child. An inappropriate Oedipal communion undermines all future development. The creative intercourse of the internal parents involves the capacity to join and separate. Fused internal parents or internal parents who do not connect contribute to a sense of barrenness and hopelessness in the personality. For Jung, individuation consists of the progressive differentiation of one's self from internal and external collectives. Psychosis is the fusion of the ego with contents of the collective unconscious. A psychotic personality exhibits a combination of inflexibility and disintegration. Neurosis occurs when an inappropriate balance between conscious and unconscious becomes fixed. The capacity of the psyche to adapt in a fluid fashion to changing circumstances is inhibited.

The concept of projective identification, in Kleinian theory, can be seen as a way of understanding the vicissitudes of communion and 'gathering'. Normal projective identification is the ground for relationship. Excessive projective identification destroys the structures of relationship and failure to engage in projective identification leads to isolation. Unconscious phantasies employed in projective identification are the elements of communication.

Jung's concept of unconscious identity performs similar tasks to those done by the concept of projective identification:

The act of making a sacrifice consists in the first place in giving something which belongs to me. Everything which belongs to me bears the stamp of 'mineness,' that is, it has a subtle identity with my ego ... The affinity

which all the things bearing the stamp of 'mineness' have with my personality is aptly characterized by Levy-Bruhl as *participation mystique*. It
is an irrational, unconscious identity, arising from the fact that anything
which comes into contact with me is not only itself, but also a symbol.
This symbolization comes about firstly because every human being has
unconscious contents, and secondly because every object has an unknown
side ... But where two unknowns come together, it is impossible to distinguish between them. The unknown in man and the unknown in the
thing fall together in one. Thus there arises an unconscious identity which
sometimes border on the grotesque.[58]

For Jung, the theurgy can be a sacrifice or a magical act. The distinction
between the two is determined by the level of consciousness:

When, therefore, I give away something that is 'mine,' what I am giving is
essentially a symbol, a thing of many meanings; but, owing to my unconsciousness of its symbolic character, it adheres to my ego, because it is part
of my personality ... Consequently the gift always carries with it a personal
intention, for the mere giving of it is not a sacrifice. It only becomes a
sacrifice if I give up the implied intention of receiving something in return
... Were the bread and wine simply given without any consciousness of
an egoistic claim, the fact that it was unconscious would be no excuse,
but would on the contrary be sure proof of the existence of a *secret* claim.
Because of its egoistic nature, the offering would then inevitably have the
character of a magical act of propitiation, with the unavowed purpose and
tacit expectation of purchasing the good will of the Deity. That is an ethi-
cally worthless simulacrum of sacrifice.[59]

There is a quantum leap when the focus of an analysis shifts from symptom
relief and acquisition of psychic payoffs to service of the psyche – psychotherapy. The sessions are at the service of the expansion and intensification
of being rather than the pursuit of discrete measurable objectives that can be
innumerated beforehand:

The Mass tries to effect a participation mystique – or identity – of priest
and congregation with Christ, so that on the one hand the soul is assimi-
lated to Christ and on the other hand the Christ figure is recollected in the
soul. It is a transformation of God and man alike, since the Mass is, at least
by implication, a repetition of the whole drama of Incarnation.[60]

Both Dionysius and Jung are often characterized as being excessively
concerned with the individual. Psychoanalytic psychotherapy is criticized as
self-centred and selfish. On the contrary, individual psychotherapy and apophatic discourse can be understood as deeply social activities:

For Denys human beings are ontologically precluded from experiences of intense interiority, the like of which are often identified with mysticism: we are not, that is, put together in such a way that appeals to an 'inner self' make any sense. In fact, the most basic religious experience that arises from the self-as-yearning, ecstasy, is an experience of being called beyond the narrow confines of the self toward the all-surpassing divine beauty … Denys's theurgical self, moreover, is not only a related self, but also necessarily an embodied self. Religious subjectivity is deeply connected with sense experience, for it is through the sensible that God attracts us to the intelligible.[61]

Jung observes, 'If we now recall to what a degree the soul has humanized and realized itself, we can judge how very much it today expresses the body also, with which it is coexistent.'[62] The individuation of the individual is of value not only to the one concerned but contributes to the life of the collective:

> So too the self is our life's goal, for it is the completest expression of that fateful combination we call individuality, and full flowering not only of the single individual, but of the group, in which each adds his portion to the whole.[63]

The EH continues with chapters on the rite of anointing, the clerical orders, the orders of those being initiated (including the 'therapeutae'), the consecration of a monk, and the rite for the dead, which will not be examined in detail here. However, the themes of those chapters add weight to the importance of the *Ecclesiastical Hierarchy* for a consideration of the apophatic elements of psychoanalysis, because it brings to light the social dimension of *apophasis*. We can describe Jung's project of cultural transformation as a kind of cultural *apophasis*. He is concerned to read contemporary history as humanity's halting efforts to wrestle with unknown futures.

There is a considerable literature on the relationship between psychoanalysis and ritual. I suggest that it may also be worthwhile to think about the liturgical dimension of psychoanalysis. I would characterize a ritual as linear and liturgy as circular. Commenting on Dionysius' account of the Eucharist in the *Ecclesiastical Hierarchy*, Golitzin notes:

> Just as this sacrament brings an illumination at once revealing and making Christ present, so the action or 'spiritual motion' to be associated with it is that of the spiral. We begin at the altar and follow the bishop out as he moves to include the whole of the Church in his censing, and then as he returns to the altar … Dionysius' *theoria* of the sacrament is at once a turning around and a gathering into that unique point, precisely a spiral. It is therefore also an image of the sanctified human intelligence both circling about, and increasingly drawn into, the mystery of God – as into the 'still point' of the poet. In as much as it is an image, so it is as well a reality.[64]

The therapist and client circle around the potency of emerging psychic contents and in the process develop a unique form of kinship. Jung describes the importance of circumambulation in the Mass as follows:

> Anyone who does not join in the dance, who does not make the circumambulation of the centre (Christ and Anthropos), is smitten with blindness and sees nothing. What is described here as an outward event is really a symbol for the inward turning of man, towards the self – for the dance can hardly be understood as an historical event. It should be understood, rather as a sort of paraphrase of the Eucharist, an amplifying symbol that renders the mystery more assimilable to consciousness, and it must therefore be interpreted as a psychic phenomenon. It is an act of conscious realization on a higher level, establishing a connection between the consciousness of the individual and the supraordinate symbol of totality.[65]

Pickstock's description of medieval liturgy resonates with another aspect of psychoanalysis – its repetitiveness and its meandering quality. She argues that 'the many repetitions and recommencements' in the liturgy are a result of the blending of oral tradition and 'an apophatic reserve which betokens our constitutive, positive, and analogical distance from God, rather than our sinfulness and humiliation. According to such a perspective, the haphazard structure of the Rite can be seen as predicated upon a need for a constant re-beginning of liturgy because the true eschatological liturgy is in time endlessly postponed.'[66] Similarly, each analytic session is a re-beginning. There is a recognition that wholeness is 'endlessly postponed'. There is no solution, cure or definitive interpretation that can be grasped with certainty in the present.

Furthermore, the ongoing process of analysis undermines presuppositions about identity. Pickstock observes that '[f]or liturgy is at once a gift *from* God and a sacrifice *to* God, a reciprocal exchange which shatters all ordinary positions of agency and reception.'[67] Is the speech of the client, the symptom, the image or the transference directed from the unconscious to the conscious, or from the conscious to the unconscious? Who within the psyche is speaking to whom? Who is acting on or reacting to whom? The therapist is listening to a choir of complexes. According to Jung, 'we are unable to distinguish whether these actions emanate from God or from the unconscious. We cannot tell whether God and the unconscious are two different entities.'[68] And 'the question as to whether the process is initiated by consciousness or by the archetype can never be answered'.[69]

A ritual has a greater sense of intentionality than liturgy. Some rituals, such as initiation rituals, aim to transform the status of the participant. For example, Turner contends that '[i]f our basic model of society is that of a "structure of positions," we must regard the period of margin or "liminality" as an interstructural situation'.[70] Psychotherapists have drawn heavily on this notion of liminality as the space between to describe psychotherapy, midlife and analytic training. In this theory liminality only has meaning in relation to structure.

In a sense a liturgy is an end in itself. It is the taking part that matters. Worship is not measured by outcomes. Torevell describes it as 'an endless and unsatiated encounter with the Unknown'.[71] There is an aspect of psychoanalysis that shares this quality. The sessions become an end in themselves. Indeed, this is an aspect of psychoanalysis that is much lampooned and criticized. There is an anxiety that it can become a self-indulgent exercise. The dwelling together of the therapist and client in a long-term therapy, like the Mass, is a participation in a special register of existence – the analytic process. At its heart it is an experience that transcends the objectives of evidence-based practice. Sullivan tries to capture the mystery of the analytic relationship:

> Simply making something intellectually conscious is not a meaningful activity … the patient will become more alive, increasingly aware of the way in which so much more than we know is always happening, and increasingly able to take the terrifying step of investigating what that 'more' might consist of … The therapist, working to ground herself in unknowing and to open herself to the fullness of the immediate moment, will experience that same shift … The truth cannot be *known*, and this truth – the fundamental mystery of life – is bearable only briefly and only in the context of a loving relationship.[72]

Torevell states that 'the liturgical soul's ascent is an endless, dramatic journey into difference, a constant traversing of the distance towards mystery'.[73] During this journey the certainties, assumptions and expectations of both the analyst and the patient undergo profound change. Knowledge based on theory becomes transformed into knowledge based on experience. Lossky describes that the movement of apophaticism in words that resonate with the experience of the psychotherapist:

> It is a tendency towards an ever-greater plenitude, in which knowledge is transformed into ignorance, the theology of concepts into contemplation, dogmas into experience of ineffable mysteries. It is, moreover, an existential theology involving man's entire being, which sets him upon the way of union, which obliges him to be changed.[74]

We are reminded of Jung's discussion of the demands made on the analyst by the transference:

> But life cannot be mastered with theories, and just as the cure of neurosis is not, ultimately, a mere question of therapeutic skill, but is a moral achievement, so too is the solution to problems thrown up by the transference. No theory can give us any information about the ultimate requirements of individuation, nor are there any recipes that can be applied in a routine manner. The treatment of the transference reveals in a pitiless light what the healing agent really is: it is the degree to which the analyst himself can cope with his own psychic problems. The higher levels of therapy involve his own reality and are the acid test of his superiority.[75]

The analyst and the patient are subject to the apophatic logic of the analytic process. In this chapter I have explored some of the resonances between Dionysius' discussion of liturgy and sacraments in *Ecclesiastical Hierarchy* and the theory and practice of psychoanalytic psychotherapy and highlighted the social dimension of *apophasis*.

Notes

1   CW11 414.
2   Hotz, Kendra G. (2000), *The Theurgical Self: The Theological Anthropology of the Pseudo-Dionysius*. PhD thesis, Emory University, p. 20.
3   EH432B.
4   Balint, Michael (1968), *The Basic Fault*. London: Tavistock Publications, p. 66.
5   CW13 482.
6   Hotz, p. 12.
7   EH 373B.
8   EH 373C.
9   EH 376A.
10 Freud's letter to Jung, 6 Decembe, 1906. William McGuire (ed.) (1974), *The Freud/Jung Letters*. Princeton: Princeton University Press, pp. 12–3. Most references to this letter read, 'psychoanalysis is in essence a cure through love', which appears on the frontispiece of Bruno Bettelheim's book, *Freud and Man's Soul* (1983), London: Chatto & Windus. In the PEP Archive this version is incorrectly attributed to McGuire's translation by writers after 1986. Bettelheim states, 'Most of the passages from Freud quoted here are taken from the *Standard Edition*. All unattributed translations are my own.' We have to assume therefore that Bettelheim's translation, which is subtly different from McGuire's has infected the scholarly rhizome of citations and footnotes.
11 Hotz, p. 14.
12 EH 376D.
13 EH 376D-377A.
14 EH 377A.
15 EH 392A.
16 EH 392A.
17 EH 393B.
18 Freud, Sigmund (2002), 'On Initiating Treatment', Alan Bance (trans.), in *Wild Analysis, New Penguin Freud*, Adam Phillips (Gen. Ed.). London: Penguin, p. 59.
19 EH 393B.
20 CW16 358.
21 EH 396A.
22 EH 397C.
23 EH 400A.
24 EH 400B.
25 EH 400C.
26 EH 401A.
27 EH 404A.
28 EH 401C.
29 EH 401C.
30 EH 404B.
31 EH 404C.
32 EH 424C-D.
33 EH 428C.
34 EH 429B.

35 EH 429C.
36 EH 432A.
37 EH 432B.
38 EH 432C.
39 EH 432C.
40 EH 432D.
41 EH 433A–B.
42 EH 433B.
43 EH 433C–D.
44 EH 436A.
45 EH 433D.
46 EH 436B.
47 EH 436D.
48 EH 437A.
49 EH 437B.
50 EH 440B–C.
51 EH 440C–441A.
52 EH 441B.
53 EH 441C.
54 EH 441D.
55 EH 444A.
56 CW11 380.
57 CW11 383*n*.
58 CW11 389.
59 CW11 390.
60 CW11 413.
61 Hotz, p. 28.
62 CW14 777.
63 CW7 404.
64 Golitzin, Alexander (1994), *Et Introibo Ad Altare Dei: The Mystagogy of Dionysius Areopagita, with Special Reference to its Predecessors in the Eastern Christian Tradition.* Thessaloniki: Analecta Vlatadon, pp. 202–3.
65 CW11 425.
66 Pickstock, Catherine (1998), *After Writing: On the Liturgical Consummation of Philosophy.* Oxford: Blackwell, p. 173.
67 Pickstock, pp. 176–7.
68 CW11 757.
69 CW11 758.
70 Turner, Victor (1987), 'Betwixt and Between: The Liminal Period in Rites of Passage', in *Betwixt and Between: Patterns of Masculine and Feminine Initiation*, L. C. Mahdi, S. Foster and M. Little (eds). La Salle, IL: Open Court, p. 4.
71 Torevell, David (2007), *Liturgy and the Beauty of the Unknown: Another Place.* Aldershot, UK: Ashgate, p. 1.
72 Sullivan, Barbara Steven (2010), *The Mystery of Analytical Work: Weavings from Jung and Bion.* London: Routledge, pp. 257–8.
73 Torevell, p. 6.
74 Lossky, Vladimir (1957), *The Mystical Theology of the Eastern Church.* Crestwood, NY: St Vladimir's Seminary Press, p. 238.
75 CW18 1172.

Chapter 9

Conclusion

This study has sought to identify apophatic elements in the theory and practice of C. G. Jung. It demonstrates that Jung's work is saturated with apophatic concepts, images and dynamics. *Apophasis* is broadly conceived to include a range of theories, linguistic practices and behaviours. It is a lens with many facets. Just as there is no single conception of the *via negativa*, there is no need to identify one single occasion for apophatic thought or practice in psychoanalysis. Apophatic intensity can be found in many different elements of the analytic encounter.

The work began with a thorough philological exposition of concepts within the *Corpus Dionysiacum*, which are integral to Dionysius' apophatic discourse: *kataphasis* (affirmation); *anagou* and *anagoge* (uplifting); *aphairesis* (abstraction); *apophasis* (unsaying, denial, negation); *hoion* (as it were); *hyper-* (above, beyond, super-); *exaireou* (to be removed from, transcend); *epekeina* (transcend, beyond); *exaiphnes* (sudden, suddenly); *ekstasis* (ecstatic, ecstasy); *apeiria* and *apeiron* (infinite, infinity, unlimited, unbound); *agnousia, agnoustos, agnoustous* and *hyper-agnoustos* (unknowing, unknowable, lack of knowledge, ignorance); *henousis* (unity, union); *theosis, theousis* and *theôsis* (deification, divinization, becoming godlike). Such a detailed taxonomy of the language of *apophasis* in the *Corpus Dionysiacum* has not been undertaken before. It provides scholars with ready access to essential references.

Jung's reception of Dionysius and Cusa have been examined in detail, as has his engagement with Neoplatonism. The study analyses Jung's uses of the concept of opposites: coincidence of opposites (*coincidentia oppositorum*), complexio oppositorum, conjunction of opposites (*coniunctio oppositorum*) and union of opposites. The problem of opposites constitutes a major site for *apophasis* in Jung's work. It was acknowledged that claims to this effect have been made by others, but this is the first time that it has been conclusively proven by an exhaustive analysis of the references to opposites in the *Collected Works*. It was suggested that the transcendent function acts as an apophatic methodology at the heart of Jung's theory.

Jung's work was looked at in relation to contemporary writers. Sells, Milem and Rorem are scholars of religion who have suggested novel frameworks for understanding *apophasis*. It is possible to find resonances with these structures in Jung's thought. Deleuze and Derrida are thinkers who have had an impact on post-Jungian theory. Apophatic features in their thought were compared with themes in Jung's work. The writings of two Jungian writers, Tacey and Dourley, who have discussed Jung and *apophasis* were examined. These explorations demonstrate that Jung's engagement with apophatic themes is in sympathy with contemporary discussions in philosophy and theology and is not anachronistic.

An impressionistic weaving of the practices described in the *Ecclesiastical Hierarchy* and aspects of the psychoanalytic psychotherapy process displayed the hidden sympathy between the two. It also raised the question of the social and cultural features of apophatic discourse. While psychotherapy has often been described as a ritual process, it was proposed that in significant respects psychoanalysis might be viewed as a liturgical practice.

There are important aspects of Jung's work that could have been usefully explored to further our understanding of the apophatic character of his thought. These include his writings on individuation, the self, the *imago dei*, the Gnostics, alchemy, Eckhart, Zen, the *Secrets of the Golden Flower*, synchronicity, amplification and the dynamics of the relationship between the ego and the unconscious.

As a case study in the application of the lens of *apophasis* to psychoanalysis, this research points beyond the work of Jung. It provides a platform for the identification of apophatic elements in the theory and practice of other schools of psychoanalysis. Theories that might benefit from being read through an apophatic lens include Freud's unrepressed unconscious, castration, resolution of the Oedipus complex and primordial images; Bion's 'O'; Lacan's real and lack; Winnicott's true self and going on being; and Klein's projective identification and depressive position. Aspects of clinical practice that may be usefully considered as part of a contemplative, apophatic tradition include evenly hovering attention, free association, approaching the session without memory or desire, boundaries of the session, therapeutic neutrality, working through and withdrawal of projections.

Further research may support the hypothesis that the concepts of *apophasis* and the *via negativa* provide a key to illuminating the family resemblance among the various schools of psychoanalysis. It may be that when one reads a piece of theory or a clinical vignette, what makes it identifiable as *analysis* is the apophatic element; that we experience the Freudian, Jungian, Lacanian, Kleinian etc. versions of psychoanalysis *as* psychoanalysis, because they all embody or enact *apophasis* each in their own particular ways. As Mortley observes, 'at the hands of the divine Denys the negative way also has an ecumenical function. More clearly than in any other thinker, the negative method of the Areopagite dissolves the differences between the dogmas of various schools.'[1] An interest in *apophasis* is emerging in psychoanalytic writing.[2] It is possible that a recognition of the apophatic, contemplative nature of psychoanalysis could provide a way through some of the current theoretical, institutional, cultural and clinical impasses in the field of psychoanalysis.

In 1960, Jung wrote to Herbert Read:

> The great problem of our time is the fact that we don't understand what is happening in the world. We are confronted with the darkness of our soul, the unconscious. It sends up its dark and unrecognizable urges. It hollows out and hacks up the shapes of our culture and its historical dominants. We have no dominants any more, they are in the future. Our values are shifting, everything loses its certainty.[3]

We might describe the current state of the world of psychoanalysis as one in which there are 'no dominants' and all of the schools have lost their certainties. In this situation it is not surprising that analysts and therapists are looking to apophatic traditions for guidance in how to think about unknowing. Jung looked to Eckhart for instruction:

> The art of letting things happen, action through non-action, letting go of oneself as taught by Meister Eckhart, became for me the key that opens the door to the way. We must be able to let things happen in the psyche.[4]

The psychotherapist sitting in his/her consulting room, listening to a patient, is often forced to recognize that he/she does not understand the analytic process, the patient or him/herself. Dionysius experienced a similar aporia:

> If God cannot be grasped by mind or sense-perception, if he is not a particular being, how do we know him? This is something we must inquire into.[5]

Notes

1 Mortley, Raoul (1986), *From Word to Silence II: The Way of Negation, Christian and Greek*. Bonn: Hanstein, p. 229.
2 See, for example: Black, David (ed.) (2006), *Psychoanalysis and Religion in the 21st Century*. London: Routledge; Rubin, Jeffery (1996), *Psychotherapy and Buddhism: Toward an Integration*. New York: Springer; Merkur, Daniel (2010), *Explorations of the Psychoanalytic Mystics*. Amsterdam: Rodopi.
3 Letter to Herbert Read, Sept. 1960.
4 CW13 20.
5 DN 869C.

Bibliography

Dionysius: Primary texts

Campbell, Thomas L. (trans.) (1981), *Dionysius the Pseudo-Areopagite: The Ecclesiastical Hierachy*. Lantham, MD: University Press of America.

de Gandillac, Maurice (trans.) (1943), *Oeuvres completes du Pseudo-Denys L'Areopagite*. Paris: Aubier.

Hathaway, Ronald F. (trans.) (1969), *Hierarchy and the Definition of Order in the 'Letters' of Pseudo-Dionysius: A Study in the Form and Meaning of the Pseudo-Dionysian Writings*. The Hague: Martinus Nijhoff.

Jones, John D. (trans.) (1980), *Pseudo-Dionysius Areopagite: The Divine Names and Mystical Theology*. Milwaukee, WI: Marquette University Press.

Luibheid, Colm (trans.) (1987), *Pseudo-Dionysius: The Complete Works*, P. Rorem (foreword, notes, trans. collaboration), R. Roques (preface), J. Pelikan, J. Leclercq and K. Froehlich (introductions). New York: Paulist Press.

McEvoy, James (trans.) (2003), *Mystical Theology: The Glosses by Thomas Gallus and the Commentary of Robert Gosseteste on 'De Mystica Theologia'*. Leuven: Peeters.

Rolt, C. E. (trans.) (1972), *Dionysius the Areopagite: The Divine Names and The Mystical Theology*. London: SPCK.

Timothey, T. (trans.) (1990), *Dionysius' Mysticism: A Modern Version of the Middle English Translation*, (Middle English translation by the author of *The Cloud of Unknowing*). York: 1st Resource.

Vives, Josep (trans.) (1994), *Pseudo-Dionis Areopagita: La Jerarquia Celeestial, La Jerarquia Eclesiastica*. Barcelona: Enciclopedia Catalana.

Jung: Primary texts

Jung, C. G. (1916), *Psychology of the Unconscious*, Beatrice Hinkle (trans.). New York: Moffat, Yard and Company.

Jung, C. G. (1939), *The Integration of the Personality*. London: Routledge & Kegan Paul.

Jung, C. G. (1963), *Memories, Dreams, Reflections*, Aniela Jaffe (ed.), R. and C. Winston (trans.). New York: Random House.

Jung, C. G. (1967), *C. G. Jung Bibliothek: Katalog, Kusnacht-Zurich*. Privately printed. Available at: http://www.goodreads.com/book/show/3198295-c-g-jung-bibliothek-katalog

Jung, C. G. (1971), *The Collected Works of C. G. Jung*, 20 vols, Sir Herbert Read, Michael Fordham and Gerhard Adler (eds), William McGuire (exec. ed.), R. F. C. Hull (trans.). Princeton, NJ: Princeton University Press.

McGuire, William (ed.) (1974), *The Freud/Jung Letters*. Princeton, NJ: Princeton University Press.

McGuire, William and R. F. C. Hull (eds) (1977), *C. G. Jung Speaking: Interviews and Encounters*. Princeton, NJ: Princeton University Press.

Other

Aberth, John (1996), 'Pseudo-Dionysius as Liberator: The Influence of the Negative Tradition on Late Medieval Female Mystics', *Downside Review*, 114(395).

Abunuwara, Kimberley (1998), 'Drawing on Levinas to Redefine Education: Making the Unknowable the New Priority', *Education*, 119(1).

Altizer, Thomas J. J. (1955), *A Critical Analysis of C. G. Jung's Understanding of Religion*. PhD thesis, University of Chicago.

Anderson, S. Michael (1984), *Therapy as Self-Emptying: Doing Pastoral Psychotherapy From an Apophatic Perspective*. DST dissertation, Emory University.

Balint, Michael (1968), *The Basic Fault*. London: Tavistock Publications.

Barnard, Leslie W. (1991), 'Asceticism in Early Syriac Christianity', *Monastic Studies II: The Continuity of Tradition*, Judith Loades (ed.). Bangor: Headstart History.

Barnes, Hazel E. (1945), 'Neo-Platonism and Analytical Psychology', *The Philosophical Review*, 54(6).

Bateman, Josiah (1857), *Things that Accompany Salvation: Nineteen Sermons, Preached in St. Ann's Church, Manchester*. London: James Nisbet and Co.

Beggiani, Chorbishop Seely (1991), *Introduction to Eastern Christian Spirituality: The Syriac Tradition*. London: University of Scranton Press.

Beierwaltes, W. (1966), 'Exaiphnes oder die Paradoxie des Augenblicks', *Philosophisches Jahrbuch* 74.

Bernauer, James (1990), *Michel Foucault's Force of Flight: Toward an Ethics for Thought*. Atlantic Highlands, NJ: Humanities Press International.

Bettelheim, Bruno (1983), *Freud and Man's Soul*. London: Chatto & Windus.

Bishop, Paul (2000), *Synchronicity and Intellectual Intuition in Kant, Swedenborg, and Jung*. Lampeter: Edwin Mellen.

Black, David (ed.) (2006), *Psychoanalysis and Religion in the 21st Century*. London: Routledge.

Blackwell, Christopher (2000), 'Apophasis', in *Demos: Classical Athenian Democracy*, JR. Scaife and A. M. Mahoney (eds). The Stoa: a Consortium for Electronic Publication in the Humanities, available at: http://www.stoa.org/projects/demos/home

Blum, Richard and Alexander Golitzin (1991), *The Sacred Athlete: On the Mystical Experience and Dionysios, its Westernworld Fountainhead*. London: University Press of America.

Boeve, Lieven (2000), 'Christus Postmodernus: An Attempt at Apophatic Christology', *The Myriad Christ: Plurality and the Quest for Unity in Contemporary Christology*, T. Merrigan and J. Haers (eds), BETL, 152. Leuven: Peeters.

Boeve, Lieven (2002), 'The Rediscovery of Negative Theology Today: The Narrow Gulf between Theology and Philosophy', *Theologie Negative* (Biblioteca del' 'Archivio di Filosofia', 59), M. Olivetti (ed.). Rome: CEDAM.

Boeve, Lieven (2004), 'Cultural Apophaticism: A Challenge for Contemporary Theology', *Rethinking Ecumenism: Strategies for the 21st Century*, Freek L. Bakker, et al (eds). Zoetermeer: Meinema.

Bond, H. Lawrence (1997), 'Introduction', *Nicholas of Cusa: Selected Spiritual Writings*. New York: Paulist.

Bostock, David (1978), 'Plato on Change and Time in the "Parmenides"', *Phronesis*, 23.

Bradley, Arthur (2004), *Negative Theology and Modern French Philosophy*. London: Routledge.

Bradley, Arthur (2006), 'Derrida's God: A Genealogy of the Theological Turn', *Paragraph*, 29(3).

Brown, Peter (1982), 'The Rise and Function of the Holy Man in Late Antiquity', in *Society and the Holy in Late Antiquity*. London: Faber and Faber.

Brown, Peter (1995), *Authority and the Sacred: Aspects of the Christianisation of the Roman World*. Cambridge: Cambridge University Press.

Burke, Kenneth (1969), *A Grammar of Motives*. Berkeley: University of California Press.

Caputo, John (1997), *The Prayers and Tears of Jacques Derrida: Religion without Religion*. Bloomington, IN: Indiana University Press.

Carabine, Deirdre (1995), *The Unknown God: Negative Theology in the Platonic Tradition: Plato to Eriugena*. Leuven: Peeters.

Carlson, Thomas A. (1998), 'The Poverty and Poetry of Indiscretion: Negative Theology and Negative Anthropology in Contemporary and Historical Perspective', *Christianity and Literature*, 17(2).

Carlson, Thomas, A. (1999), *Indiscretion: Finitude and the Naming of God*. Chicago: University of Chicago Press.

Carlson, Thomas (2008), *The Indiscrete Image: Infinitude and Creation of the Human*. Chicago: Chicago University Press.

Cartledge, Paul, Paul Millett and Stephen Todd (2002), *Nomos: Essays in Athenian Law, Politics and Society*. Cambridge: Cambridge University Press.

Casarella, Peter, J. (ed.) (2006), *Cusanus: The Legacy of Learned Ignorance*. Washington, DC: Catholic University of America Press.

Chkheidze, Paata (1994), 'Morality and Ethics According to Shota Rustaveli's Epic "The Knight in the Panther's Skin"', in *National Identity as an Issue of Knowledge and Morality: Georgian Philosophical Studies I*, N. V. Chavchavdze, G. Nodia and P. Peachey (eds). Washington, DC: The Council for Research in Values and Philosophy.

Chodorow, Joan (ed.) (1997), *Jung on Active Imagination*. London: Routledge.

Christianson, G. and T. Izbicki (eds) (1996), *Nicholas of Cusa on Christ and the Church*. Leiden: Brill.

Coakley, Sarah (2008), 'Introduction: Re-Thinking Dionysius the Areopagite', *Modern Theology* 24(4).

Coles, Alasdair Charles (2003), *The Treatment of Matter and Divinisation Language in the Ecclesiastical Hierarchy of Pseudo-Dionysius as a Basis for Evaluating his Sacramental Theology*. PhD thesis, Heythrop College, University of London.

Corrrigan, Kevin (1996), '"Solitary" Mysticism in Plotinus, Proclus, Gregory of Nyssa, and Pseudo-Dionysius', *Journal of Religion*, 76(1).

Corrigan, Kevin and L. Michael Harrington, 'Pseudo-Dionysius the Areopagite', in *The Stanford Encyclopedia of Philosophy*, available at: http://plato.stanford.edu/entries/pseudo-dionysius-areopagite/

Counet, Jean-Michel, (2004), 'The Meaning of Apology and Reconciliation for an Apophatic Theology', in *Conflict and Reconciliation: Perspectives on Nicholas of Cusa*, Inigo Bocken (ed.). Leiden: Brill.

Cranz, F. Edward (2000), 'The (Concept of the) Beyond in Proclus, Pseudo-Dionysius, and Cusanus', in *Nicholas of Cusa and the Renaissance*, T. Izbici and G. Christianson (eds). Aldershot: Ashgate.

Cranz, F. Edward (2000), 'Nicolaus Cusanus and Dionysius Areopagita', in *Nicholas of Cusa and the Renaissance*, T. M. Izbicki and G. Christianson (eds). Aldershot, UK: Ashgate.

Cranz, F. Edward (2000), 'Cusanus' Use of Pseudo-Dionysius', in *Nicholas of Cusa and the Renaissance*, T. M. Izbicki and G. Christianson (eds). Aldershot, UK: Ashgate.

Davies, Oliver (2001), 'Thinking Difference: A Comparative Study of Gilles Deleuze, Plotinus and Meister Eckhart', in *Deleuze and Religion*, Mary Bryden (ed.). London: Routledge.

de Certeau, Michel (1992), *The Mystic Fable*. Chicago: University of Chicago Press.

de Gaynesford, Maximilian (2001), 'Bodily Organs and Organisation,' in *Deleuze and Religion*, Mary Bryden (ed.). London: Routledge.

Dehing, Jef (1993), 'The Transcendent Function: A Critical Re-Evaluation', in *The Transcendent Function: Individual and Collective Aspects: Proceedings of the Twelfth International Congress for Analytical Psychology*, Mary Ann Mattoon (ed.). Einsiedeln, Switzerland: Daimon Verlag.

Deleuze, Gilles (1995), *Negotiations, 1972–1990*, Marin Joughin (trans.). New York: Columbia University Press.

Deleuze, Gilles and Felix Guattari (1987), *A Thousand Plateaus: Capitalism and Schizophrenia*. London: Continuum.

Derrida, Jacques (1967), 'Differance', in *Margins of Philosophy*, (1982), A. Bass (trans.). Chicago: University of Chicago Press.

Derrida, Jacques (1992), 'How to Avoid Speaking: Denials', in *Derrida and Negative Theology*, Howard Coward and Toby Foshay (eds). Albany, NY: SUNY Press.

Derrida, Jacques (1992), 'Post-Scriptum: Aporias, Ways and Voices', in *Derrida and Negative Theology*, Howard Coward and Toby Foshay (eds). Albany, NY: SUNY Press.

Derrida, Jacques (1995), *On the Name*, Stanford: Stanford University Press

Dourley, John (1981), *The Psyche as Sacrament: A Comparative Study of C. G. Jung and Paul Tillich*. Toronto: Inner City Books.

Dourley, John (1984), *The Illness That We Are: A Jungian Critique of Christianity*. Toronto: Inner City Books.

Dourley, John P. (1992), *A Strategy for a Loss of Faith: Jung's Proposal*. Toronto: Inner City Books.

Dourley, John (1995), *Jung and the Religious Alternative: The Rerooting*. Lampeter, UK: Edwin Mellen.

Dourley, John (2006), *The Intellectual Autobiography of a Jungian Theologian*. Lewiston, NY: Edwin Mellen.

Dourley, John (2008), *Paul Tillich, Carl Jung and the Recovery of Religion*. London: Routledge.

Dourley, John (2010), *On Behalf of the Mystical Fool: Jung on the Religious Situation*. London: Routledge.

Duclow, Donald F. (1972), 'Pseudo-Dionysius, John Scotus Eriugena, Nicholas of Cusa: An Approach to the Hermeneutic of the Divine Names', *International Philosophical Quarterly*, XII.

Duclow, Donald F. (1974), 'Gregory of Nyssa and Nicholas of Cusa: Infinity, Anthropology and the *Via Negativa*', *The Downside Review*, 92(309).

Duclow, Donald (1994), 'Isaiah Meets the Seraph: Breaking Ranks in Dionysius and Eriugena?', in *Eriugena: East and West*, Bernard McGinn and Willemien Otten (eds). Notre Dame, IN: University of Notre Dame Press.

Eliade, Mircea (1965), 'Mephistopheles and the Androgyne', in *The Two and The One*. London: Harvill.

Ellenberger, Henri (1957), 'The Unconscious Before Freud', *Bulletin of the Menninger Clinic*, 21(1): 3–15.

Ellenberger, Henri (1970), *The Discovery of the Unconscious: The History of Dynamic Psychiatry*. New York: Basic Books.

Esposito Buckley, Lisa Marie (1992), 'Ecstatic and Emanating, Providential and Unifying: A Study of Pseudo-Dionysian and Plotinian Concepts of Eros', *Journal of Neoplatonic Studies*, I(1).

Esposito, Lisa Marie (1997), *Pseudo-Dionysius: A Philosophical Study of Certain Hellenic Sources*. PhD thesis, University of Toronto.

Finlan, S. and V. Kharlamov (eds) (2006), *Theosis: Deification in Christian Theology*, Princeton Theological Monograph Series. Eugene, OR: Pickwick Publications.

Fisher, Jeffrey (2001), 'The Theology of Dis/similarity: Negation in Pseudo-Dionysius', *Journal of Religion*, 81(4).

Fitzpatrick, Sean Joseph (2000), *Saying and Unsaying Mysticism: The Problem of Defining Mysticism in the Social Sciences*. PhD thesis, Rice University.

Frank, S. L. (1983), *The Unknowable: An Ontological Introduction to the Philosophy of Religion*. Athens, OH: Ohio University Press.

Franke, William (2004), 'A Philosophy of the Unsayable: Apophasis and the Experience of Truth and Totality', *Analecta Husserliana*, 83.

Franke, William (2007), *On What Cannot be Said: Apophatic Discourses in Philosophy, Religion, Literature and the Arts: Vol. 1, Classic Formulations*. Notre Dame, IN: Notre Dame University Press.

Franke, William (2007), *On What Cannot be Said: Apophatic Discourses in Philosophy, Religion, Literatue and the Arts: Vol. 2, Modern and Contemporary Transformations*. Notre Dame, IN: Notre Dame University Press.

Freud, Sigmund (2002), 'On Initiating Treatment', Alan Bance (trans.), in *Wild Analysis, New Penguin Freud*, Adam Phillips (Gen. Ed.). London: Penguin.

Gersh, Stephen (1978), *From Iamblichus to Eriugena: An Investigation of the Prehistory and Evolution of the Pseudo-Dionysisan Tradition*. Leiden: Brill.

Gersh, Stephen (2006), *Neoplatonism after Derrida*. Leiden: Brill.

Golitzin, Alexander (1994), 'Hierarchy Versus Anarchy? Dionysius Arepagita, Symeon the New Theologian, Nicetas Stethatos, and Their Common Roots in Ascetical Tradition', *St. Vladimir's Theological Quarterly*, 38(2).

Golitzin, Alexander (1994), *Et Introibo Ad Altare Dei: The Mystagogy of Dionysius Areopagita, with Special Reference to its Predecessors in the Eastern Christian Tradition*. Thessaloniki: Analecta Vlatadon.

Golitzin, Alexander (2001), 'Revisiting the "Sudden": Epistle III in the *Corpus Dionysiacum*', *Studia Patristica*, 37.

Golitzin, Alexander (2003), '"Suddenly, Christ": The Place of Negative Theology in the Mystagogy of Dionysius Areopagites', in *Mystics: Presence and Aporia*, Michael Kessler and Christian Sheppard (eds). Chicago: University of Chicago Press.

Goudsmit, Arno L. (1998), *Towards a negative understanding of psychotherapy*. PhD thesis Rijksuniversiteit Groningen.

Gregory of Nyssa (1965), 'On the Making of Man', *Gregory of Nyssa: Dogmatic Treatises, etc.*, W. Moore and H. A. Wilson (trans.), in *Nicene and Post-Nicene Fathers of the Christian Church*, Vol. 5 Series II, P. Schaff and H. Wace (eds). Grand Rapids, MI: Eerdmans.

Grinberg, Leon (1969), 'New Ideas: Conflict and Evolution', *International Journal of Psychoanalysis*, 50: 517–28.

Gross, Jules (2002), *The Divinization of the Christian According to the Greek Fathers*. Anaheim, CA: A & C Press.

Gundry, Mark (2006), *Beyond Psyche: Symbol and Transcendence in C. G. Jung*. New York: Peter Lang.

Hager, F. -P. (1993), 'Infinity and Simplicity of God in Plotinus, Proclus and Pseudo-Dionysius', *Journal of Neoplatonic Studies*, 2(1).

Hallward, Peter (2010), 'You Can't Have It Both Ways: Deleuze or Lacan', in *Deleuze and Psychoanalysis: Philosophical Essays on Deleuze's Debate with Psychoanalysis*, Leen de Boole (ed.). Leuven: Leuven University Press.

Hamilton, J. W. (1969), 'Object Loss, Dreaming, and Creativity: The Poetry of John Keats', *Psychoanalytic Studies of the Child*, 24.

Hankey, Wayne J. (1997), '"Ad intellectum rationcinatio": Three Procline Logics, *The Divine Names* of Pseudo-Dionysius, Eriugena's *Periphyseon* and Boethius' *Consolatio philosophiae*', *Patristic Studies*, 24.

Harries, Karsten (2001), *Infinity and Perspective*. Cambridge, MA: MIT Press.

Hart, Kevin (1989), *The Trespass of the Sign: Deconstruction, Theology, and Philosophy*. Cambridge, Cambridge University Press.

Hay, David M. (1998), 'The Veiled Thoughts of the Therapeutae', in *Mediators of the Divine: Horizons of Prophecy, Divination, Dreams and Theurgy in Mediterranean Antiquity*, Robert M. Berchman (ed.). Atlanta, GA: Scholars Press.

Henderson, David (1998), 'Solitude and Solidarity: A philosophy of supervision', in *Psychoanalytic and Jungian Supervision*, Petruska Clarkson (ed.). London: Whurr.

Henderson, David (1999), 'From Shaman to Therapist', *Therapy on the Couch*, Susan Greenberg (ed.), David Henderson (consulting editor). London: Camden Press.

Henderson, David (1999), 'The Medium is the Message', unpublished paper.

Herbert, Jack (2001), *The German Tradition: Uniting the Opposites: Goethe, Jung and Rilke*. London: Temenos Academy.

Herold, Christine (2006), 'One Mind: Jung and Meister Eckhart on God and Mystical Experience', *Journal of Jungian Scholarly Studies*, 2(4).

Hillman, James (1975), *Re-Visioning Psychology*. New York: Harper & Row.

Homans, Peter (1995), *Jung in Context: Modernity and the Making of Psychology*. Chicago: University of Chicago Press.

Hood, Ralph W. (1976), 'Conceptual Criticisms of Regressive Explanations of Mysticism', *Review of Religious Research*, 17(3).

Hopkins, Jasper (1983), *Nicholas of Cusa's Metaphysic of Contraction*. Minneapolis, MN: Arthur J. Banning Press.

Hopkins, Jasper (1985), *Nicholas of Cusa's Dialectical Mysticism*. Minneapolis, MN: Arthur J. Banning Press.

Hopkins, Jasper (2006), 'Nicholas of Cusa's Intellectual Relationship to Anselm of Canterbury', in *Cusanus: The Legacy of Learned Ignorance*. Washington, DC: Catholic University of America Press.

Hotz, Kendra G. (2000), *The Theurgical Self: The Theological Anthropology of the Pseudo-Dionysius*. PhD thesis, Emory University.

Hudson, Nancy Joyce (1999), *Theosis in the Thought of Nicholas of Cusa: Origin, Goal, and Realized Destiny of Creation*. PhD thesis, Yale University.

Hudson, Nancy (2005), 'Divine Immanence: Nicholas of Cusa's Understanding of Theophany and the Retrieval of a "New" Model of God', *Journal of Theological Studies*, 56(2).

Humbert, Elie (1988), *C. G. Jung: The Fundaments of Theory and Practice*. Wilmette, IL: Chiron.

Iamblichus (1999), *On the Mysteries*, X.VI, Thomas Taylor (trans.). Frome, UK: Prometheus Trust.

Jonas, Hans (1963), *The Gnostic Religion*. Boston: Beacon Press.

Jordan, Elijah (1911), 'The Unknowable of Herbert Spencer', *Philosophical Review*, 20(3).

Karlsson, Gunnar (2000), 'The Question of Truth Claims in Psychoanalysis', *Scandinavian Psychoanalytic Review*, 23: 3–24.

Kenny, John Peter (1993), 'The Critical Value of Negative Theology', *Harvard Theological Review*, 86(4).

Kerslake, Christian (2002), 'The Vertigo of Philosophy: Deleuze and the Problem of Immanence', *Radical Philosophy*, No. 113.

Kerslake, Christian (2004), 'Rebirth Through Incest: On Deleuze's Early Jungianism', *Angelaki: Journal of the Theoretical Humanities*, 9 (1).

Kerslake, Christian (2006), 'Insects and Incest: From Bergson and Jung to Deleuze', available at: http://multitudes.samizdat.net/Insects-and-Incest-From-Bergson

Kerslake, Christian (2007), *Deleuze and the Unconscious*. London: Continuum.

Kerslake, Christian (2009), 'Deleuze and the Meanings of Immanence,' available at: http://www.after1968.org/app/webroot/uploads/kerslake-paper(1).pdf

Koch, H. (1895), 'Der Pseudo-Epigraphische Character der Dionysischen Schriften', *Theologische quartalschrift*, 77.

Lambert, Kenneth (1972), 'Books and Journals: Recent Publications in Journals', *Journal of Analytical Psychology*, 17.

Lampe, G. W. H. (1961), *Patristic Greek Lexicon*. Oxford: Clarendon.

Land, Nick (2011), *Fanged Noumena: Collected Writings 1987–2007*. Falmouth, UK: Urbanomic.

Lewy, Hans (1978), *Chaldean Oracles and Theurgy: Mysticism Magic and Platonism in the Later Roman Empire*. Paris: Etudes Augustiniennes.

Liddell, H. G. and Scott, R. (1940), *Greek–English Lexicon*. Oxford: Clarendon.

Lilla, Salvatore R. C. (1980), 'The Notion of Infinitude in Ps.-Dionysius Areopagita', *Journal of Theological Studies*, 31(1).

Lilla, Salvatore (2001), 'Brief Notes on the Greek *Corpus Areopagiticum* in Rome during the Early Middle Ages', *Dionysius*, 59: 201–14.

Lossky, Vladimir (1957), *The Mystical Theology of the Eastern Church*. Crestwood, NY: St Vladimir's Seminary Press.

Louth, Andrew (1992), *The Origins of the Christian Mystical Tradition from Plato to Denys*. Oxford: Oxford University Press.

Luther, Martin, *Luther's Works*, 13: 110–11.

MacLennan, Bruce (2003), 'Evolution, Jung, and Theurgy: Their Role in Modern Neoplatonism', available at: http://www.cs.utk.edu/~mclennan

Marion, Jean-Luc (2001), *The Idol and Distance*. New York: Fordham University Press.

Marion, Jean-Luc (2005), '*Mihi magna quaestio factus sum*: The Privilege of Unknowing', *Journal of Religion*, 85(1).

McCort, Dennis (2001), *Going Beyond the Pairs: The Coincidence of Opposites in German Romanticism, Zen and Deconstruction*. Albany, NY: SUNY Press.

McGinn, Bernard (1992), *The Foundations of Mysticism: Origins to the Fifth Century*. London: SCM Press.

McGinn, Bernard (1995), *The Growth of Mysticism: From Gregory the Great to the Twelfth Century*. London: SCM Press.

McGinn, Bernard (1998), *The Flowering of Mysticism: Men and Women in the New Mysticism – 1200–1350*. New York: Crossroads.

McGinn, Bernard (2009), 'Three forms of Negativity in Christian Mysticism', in *Knowing the Unknowable: Science and Religions on God and the Universe*, J. Bowker (ed.). London: Tauris.

Merkur, Daniel (2010), *Explorations of the Psychoanalytic Mystics*. Amsterdam: Rodopi.

Milem, Bruce (2007), 'Four Theories of Negative Theology', *Heythrop Journal*, 48.

Miller, Clyde Lee (2003), *Reading Cusanus: Metaphor and Dialectic in a Conjectural Universe*. Washington, DC: Catholic University of America Press.

Miller, Jeffery C. (2004), *The Transcendent Function: Jung's Model of Psychological Growth Through Dialogue with the Unconscious*. Albany, NY: SUNY Press.

Morel, Ferndinand (1918), *Essai sur l'Introversion Mystique: Etude Psychologique de Pseudo-Denys l'Areopagite et de Quelques Autres cas de Mysticism*. Geneva: Librairie Kundig.

Mortley, R. (1982), 'The Fundamentals of the Via Negativa', *American Journal of Philology*, 103(4).

Mortley, Raoul (1986), *From Word to Silence: I The Rise and Fall of Logos*. Bonn: Hanstein.

Mortley, Raoul (1986), *From Word to Silence: II The Way of Negation, Christian and Greek*. Bonn: Hanstein.

Nagy, Marilyn (1991), *Philosophical Issues in the Psychology of C. G. Jung*. Albany, NY: SUNY Press.

Nef, Frederic (2005), 'Contemplation', in *Encyclopedia of Christian Theology*, Jean-Yves Lacoste (ed.). London: Routledge.

Nicholas of Cusa (1954), *Of Learned Ignorance*, Germain Heron (trans.). London: Routledge & Kegan Paul.

Nicholas of Cusa (1997), *Nicholas of Cusa: Selected Spiritual Writings*, H. Lawrence Bond (trans.). New York: Paulist.

O'Meara, Dominic J. (2003), *Platonopolis: Platonic Political Philosophy in Late Antiquity*. Oxford: Clarendon.

Otten, W. (1999), 'In the Shadow of the Divine: Negative Theology and Negative Anthropology in Augustine, Pseudo-Dionysius and Eriugena', *Heythrop Journal*, 40: 438–55.

Paper, Jordan (2004), *The Mystic Experience: A Descriptive and Comparative Analysis*. Albany, NY: SUNY Press.

Pauson, Marian (1988), *Jung the Philosopher: Essays in Jungian Thought*. New York: Peter Lang.

Perczel, Istvan (2000), 'Pseudo-Dionysius and the Platonic Theology: A Preliminary Study', in *Proclus et la Theologie Platonicienne*, Segonds and Steel (eds). Leuven: Leuven University Press.

Perl, Eric D. (1997), 'The Metaphysics of Love in Dionysius the Areopagite', *Journal of Neoplatonic Studies*, 6(1).

Peters, F. E. (1967), *Greek Philosophical Terms: A Historical Lexicon*. New York: New York University Press.

Pickstock, Catherine (1998), *After Writing: On the Liturgical Consummation of Philosophy*. Oxford: Blackwell.

Pietkainen, Petteri (1999), *C. G. Jung and the Psychology of Symbolic Forms*. Helsinki: Academia Scientiarum Fennica.

Plaut, Fred (1972), 'W. R. Bion: Attention and interpretation. A scientific approach to insight in psychoanalysis and groups. London, Tavistock, 1970. pp. 136. £1.50.' *Journal of Analytical Psychology*, 17.

Proclus (1963) *The Elements of Theology*, E. R. Dodds (trans.). Oxford: Clarendon.

Proclus, *Parmenides*. 1073, 11.

Rayment-Pickard, Hugh (2003), *Impossible God: Derrida's Theology*. Aldershot, UK: Ashgate.

Rist, John M. (1966), 'A Note on Eros and Agape in Pseudo-Dionysius', *Virgiliae Christianae*, 20, Amsterdam.

Robertson, Robin (1995), *Jungian Archetypes: Jung, Godel, and the History of Archetypes*. York Beach, ME: Nicholas-Hays.

Robertson, Robin (2002), 'Stairway to Heaven: Jung and Neoplatonism', available at: http://www.angelfire.com/super/magicrobin/STAIRWAY.htm

Rorem, Paul (1982), 'Iamblichus and the Anagogical Method in Pseudo-Dionysian Liturgical Theology', in *Studia Patristica*, Vol. XVII, Part One, Elizabeth A. Livingstone (ed.). Oxford: Pergamon Press.

Rorem, Paul (1986), 'The Uplifting Spirituality of Pseudo-Dionysius', in *Christian Spirituality: Origins to the Twelfth Century*, B. McGinn and J. Meyendorff (eds). London: Routledge.

Rorem, Paul (2008), 'Negative Theologies and the Cross', *Harvard Theological Review*, 101(3–4).

Rorem, Paul and John C. Lamoreaux (1998), *John of Scythopolis and the Dionysian Corpus: Annotating the Areopagite*. Oxford: Oxford University Press.

Rubenstein, Mary-Jane (2008), 'Dionysius, Derrida, and the Critique of "Ontotheology"', *Modern Theology*, 24(4).

Rubin, Jeffery (1996), *Psychotherapy and Buddhism: Toward an Integration*. New York: Springer.

Saffrey, Henri-Dominique (1982), 'New Objective Links Between the Pseudo-Dionysius and Proclus', in *Neoplatonism and Christian Thought*, E. J. O'Meara (ed.). Albany, NY: SUNY Press.

Salman, Sherry (1993), 'Response: Fermenting the Dialectic into Psychological Process', in *The Transcendent Function: Individual and Collective Aspects: Proceedings of the Twelfth International Congress for Analytical Psychology*, Mary Ann Mattoon (ed.). Einsiedeln, Switzerland: Daimon Verlag.

Sandler, Donald F. (1993), 'Response', in *The Transcendent Function: Individual and Collective Aspects: Proceedings of the Twelfth International Congress for Analytical Psychology*, Mary Ann Mattoon (ed.). Einsiedeln, Switzerland: Daimon Verlag.

Saward, John (1974), 'Towards an Apophatic Anthropology', *Irish Theological Quarterly*, 41.

Seem, Mark (1984), 'Introduction,' in *Anti-Oedipus: Capitalism and Schizophrenia*, G. Deleuze and F. Guattari. London: Continuum.

Sells, Michael A. (1994), *Mystical Languages of Unsaying*. Chicago: University of Chicago Press.

Sells, Michael A. and James Webb (1997), 'Lacan and Bion: Psychoanalysis and the Mystical Language of "Un-Saying"', *Journal of Melanie Klein and Object Relations*, 15(2): 243–64.

Semetsky, Inna (2004), 'The Complexity of Individuation', *International Journal of Applied Psychoanalytic Studies*, 1(4).

Semetsky, Inna (2006), *Deleuze, Education and Becoming*. Rotterdam: Sense Publishers.

Semetsky, Inna (2009), 'Practical Mysticism and Deleuze's Ontology of the Virtual' (with T. Lovat), *Cosmos and History: The Journal of Natural and Social Philosophy*, 5(2).

Semetsky, Inna and Joshua Ramey (2012), 'Deleuze's Philosophy and Jung's Psychology: Learning and the Unconscious', in *Jung and Educational Theory*, Inna Semetsky (ed.). Bognor Regis, UK: Wiley-Blackwell.

Shelburne, Walter A. (1988), *Mythos and Logos in the Thought of Carl Jung: The Theory of the Collective Unconscious in Scientific Perspective*. Albany, NY: SUNY Press.

Sherry, Richard (1550), *A Treatise of Schemes and Tropes*. London: John Day.

Smith, Mark Trevor (1993), *'All Nature is but Art': The Coincidence of Opposites in English Romantic Literature*. West Cornwall, CT: Locust Hill Press.

Solomon, Hester McFarland (1993), 'Hegel's Dialectical Vision and the Transcendent Function', in *The Transcendent Function: Individual and Collective Aspects. Proceedings of the Twelfth International Congress for Analytical Psychology*, Mary Ann Mattoon (ed.). Einsiedeln, Switzerland: Daimon Verlag.

Spearritt, Placid (1970), 'The Soul's Participation in God According to Pseudo-Dionysius', *The Downside Review*, 88(293).

Stagoll, Cliff (2005), 'Becoming', in *The Deleuze Dictionary*, A. Parr (ed.). New York: Columbia University Press.

Stang, Colin (1974), 'Plato and the Instant', *Proceedings of the Aristotelian Society*, Suppli. Vol. 48.

Stephenson, Craig E. (2009), *Possession: Jung's Comparative Anatomy of the Psyche*. London: Routledge.

Stiglmayr, J. (1895), 'Der Neuplatoniker Proclus als Vorlage des Sogen: Dionysius Areopagiten in der Laehre vom Ubel', *Historisches Jahrbuch*, 16.

Stiglmayr, J. (1909), 'Dionysius the Pseudo-Areopagite', *The Catholic Encyclopedia*. New York: Robert Appleton.

Stobach, Niko (1998), *The Moment of Change: A Systematic History in the Philosophy of Space and Time*. Dordrecht: Kluwer.

Sullivan, Barbara Steven (2010), *The Mystery of Analytical Work: Weavings from Jung and Bion*. London: Routledge.

Swenson, David F. (1905), 'The Category of the Unknowable', in *Journal of Philosophy, Psychology and Scientific Methods*, 2(19).

Tacey, David (2007), 'The Gift of the Unknown: Jung(ians) and Freud(ians) at the End of Modernity', *European Journal of Psychotherapy and Counselling*, 9(4).

Tacey, David (2008), 'Imagining Transcendence at the End of Modernity: Jung and Derrida', in *Dreaming the Myth Onwards: New Directions in Jungian Therapy and Thought*, Lucy Huskinson (ed.). London: Routledge.

Taylor, Warren (1938), 'A Note on English Figures of Speech', *Modern Language Notes*, 53(7).

Tomasic, Thomas Michael (1969), 'Negative Theology and Subjectivity: An Approach to the Tradition of the Pseudo-Dionysius', *International Philosophical Quarterly*, 9.

Tomasic, Thomas Michael (1988), 'The Logical Function of Metaphor and Oppositional Coincidence in the Pseudo-Dionysius and Johannes Scottus Eriugena', *Journal of Religion*, 68(3).

Torevell, David (2007), *Liturgy and the Beauty of the Unknown: Another Place*. Aldershot, UK: Ashgate.

Treiger, Alexander (2001), *On the Arabic Version of Ps.-Dionysius the Areopagite's 'Mystical Theology'*. MA dissertation, Hebrew Union University, Jerusalem.

Turner, Denys (1995), *The Darkness of God: Negativity in Christian Mysticism*. Cambridge: Cambridge University Press.

Turner, Denys (2005), 'How to Read the Pseudo-Denys Today?' *International Journal of Systematic Theology*, 7(4).

Turner, Victor (1987), 'Betwixt and Between: The Liminal Period in Rites of Passage', in *Betwixt and Between: Patterns of Masculine and Feminine Initiation*, L. C. Mahdi, S. Foster and M. Little (eds). La Salle, IL: Open Court.

Van Den Daele, Albert (1941), *Indices Pseudo-Dionysiani*. Leuven: Bibliothèque de l'Université.

Vansteenberghe, Edmond (1920), *Le Cardinal Nicolas de Cues*. Paris: H. Champion.

Walker, Andrew George (1979), *Two Versions of Sociological Discourse: The Apophatic and Cataphatic Grounds of Social Science*. PhD dissertation, Goldsmiths College, University of London.

Watts, Pauline Moffitt (1987), 'Pseudo-Dionysius the Areopagite and Three Renaissance Neoplatonists: Cusanus, Ficino, and Pico on Mind and Cosmos', in *Supplementum Festivum: Studies in Honor of Paul Oskar Kristeller*, J. Hankins, J. Monfasani and F. Purnell, Jr. (eds). Binghamton, NY: Medieval and Renaissance Texts and Studies.

Whyte, L. L. (1978), *The Unconscious Before Freud*. London: Julian Friedmann.

William of St. Thierry (1998), *The Way of Divine Union*, Basil Pennington (trans.). Hyde Park, NY: New City Press.

Williams, A. H. (1966), 'Keats' "La Belle Dame Sans Merci": The Bad-Breast Mother', *American Imago*, 23.

Withim, P. (1969–70), 'The Psychodynamics of Literature', *Psychoanalytic Review*, 56D.

Wolosky, Shira (1995), *Language Mysticism: The Negative Way of Language in Eliot, Beckett, and Celan*. Stanford, CA: Stanford University Press.

Yannaras, Christos (2005), *On the Absence and Unknowability of God: Heidegger and the Areopagite*. London: T & T Clark.

Zembylas, Michalinos (2005), 'A Pedagogy of Unknowing: Witnessing Unknowability in Teaching and Learning', *Studies in Philosophy and Education*, 24(2).

Zizek, Slavoj (2004), 'Notes on a Debate "From Within the People"', *Criticism*, 46(4).

Dictionaries and encyclopaedias

The Hutchinson Dictionary of Difficult Words. Helicon Publishing, 1998.

The American Heritage Dictionary of the English Language, Fourth Edition. Houghton Mifflin, 2000.

http://www.britannica.com

http://www.mathacademy.com

Index